A TRAVELER'S GUIDE TO
NORTH AMERICAN GARDENS

A TRAVELER'S GUIDE TO
North AMERICAN GARDENS

BY HARRY BRITTON LOGAN

CHARLES SCRIBNER'S SONS

NEW YORK

Library of Congress Cataloging in Publication Data

Logan, Harry Britton, 1910–
   The traveler's guide to North American gardens.

   1. Gardens—United States.   2. Gardens—North
America.   I. Title.
SB466.U6L63   917′.04′53   73–1103
ISBN 0–684–13493–4

1 3 5 7 9 11 13 15 17 19 V/C 20 18 16 14 12 10 8 6 4 2

For Lyn

Contents

A TRAVELER'S GUIDE TO NORTH AMERICAN GARDENS

Alabama

AUBURN: *Auburn Arboretum and Gardens, Auburn University, 36830.* On the university campus is the Garden of Memory (miscellaneous annuals and shrubs), the Centennial Garden (roses and annuals), and the Collection Garden. An arboretum ($7\frac{1}{2}$ acres) is in the formative stage. There is also an Agricultural Experiment Station. Open only during school hours; visitors should check with the main office.

BIRMINGHAM: *Birmingham Botanical Garden, 2610 Lane Park Drive, 35203.* Within 67 acres are a Japanese Garden, a Zen Garden, waterfalls, and a tea house. Special plant groups of roses, iris, day-lilies, wildflowers. The arboretum has azaleas, dogwood, some unusual trees and shrubs, and a nature trail. The 85-foot conservatory has orchids and other rare plants; and fall-winter-spring exhibitions of chrysanthemums, poinsettias, and Easter lilies. Daily, 9:00 A.M.–5:30 P.M. Possibly a fee. When in Birmingham don't overlook the formal gardens in *Vulcan Park on Red Mountain*; the charming 19th-century garden at *Arlington House, 331 Cotton Avenue,* tulips, buttercups, and other plants against a background of boxwood hedges and huge magnolias; the rose garden at *Avondale Park;* the *Camellia Show* in February; the *Dogwood Trail Caravan*, the *Rose Trail*, the *Garden Pilgrimages* in spring (dates are available at the Chamber of Commerce); and the *Vestavia Baptist Church and Gardens, 3600 Vestavia Drive,* on top of Shades Mountain. The gardens are designed for continuous bloom around a copy of the temple of Vesta modified for use as a church. Daily, 8:30 A.M.–4:30 P.M.

CULLMAN: *Ave Maria Grotto, St. Bernard College, 35138.* More than 150 mini-replicas of world-famous religious buildings set in a 4-acre park on the college campus. Daily, 7:00 A.M.–sunset. Fee.

If there is time, walk the nature trail at nearby *Hurricane Creek Park.* Daily, sunrise–sunset. Fee.

FORT PAYNE: *De Soto Park (Little River Canyon).* Spectacular falls and spectacular spring blooms of

Opposite: *Bellingrath Gardens.* Above: *Ave Maria Grotto*

3

Oriental Gardens   Opposite, top: *University of Alabama*

mountain laurel, rhododendron, wild azalea, redbud, other shrubs and wildflowers. Daily, 8:00 A.M.–sunset.
GADSEN: *Noccalula Falls Botanical Gardens.* Parks with seasonal flowers: tulips, hyacinths planted among dogwood. Best season, April through May. Daily, 8:00 A.M.–sunset.
HODGES: *Rock Bridge Canyon.* Sub-tropical plants set among waterfalls and springs. Wildflower festival in early May, but especially exciting are the mountain laurels, ferns, arbutus, hydrangeas, hollies, and other indigenous flowering shrubs. Daily, sunrise–sunset. Fee.
MOBILE: *Earle W. Long's Gardens, 250 Tuthill Lane, Spring Hill.* Ten acres of massed camellias and azaleas in landscaped ravines, blooming from September through March. A featured spot in the Azalea Trail. Fee.
Oakleigh House, 350 Oakleigh Place. Remarkable azaleas beneath moss-festooned oaks. Weekdays, 10:00 A.M.–4:00 P.M. Sunday, 2:00 P.M.–4:00 P.M. Closed Christmas week and legal holidays.
Clark Gardens, 2100 Forest River Drive (12 miles south of Mobile via Route 163). Thick growths of pine, hardwood, dogwood; pine walks edged with azaleas and camellias,

and interspersed with native shrubs—holly, myrtle, shadbury, and more. Spring is colorful; fall is picturesque. Daily, 8:00 A.M.–sunset. Fee.
Other excellent gardens in Mobile: at the Tacon-Gordon House, the Tuthill Home, the Georgia Cottage in a setting of oaks and magnolias. And very important: the *Azalea Trail,* a 35-mile floral extravaganza from mid-February through March. The Chamber of Commerce has information about these gardens and others.
MONTGOMERY: *Jasmine Hill Gardens (near Wetumpka).* Extensive gardens designed to feature statues and fountains. There are pools and avenues of flowering cherries. Daily, summer, 7:00 A.M.–5:00 P.M.; winter, 7:00 A.M.–4:30 P.M. Don't overlook the *Ordman-Shaw Historic District, 309 Hull Street.* Tuesday–Saturday, 9:30 A.M.–4:00 P.M.; Sunday, 1:30 P.M.–4:00 P.M. Fee. Or the *Governor's Mansion, 1142 South Perry Street;* extensive and informal landscaping with camellias. The State Capitol grounds in spring. The White House of the Confederacy. Daily, 9:00 A.M.–4:30 P.M. Closed Saturday and major holidays.
NATURAL BRIDGE: *Natural Bridge Park.* Ravines

Ivy Green

with ferns and wildflowers, mountain laurel and snow-ball bushes; giant magnolias (14-inch blooms). Daily, 8:00 A.M.–sunset. Fee.

PHIL CAMPBELL: *Dismals Wonder Gardens.* Rare and exotic native ferns and wildflowers in a sunken garden. Waterfalls and streams in a primeval setting. Mountain laurel, mountain camellia, wild hydrangea, dogwood, and the largest fragrant decumaria known. Daily, 8:00 A.M.–sunset. Fee.

THEODORE: *Bellingrath Gardens and Home, 36582.* A world-famous garden of 65 acres; and probably the most spectacular in the south. Azaleas, 200 species and varieties among 250,000 plants (some over 150 years old). An arboretum of 4,000 camellias, all labeled. At least 70 varieties of native trees: pines, most oak species, magnolias, yaupon, cherry, sourwood, blackgum, and others. An Oriental-American garden with pools and flamingos (the estate is a bird sanctuary). There are monthly displays beginning in September with the largest massing of chrysanthemums in the world. Early and late camellias from September to April. Huge beds of poinsettias in December. Azaleas from mid-January to early April. And also in April: dogwood, mountain laurel, roses, spirea, and tulips. May: hydrangeas and gardenias. Other months are well represented with lilies, day-lilies, and water-lilies; a thousand African violets in a rock garden of ferns and streams; oleanders, crape myrtle, holly, hydrangea, hibiscus, sweet olive, fuscata, althea, wisteria. A giant bamboo grove, and many exotic foliage plants: acalypha, caladium, pandanus, crotons, ferns, dracaena. And always masses of colorful annuals. The conservatory has excellent collections of orchids and bromeliads. Daily, 7:00 A.M.–dusk. Fee.

TUSCALOOSA: *Oriental Gardens, River Road.* The national headquarters of the Gulf States Paper Corporation. Gardens and buildings designed in the classic Japanese manner. A reflection pool, rock gardens, flower-bordered walks, and many well-grown azaleas, and flowering shrubs. An extraordinary blending of outdoors (gardens) and indoors (offices). Weekdays, 4:30 P.M.–7:00 P.M. Saturdays and holidays, 8:00 A.M.–7:00 P.M. Sunday, 1:30 P.M.–7:30 P.M.

University of Alabama Arboretum, University Boulevard. A

60-acre field and woodland tract three miles east of the campus. Extensive nature trails and a considerable number of native trees, colorful shrubs, flowers, and ferns. The campus has a well-landscaped historic district, including the Gorgas House, the President's Home, the Friedman Library, the University Club. The campus ordinarily may be visited when the university is in session. Daily, 10:00 A.M.–12:00 A.M. and 2:00 P.M.–5:00 P.M. Sunday, 2:00 P.M.–4:00 P.M. When in Tuscaloosa don't overlook the gardens of the *Old Tavern on 28th Street.* Tuesday-Sunday, 1:00 P.M.–5:00 P.M. Fee.

TUSCUMBIA: *Ivy Green, 300 West North Common Street.* The birthplace of Helen Keller set within boxwood, crape myrtle, magnolia, southern smilax, iris, and ivy.

Plans have been completed to develop a Memorial Garden. Weekdays, 8:30 A.M.–5:00 P.M. Sunday, 1:00 P.M.–5:00 P.M. Closed October to March. Fee.

VANCE: *Bama Scenic Rock Gardens.* Prehistoric rock houses, woodlands and wildflowers among fanciful rock formations. Daily, May to October, 8:00 A.M.–sunset. Worth visiting is *Pope's Tavern, Florence.* Daily except Monday, 9:00 A.M.–12:00 P.M. and 2:00 P.M.–5:00 P.M. Sunday, 2:00 P.M.–5:00 P.M. Fee. *Magnolia Grove (Hobsen Memorial), Main Street, Greensboro.* Daily, 9:00 A.M.–12:00 P.M. and 2:00 P.M–5:00 P.M. Contribution. The *"Camellia City" of Greenville* and its spring camellia show. These and many others, including local garden pilgrimages, are on lists available from the Bureau of Publicity, State of Alabama, Montgomery, Alabama, 36104.

Alaska

There are few gardens in Alaska, as we think of them in the continental limits of the United States. With less than a hundred days of growing weather, they are limited to riotous displays of annuals around some private homes. The city of Anchorage maintains 1,400 acres of city parks; and about 32,000 plants are transferred from greenhouse to the parks and public buildings and floral street baskets. The Parks and Recreation Department operates an 18,000-square-foot greenhouse as an educational facility as well as a growing facility. And the University of Alaska Extension Service has a trial ground for ornamentals. So, between these operations and the growing influence of the Federation of Garden Clubs, gardening is becoming more professional and more widely practiced.

But travelers to Mt. McKinley, crossing from Anchorage to the National Park, can see during the short spring thousands upon thousands of wildflowers: anemones and arnica, baby's breath and several kinds of bog orchids, bunchberry, daisy, and dogwood; forget-me-nots,

gentian, harebell, larkspur, lupine, monkshood, paintbrush, valerian, saxifrage, and sweet peas, asters, sedums by the dozens, and stonecrop; heliotrope and 300 others as listed in the University of Alaska's brief guide book of the area.

Mt. McKinley National Park has even a greater variety of wildflowers. Now connected by good roads or public transportation with both Anchorage and Fairbanks, the park provides reasonable access to nearly two million virgin acres, much of which is a "garden" by any definition. Special services provide trips to the lower slopes, which are covered with shrubs and wildflowers, alpine tundra plants and—so say the park naturalists— "hundreds, perhaps thousands of 'garden' spots." The park plant check list describes over 500 flowering plants and shrubs, from aconitum and alpine azaleas through buttercups and heather, marigolds and arctic poppies, rhododendrons and ranunculuses to valerian and wintergreen. The park is open daily from June 1 to about mid-September.

Organ Pipe Cactus National Monument

Arizona

AJO: *Organ-Pipe Cactus National Monument, 85321* (west of Tucson, about 142 miles, via routes 86 and 85). Sometimes wilderness areas, or deserts, are so lovely and seemingly so skillfully arranged by nature that man cannot improve them. This is so at the 300,000-acre (516 square miles) Organ-Pipe Cactus National Monument. There are many thousands of this unique cactus, the nation's second largest, whose flowers are brilliant, and whose fruits are eaten or the juice fermented. Other cacti in the area that have been identified (more than 30 species) include the rare senita, whisker cactus, teddybear cholla, many varieties of prickly pear, saguaro; there are succulents, ocotillo, paloverde, mesquite, ironwood, mountain mahogany. And oaks, agaves, Arizona rosewood, galleta, brittlebush, broom, jojoba, acacia, jumping bean sapium, juniper, and 200 more plants—all catalogued. In spring if the rains are good, there is an abundance of wildflowers; but the cacti will flower willy-nilly. Daily, sunrise–sunset; but check in at the visitor center.

MESA: *Mormon Temple Gardens, 525 East Main Street.* Many species of attractive cacti, flower gardens and unusual trees and shrubs within 20 acres of well-landscaped grounds. There are sunken gardens, fountains, reflecting pools, and many citrus, palms, and cedars—all arranged to provide a beautiful desert setting for the temple. Daily, 8:00 A.M.–9:00 P.M.

PHOENIX: *Desert Botanical Garden, 6400 East McDowell Road, 85010* (located in Papago Park). Agaves, cacti, dry-climate trees and shrubs from all over the world, including desert fern tree, creosote bush, acacia, boojam tree, honey mesquite, paloverde tree, desert spoon plant, and many yuccas, aloes, cassia, as well as some pleasant sage. About 4,500 specimens arranged within 120 acres of desert land. A lathhouse display of cacti and succulents from the deserts of the world. Nature trails and monthly desert excursions. April is the best month to see the cacti flowers; wildflowers, from February to April; desert shrubs, from late April through May: Daily, 9:00 A.M.– 5:00 P.M.

Encanto Park, 2705 North 15th Avenue. Exotic trees and shrubs—all labeled—collected by the Phoenix Parks Department; a sort of tree "walk," Mexican palms, African sumac, limequats, jasmine, bottle trees, and

Mormon Temple Gardens

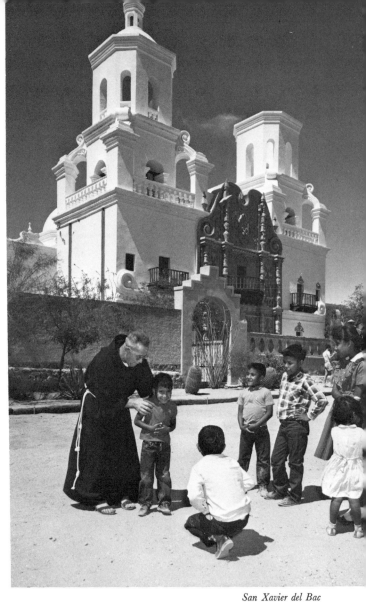

San Xavier del Bac

others, including natives. Daily, sunrise–sunset.
Valley Garden Center, 1809 North 15th Avenue. About 3,000 roses in the rose test center, seasonal flowers, and three demonstration gardens—tropical, low-maintenance, fun. Daily, 8:00 A.M.–5:00 P.M.
The state capitol grounds.
Tropic Garden Zoo, 6232 North 7th Street. It has good tropical trees and shrubs, all labeled. Monday through Saturday, 9:30 A.M.–5:00 P.M. Fee.
While in Phoenix visit the *Japanese Flower Fields on Baseline Road between 36th and 40th Streets.* A color-saturated area.
SUPERIOR: *Boyce Thompson Southwestern Arboretum, 85273.* Though privately owned and endowed, now operated by the University of Arizona as an outdoor laboratory of desert plants. Of the 1,200 acres, 20 acres are an arboretum and open to the public. Among the dry-climate—drought-resistant—plants (10,000 flowering plants, shrubs, trees from all over the world) is a large collection of succulents, as well as cacti; and eucalyptus, palms, oleander, bottlebrush, osteomeles, lysiloma, African sumac, some excellent acacias; fruit

Desert Botanical Garden

Arizona-Sonora Desert Museum

trees such as Natal plum, jujube, guava, etc. Daily, 8:00 A.M.–4:40 P.M. Closed New Year's Day, Independence Day, Labor Day, Veteran's Day, Thanksgiving, and Christmas.

TUCSON: *Arizona-Sonora Desert Museum, Tucson Mountain Park* (14 miles west of Tucson via Route 86—Speedway). Mailing address: Box 5607, Tucson, 85703. Species and varieties of most desert plants native to Arizona, especially to the Sonora Desert region. Special exhibits include a desert demonstration garden, the Haag Memorial Cactus Garden, the Saguaro Ramada, natural history displays with living plants and animals that also can be seen from underground tunnels—revealing their hiding places—and a unique watershed exposition. Daily, 9:00 A.M.–sunset. Fee.

Saguaro National Monument, Tucson Mountain Section (west from Tucson via Speedway Boulevard and Gates Pass Road). The dense forest of saguaros in this 15,500-acre section of the monument (there are two separate sections some distance apart) are the "kings of the cactus world," and, are best seen in this section. Flowering is in May, give or take a few weeks. The monument consists of

four distinct plant communities: the lower desert (saltbrush, etc.), higher desert (saguaros and other cacti), woodland (juniper), and forest (oaks and pines). The July temperatures range from 96° F down to 68° F as one moves upward. Some typical plants are barrel cactus, hedgehog cactus, cholla, paloverde, ocotillo, catclaw, pincushion cactus, acacia, and desert flowers. The arboretum checklist includes nearly a thousand species and varieties. Flowering begins in March, is especially abundant from April to May, with some cacti flowering in August and September. Check in at the visitor center for complete information. Daily.

San Xavier del Bac Mission (9 miles southwest of Tucson via Mission Road). Often called the "white dove of the desert," the mission is not only the loveliest of all similar structures, but has an outstanding mission garden, using with marvelous effect native materials of mesquite and cholla along with figs, lemons, pomegranates, and almonds, and has courtyards redolent with fragrant herbs. Daily; the mission is open from sunrise to sunset and holds regular services.

When visiting Arizona, find time to walk around the

campus of the two universities, *Arizona State University at Tempe* and the *University of Arizona at Tucson*. Both are open during the school terms and are beautifully landscaped with palms, olives, citrus, African sumac, mulberry, pine, and seasonal flowers. Don't overlook the wildflowers in many of the *state parks*, or *Oak Creek Canyon at Sedona*. The *Tumacacori National Monument below Tucson* has a mission garden court. The *Chiricahua National Monument at Dos Cabezas Star Route, Wilcox*, is a sort of island mountain surrounded by an arid "sea" of grassland. The nature trail is vivid with canyon grape, alligator juniper, skunkbush, oak, yucca, pine, agave, cypress, madrone, chokecherry, indigo bush, honeysuckle—even cacti and several hundred more identified plants. Visit *Sharlott Hall Museum Garden in Prescott* and *Lake Havasu City*, an authentically groomed English village "dropped" into the desert.

A desert spring is unbelievably beautiful and many resorts have spectacular flower gardens—which go quickly after the first week of 100°-plus temperatures. But for that short period, as someone once wrote: "The blossoms and rocks [are] lovelier than orchids and gems."

Boyce Thompson Southwestern Arboretum

Arkansas

ARKADELPHIA: *Henderson State College, 100 Henderson Street, 71923.* Wild roses and giant water oaks on the campus.

HOT SPRINGS: *Hot Springs National Park.* Bath House Row is the city's quaintly derisive name for the spa's Grand Promenade, where holly and magnolia edge the landscaped walks, streets, and a pleasant park. The several self-guiding trails start from the visitor center at Reserve Avenue and Central Avenue, and introduce visitors to a wide variety of native Arkansas plants; more than 250 flowering shrubs and plants are listed by the center, together with their blooming period (from April to October). Daily, during the daylight hours.

LITTLE ROCK: *Arkansas Territorial Capitol Restoration, 214 East 3rd Street.* Thirteen restored buildings from the nineteenth century occupy nearly a city block; the flower and herb gardens have regained much of their original appearance. Daily, April through September, 9:30 A.M.–5:00 P.M.; balance of year, 10:00 A.M.–4:30 P.M. Sunday, 1:00 P.M.–5:00 P.M. Closed Easter, Thanks-giving, and Christmas. Fee.

MENA: *Queen Wilhelmina State Park.* The garden of tulips on Rich Mountain—one of the highest in the state, 3,000 feet—was begun as a resort. There are ruins of a castle once allegedly built for Queen Wilhelmina with Dutch funds. The Dutch still provide thousands of tulip bulbs, which can be seen from a scenic drive leading to this tulip-blooming mountaintop. Daily in spring.

PARAGOULD: *Crowleys Ridge State Park.* In the spring the redbud trees and, especially, the dogwood put on a vivid display of color throughout the park's 265 acres. Daily, to sunset.

RUSSELLVILLE: *Ozark-St. Francis National Forests, 72801.* Unusual geologic features provide sheltered areas for a variety of wildflowers, particularly the 50-acre patch of wild azaleas. There is also a good stand of native hardwoods near the Alum Cove Scenic Area, excellent dogwood and redbud, and summer-blooming wildflowers. Daily, to sunset.

Arkansas Territorial Capitol

California

ARCADIA: *Los Angeles State and County Arboretum, 301 North Baldwin Avenue 91006*. Once part of Rancho Santa Anita and, later, the Lucky Baldwin estate, this botanic garden of 127 acres occupies a historic spot. There are several pleasantly old buildings, and 200 peacocks (from a strain imported from India around the turn of the century) roam the grounds near the lagoon, ponds, and waterfalls. While there are many plants from all continents, the special collections include acacia, bottlebrush, eucalyptus, cassia, ficus, holly, juniper, magnolia, oak, and palms. Although the large gardens are laid out to simulate geographic areas, there are also smaller gardens of roses, Biblical plants, annuals, perennials, and a braille garden, as well as demonstration areas for turf and ground covers and demo-gardens for homeowners. The greenhouses, several of which are used for display, have a good collection of orchids and begonias. A number of specialist garden clubs hold their annual shows in the gardens, as does the Orchid Society and the Cactus Society. The arboretum tests and introduces new plants as well as accomplishing research in such problems as smog and insect pests. Each season is prominently represented with plants in bloom. Daily, summer, 8:00 A.M.–5:00 P.M.; winter, 8:30 A.M.–5:00 P.M. Greenhouse: daily, 10:00 A.M.–4:00 P.M. Closed Christmas.

ATHERTON: *Isobrook Palmer Park Foundation, 150 Watkinson, 94025*. An educational center with about 11 acres of gardens.

BERKELEY: *Municipal Rose Garden, Codornices Park, Euclid Avenue and Bayview Place, 94703*. About 4,000 roses; also rhododendrons, native shrubs, and trees. Daily, sunrise–sunset.

Regional Park Botanic Garden, Charles Lee Tilden Regional Park, 94708. The emphasis is largely on native Californian plants: red fir, Santa Lucia fir, Santa Cruz ironwood, red oak, sequoia, redwood, and wildflowers. Special gardens are set aside for alpine, mountain meadow, and dune plants. There are special collections of ceanothus, broad-leaved trees, and conifers. The garden lists 1,500 species and varieties in a 7-acre plot (out of 3,000 acres for the entire park). The best months are April and May. Daily, 10:00 A.M.–5:00 P.M.

University of California Botanic Garden, Centennial Road, 94720. The 25-acre garden is one of the major university

Below, and opposite: *Los Angeles State and County Arboretum*

botanic gardens in the country. The largest area is devoted to a group of native Californian plants and an herb garden. The largest individual garden is that for cacti and succulents, many of which have been imported from South America and South Africa. The southeast Asian, Australasian, and North American economic plant sections are being developed. The rhododendrons are noted for the mild-climate species brought originally from south China. The orchid house is particularly rich in South American orchids from the Andean region, tropical ferns, and economically important plants. All in all, about 12,000 species and varieties are represented, and may best be seen during April and May. Daily, summer, 9:00 A.M.–5:00 P.M.; winter, 9:00 A.M.– 4:00 P.M. At *Russell Tree Farm Bodega Head* and *Sage Hen Creek* are subsidiary gardens for research; qualified individuals can make arrangements with the university's Department of Botany to visit them.

Blake Garden, 70 Rincon Road Kensington 94707, is a 10-acre estate under the direction of the university's Department of Landscape Architecture. It is a superb showplace of good planting design and contains a number of rare plants and a Children's Adventure Garden. It is not a public garden but is open to interested individuals and groups by appointment only. Write to the Superintendent.

BOLINAS: *Bolinas Mesa Garden, Mesa Road.* Outstanding fuchsias. Another horticultural attraction is the *Sharon Home.* Daily, during business hours.

CAPITOLA: *Vetterle and Reinelt Begonia Gardens.* One of the largest nurseries specializing in tuberous begonias under lath. The area and the climate are geographically perfect for these flowering plants. July and August are good months to see the tuberous begonias, later for the delphiniums—the Pacific hybrids so justly famous that were developed at the nursery. Daily, during business hours. Closed Christmas and Easter.

CLAREMONT: *Rancho Santa Ana Botanic Garden, 1500 North College Avenue, 91711.* Although affiliated with the Pomona College graduate program, the garden is privately endowed, and is devoted to the study and exhibition of indigenous plants. More than 1,300 species and varieties of California plants (representing 19 plant communities) are grown on 83 acres of foothill land.

University of California Botanical Garden (Berkeley)

Mendocino Coast Botanical Gardens

Among many plants are: bush anemone, desert willow, manzanitas, wild lilacs, Oregon grape, desert willow, redbud, hawthorn, oaks, maples, pines, cedars, sage, yucca; numerous species of wildflowers in a dune garden; and special places for such flowering plants as columbine, penstemon, mariposa lilies, monkey flowers, cactus, and succulents. There is a garden of native plants for home landscaping; auto roads and nature trails. It is best visited from mid-February to mid-June. Daily, 8:00 A.M.–5:00 P.M.

COSTA MESA: *Orange County Memorial Garden Center, Fair Grounds, 92626.* A Memorial Garden and garden workshops.

DAVIS: *University Arboretum, University of California at Davis, 95616.* Situated along a two-mile strip of the Putah Creek, the 67-acre arboretum has served the students of the university as both a park and a research station. It has 17 plant areas devoted to both native plants and exotics. It contains myrtle and eucalyptus, members of the heath family. The Weier Redwood Grove is there; and native ornamentals, Australian plants, desert shrubs and trees; conifers, Shield's grove

of oaks, a cypress grove, foothill natives (Sierra Nevada and Coast ranges), ground covers, an iris garden, Guadalupe cypress, acacia, and Asian exotics. Heaviest flowering is in the spring. Daily during the school term.

ENCINITAS: *Commercial flower fields* along Highway 5 between Encinitas, Escondido, Leucadia, and up toward La Jolla. Some of America's largest flower growers have extensive fields along this highway or near it. There are large fields of poinsettias, for example.

Quail Botanic Garden, 230 Quail Gardens Drive, 92024. A 26-acre estate oriented toward home gardening, emphasizing subtropical flowering plants and vines and native California plants that have a potential for beauty as well as for commercial value. Features include a shade house and a greenhouse. The 1,000 or so varieties of plants represented are divided into 12 geographical sections among which are wildflowers, puyas, bromeliads, orchard trees, acacias, azaleas, cacti and succulents, and some fine specimen trees. The gardens are well arranged for leisurely walks. March to May are especially good months. Daily, 8:00 A.M.–5:00 P.M.

ESCONDIDO: *Thurman's Hybrids, Old Castle Road.*

Blake Garden

Tropic World, Jesmond Dean Road.
FORT BRAGG: *Mendocino Coast Botanical Gardens, Coast Highway (Route 1), 95437.* This was the retirement project of a landscape nurseryman who converted a peat bog and a rain forest into 47 acres of beautiful gardens, both formal and natural. It contains three thousand hybrid rhododendrons, many plants of heather and wild lilac, fuchsias, azaleas, acres of dahlias (30,000 plants), tulips, tuberous begonias, foxgloves that are majestic in their height, cistus, gladioli, and many others, including a wildflower display. The natural area is carefully landscaped with ornamentals, threaded with several miles of woodland trails and natural settings for ferns, yellow violets, and similar plants. Trout streams, a rain forest, canyons, and seacoast add to the scenic effect. Bulbs bloom around February-March, rhododendrons in April-May, dahlias from mid-July to October—making the summer months very colorful. Daily, 8:30 A.M.–5:00 P.M. in winter; otherwise the closing hour is 6:00 P.M. Closed Thanksgiving, Christmas, and New Year's Day. Fee.
FRESNO: *Roeding Park, West Belmont Avenue and Route 99.*
GRANTS PASS: *Commercial gladiola fields* reach their peak brilliance from late July to early August.
IRVINE: *Irvine Arboretum, University of California, 92664.* Roses, succulents, citrus trees, and orchids on 62 acres. Daily, sunrise to sunset.
LA CANADA: *Descanso Gardens, 1418 Descanso Drive, 91011.* Originally part of the great Rancho San Raphael, and begun as a private 150-acre estate, Descanso Gardens has long been famous for its camellias (100,000 plants representing more than 600 varieties). Roses, of course, have long been a Descanso favorite (600 varieties); as is certainly, the "History of the Rose" garden, where all known, or presently available, roses from Biblical times to the present may be seen. Among the 1,500 plant species and cultivars in the garden are azaleas, cymbidiums, iris, begonias, fuchsias, rhododendrons, daffodils, California natives. There is also a nature trail and a hiking trail. Near the entrance gate is an Oriental pavilion, where tea is served, and, nearby, a Japanese Garden and a Chinese Garden (one of the two in the state or three elsewhere). Colorful flowers may be found the year round, although January through April is favored

by most visitors. Daily, 8:00 A.M.–5:30 P.M. Closed Christmas.

LA VERNE: *Cecil Houdyshel Nurseries, 3rd Street.*

LOMPOC: *A center for many commercial seed and plant growers.* Nearly 2,000 acres of land in the area grow millions of flowering plants that light up the valley floor in a most extraordinary display of color. The carpet of flowers may be seen from miles away, and driving around the fields is a breath-taking experience. Award-winning plants grow side by side with standards and with newly conceived hybrids. Many of the seed nurseries permit visits during the working days, but they must be personally arranged for by each touring party, and considerable courtesy should be exercised.

LONG BEACH: *El Dorado Nature Center, El Dorado Park East, between Spring and Willow Streets.* The nature center is an 80-acre tract, a natural area devoted to establishing an awareness of the interdependence of man and nature. Self-guided tours are offered Saturday and Sunday, 1:00 P.M.–5:00 P.M. Groups may make arrangements in advance (tel. 425-8569) at least two weeks beforehand. Staff naturalists are always available to answer questions.

Rancho Los Alamitos, Palo Verde Avenue. A remarkable home and garden dating back to the Spanish colonial days. The cactus garden, the courtyard of succulents, and the fountain area all have a look of old Spain about them. The arbor, grotto, Friendship Garden, formal terrace, and informal native ornamentals reflect a later but no less colorful period in the history of the home. Wednesday through Sunday, 1:00 P.M.–5:00 P.M. Closed legal holidays.

LOS ANGELES: *Brand Park.* A Memory Garden of trees and shrubs popular in colonial California. Honeysuckle, lilac, olive, pepper trees, palms, and pomegranates. Daily.

Exposition Park, South Figueroa Street. Quite likely one of the world's largest rose gardens, with 16,000 rose bushes, 160 varieties, and 22 All-American rose beds, all within a 7-acre sunken garden. Daily, 8:30 A.M.–sunset.

University of California at Los Angeles Botanical Garden, Hilgard and Le Conte Avenues, 90024. UCLA has operated the garden since 1929 on 8 acres of land, filling them with more than 3,500 species and cultivars, including

Muir Woods National Monument

Native Plant Botanic Garden

Rancho Los Alamitos

many that are horticulturally popular. The collection is composed principally of aloes, acacias, eucalyptus, calistemon, melaleuca, and a well-represented California section. The desert garden and the native plant garden are well worth the visit. Weekdays, 8:00 A.M.–5 P.M.; Saturday and Sunday, 10:00 A.M.–4:00 P.M.. Closed holidays.

A nearby *Japanese Garden*, operated by the university, is open only by appointment on Tuesdays and Wednesdays, but first check in at the university's visitor center. *Orcutt Ranch Park and Garden Center, 23555 Justice Street, Canoga Park*. Grapefruit and oranges on 13 acres, 6 acres of formal gardens, and 5 acres of children's gardens; nature study areas. Daily, to sunset.

Wattles Park, 1824 North Curson Avenue, Hollywood. Fifty acres of a natural area; and the site of a Japanese Garden and teahouse donated by the city of Nagoya.

LUCERNE VALLEY: *Tegelberg Cactus Gardens, South Camp Rock Road*. One of the best cactus and succulent growers, who welcome visitors during business hours on weekdays.

MILL VALLEY: *Edgewood Botanic Garden, 436 Edgewood Avenue, 94941*. The gardens face Mt. Tamalpais and specialize in the display of California woody plants and shrubs, particularly from the Marin County area, although other natives are also exhibited. In addition to rhododendrons and azaleas used for color, a total of 177 different named varieties of plants are listed, of which 59 were introduced to California and 118 are natives. There are excellent specimens of ceanothus, berberis, wild ginger, Western burning bush, mountain dogwood, cypress, madrone and manzanita, ferns, iris, maple, California bay, oaks, pines, Judas tree, mountain mahogany, California nutmeg, as well as wildflowers.

OAKLAND: *Japanese Garden, 666 Bellvue Avenue, 94610*. A very choice selection of plants in a well-landscaped garden strictly designed in the classic Japanese manner. Daily, to sunset.

Lakeside Park Trial and Show Gardens, also at the above address. The Garden Center in the middle of the park is a good place to start most visits. About 45 garden clubs and plant societies make use of the building. The Trial Garden and the Show Garden display many of the ornamentals and flowering plants that are suitable for the Oakland area. Fuchsias, tuberous begonias, dahlias, chrysanthemums, camellias, and rhododendrons are successively featured from February through October and November. Daily, 10:00 A.M.–4:30 P.M.

OAKLAND: *Joseph McInnes Memorial Botanical Gardens, Mills College, Seminary Avenue and MacArthur Boulevard, 94613.* California and Pacific Basin plants. Four acres of charming, well-arranged plantings that are an excellent introduction to some California natives. Daily during the school term.

Native Plant Botanic Garden, Tilden Regional Park. California's largest native plant botanic garden. The 6½ acres, readily expandable as needed in the future, contain 1,500 species that are gathered together in geographic sections. It is possible to take a simulated 1,000-mile botanical hike from the Arizona to the Oregon border, visiting in microcosm plants from the Redwood Section, the Shasta-Cascade, the Sierran Meadows, the Foothills, Santa Lucia, the Sierra Madre Desert, and the Channel Islands. January is a period of many blooms (natives do bloom early!), then blossoms appear monthly in succession through July. Late summer in the botanic garden is a resting period. There are no "keep off the grass" signs; visitors are encouraged, for study puposes, to pinch, clip, crush, and sniff leaves as a legitimate way of learning much about plants. Plants, in this botanic garden, are a renewable resource, but visitors are definitely put on their honor not to exceed propriety.

The Oakland Museum (near the city center). An astonishingly beautiful building arranged in terraces on different levels, each of which is landscaped with trees (16 species), shrubs (27 kinds), ground covers (6 varieties), vines (5 types), and aquatics (6 species). This is sort of miniature urban botanical garden, since all of the plant materials used have proved remarkably resistant to urban pollution. Some of the plants are native Californians, others come from similar climates around the world. Oak, cedar, ironbark, acacia, Natal plum, Mexican orange, myrtle, photinia, sand strawberry, Algerian ivy, etc. Daily, year round; check with the museum for the schedule of hours.

OROVILLE: *Boynton-Stapleton House and Garden, 1681 Bird Street, 95965.* A "Queen Anne" house, now a law office, whose architecture and gardens—largely of

Piedmont Park Cherry Tree Walk

camellias and azaleas—are eye-stoppers. Visitors are shown around daily during the week from about 10:00 A.M. to 4:00 P.M.

Chinese Temple Garden, 1505 Broderick Street, 95965. One of the two Chinese temple gardens in the state. The plants in the courtyard are all of Chinese origin: tallow trees, gingko, persimmon, loquat, Chinese flame trees, dawn redwood, pine, peach, plum, bamboo, and pomelo grapefruit. All have some significance or virtue in the Chinese mythology of gardening. Within the area of the temple are other more usual plants—still definitely Chinese: rhododendrons, ginger, peony, Chinese lily, dwarf pomegranate.

The Lott House, 1067 Montgomery Street, 95965. An old-fashioned landscaped garden. This house, along with the several other Oroville installations, can make up a pleasant afternoon visit to the town.

PALM SPRINGS: *Moorten's Desertland Gardens, 92262.* Joshua trees and saguaro cacti can be pleasantly seen within a smaller area than in the national monument parks. There is also a good collection of desert cacti.

PALOS VERDES PENINSULA: *South Coast Botanic Garden, 26701 Rolling Hills Road, 90274.* The garden, which is relatively new (1961), is built on a trash landfill that was previously a mine for diatomaceous earth used in pottery. Leveled and surfaced with good earth, the area was redeveloped as a useful and ornamental public botanic garden. The youth-oriented practice gardens are particularly noteworthy. The primary collections (2,030 species and varieties) are California natives, legumes especially, and ficus, rose, myrtle, and protea. Part of the ground is devoted to ecological problems such as land erosion (capeweed and South African trailing daisies were developed) or to introducing new plants (*Chrysanthemum frutescens Palos Verdes*), and studying the habits and requirements of native plants— pines and flowering fruit trees. Daily, 8:00 A.M.–5:00 P.M., Standard Time; 8:00 A.M.–5:30 P.M., Daylight Saving Time.

PIEDMONT: *Cherry Tree Walk, Piedmont Park, Highland Avenue, 94611.* A small grove of redwoods, a large old wisteria, a Japanese rock creek with old footbridges, a wooded canyon with foot paths. But the real surprise is the many flowering cherries along a walkway now known

Oakland Museum Gardens

Marin Art and Garden Center

Eddy Arboretum

as the Cherry Tree Walk. The walk and the surrounding grounds are lighted, overhead and from the ground. Ask at the Community Center building about the visiting hours.

PLACERVILLE: *The Institute of Forest Genetics and the Eddy Arboretum, Carson Road, 95667.* Emphasis is on the improvement of Western forest trees, pines, true firs, and other commercially valuable tree crops. The mild climate and the range of elevations make it possible to grow a wide variety of species and hybrids. Research here has profoundly influenced commercial tree culture. Ninety hybrids have been produced, some amazingly fast-growing and frost- and drought-resistant (Monterey pine crossed with knobcone pine). Another cross (Jeffrey pine with Coulter pine) is resistant to the reproduction weevil. And a cross of pitch pine and loblolly pine is used to improve deteriorating forests—not to mention parks and homes as well. There are seed production areas, seed orchards, and reproductive and disease prevention laboratories. Visit the institute in the spring and watch the field work, particularly the pollination processes. See-through bags attached to the boughs are filled with

pollen injected with a hypodermic syringe. The *Eddy Arboretum* within the institute's grounds is a sort of garden of pines from all over the world. Of the 95 species originally planted, 70 survive. Some of the successful hybrids are planted in the arboretum, and some of the freaks as well. The latter show striking abnormalities, some of which have a useful potential. Monday through Friday, 8:00 A.M.–4:30 P.M. Closed legal holidays.

RESEDA: *Abby Garden, 18007 Topham Street, 91335.* A remarkable commercial nursery of cacti and succulents, the largest collection of species in the country, whose owners publish the *Cactus and Succulent Journal.* Open to the public only on Saturdays during business hours.

RIVERSIDE: *University Botanic Gardens, University of California, 92502.* Operated by the School of Biological and Agricultural Sciences, it is a southern campus of the university at Berkeley. The 37-acre gardens are quite new and still in the development stages. Largely, at present, there are only dry-climate plants and Australian species. Daily during the school term.

ROSS: *Marin Art and Garden Center, Sir Francis Drake Boulevard and Laurel Grove Avenue, 94957.* A cooperative

Sea World Japanese Gardens

Chinese Temple Garden

group that operates the center as a garden, an art gallery, and a sales department of art products. The large garden area (8 acres) is almost an arboretum, with some of the special plants and trees preserved from previous owners of the property. Among the memorial trees is a great sequoia, a much-photographed 100-year old magnolia, a dawn redwood, a pleasant Japanese maple near the fountain, an enormous black oak, and a golden locust. Many other specimens will become memorials in time. There is a Memory Garden of miscellaneous plants and an excellent area of rhododendrons and other horticultural plantings. A wisteria walkway—used for orchid displays—is a pleasant place to rest and contemplate the gardens. Check with the center for visiting hours; usually daily, about 9:00 A.M.–5:00 P.M.

ROSSMOOR: *Stanley Dollar Arboretum, Walnut Creek.*

SACRAMENTO: *C. M. Goethe Arboretum, Sacramento State College, 6000 Jay Street, 95819.* Seven acres of California shrubs and trees. Check with the college for visiting hours.

State Capitol grounds, adjacent to the buildings. Thirty-three acres of landscaping, with camellias as a feature and 5,000 other plants—including seasonal displays of tulips, annuals, and other bedding plants. Daily, sunrise–sunset.

SAN DIEGO: *Balboa Park, Laurel Street and Sixth Avenue.* Begun in 1868 and intermittently improved during exposition years, the 1,820-acre park—now one of the largest and best in the country—offers a wide variety of leisure services. Many of the buildings are holdovers from earlier days and provide a Spanish-Moorish-Mayan look among the formal garden areas. There are more than 800 species and cultivars represented, and an unknown total of plants. Gardens: Casa del Rey Moro garden closely resembles its prototype in Ronda, Spain; the Formal Garden is a good example of an English garden planted with a wide variety of cultivars; the Alcazar Garden has walks with arches, fountains, and a planting area patterned after the Alcazar in Seville; the Lily Pond and reflecting pools have lilies, lotus, and accessory water plants; a Desert Garden is being rebuilt to make it one of the most extensive in the country; a Rose Garden, joined with a huge bed of annuals, blooms for ten months out of the year. Camellias line El Prado Drive and the park's other thoroughfares,

Balboa Park

Balboa Park

and fill Camellia Canyon. Floral exhibits are put on almost monthly with fuchsias, begonias, calendulas, zinnias, pansies, marigolds, stocks, petunias, and snapdragons. The permanent collections in the Botanical Building—the park's conservatory—are outstanding, containing over 500 species and cultivars of shade and tropical plants, particularly ferns. The Botanical Building itself is a good example of a conservatory constructed for both glass and lath units, and was formerly an iron railroad station, which was moved to the park and modified for its present use. Exhibits in the building change constantly. Poinsettias, Easter lilies, gloxinias, hydrangeas, cinerarias, tuberous begonias, rubrum lilies, and caladiums and similarly leaved exotics. Most garden clubs and specialist plant societies in the San Diego area plan their shows at the park, either in the Conference Building or the Majorca Room of Casa del Prado; there are 36 shows between January and October. Each weekend, garden clubs rotate as hosts of a garden demonstration and clinic for home gardeners. Balboa Park: daily, sunrise–sunset. Botanical Building: daily except Friday, 10:00 A.M.–4.30 P.M.

Balboa Zoo (officially the San Diego Zoological Gardens) encompasses 128 acres and 5,000 animals, and is planted with rare tropical trees and shrubs—one of the world's finest collections—some of which are used as food for exotic animals. In themselves these plants are worth a great deal of attention from gardeners. The rain forest in the zoo is often a greater attraction than the animals that inhabit it. Frangipani, cup of gold, jacaranda, silk oak, elephant's-foot tree, viper's bugloss, Canary Island palm, rice-paper plant, giant Burmese honeysuckle. Daily, winter, 9:00 A.M.–4:00 P.M.; spring, 9:00 A.M.–5:00 P.M.; summer, 9:00 A.M.–6:00 P.M. Fee.

Rosecroft Begonia Gardens, 510 Silvergate Avenue, Point Loma. An acre and a half of tuberous begonias grown under lath, and exhibited among fountains and waterfalls. The fern collection in the fern glen is remarkably complete and is combined with streptocarpus as well as begonias, azaleas, camellias, and clivias. Bromeliads are well represented, and there are 150 fuchsia cultivars. Daily, 9:00 A.M.–4:00 P.M. Fee.

Sea World, 1720 South Shore Road, 92109. A botanical tour of Sea World will turn up about 115 species of exotic plants on 80 acres of groomed parkland. A lagoon is surrounded with Natal plum hedges and ground covers of trailing African daisies, ivy, and petunias. There are beds of pansies, celosia, and marigolds, as well as Cajeput trees, fountains, and a Japanese village. The most expensive plant is a single palm—*Phoenix reclinata*—valued at $8,000; the entire planting is estimated at $2.5 million dollars. The tidal pools at the marine park feature California marine life in their natural environments. Daily, 10:00 A.M.–dusk. Fee.

SAN FRANCISCO: *Garden Plaza, 555 Market Street.* A major contribution by the Standard Oil Company to urban beautification. The restoration of the Ghiradelli complex is another accomplishment toward making cities livable again.

Strybing Arboretum, 9th Avenue and South Drive, Golden Gate Park, 94122. An arboretum in one of the most interesting and beautiful parks in the world, a former sand barren transformed into a 1,000-acre park of Monterey pines and well-grown flowering ornamentals, of which 40 acres are assigned to the arboretum. The extraordinary range of subtropical and temperate plants is the result of an excellent climate that forms a series of microclimates rarely found outside of Florida and similar places. Alaska cedar flourishes near New Zealand Christmas trees and Campbell's magnolia from the 7,000-foot level of the Himalayas. Over 3,000 species and cultivars are grown, many from such diverse countries as South Africa, New Zealand, Australia, Central America, Mexico, South America, China, Japan, and Malaysia. There are good collections of rhododendrons, echeverias and other succulents, conifers, cotoneasters, crab apples, and one of the world's best groups of magnolias. A Shakespeare Garden, a Garden of Fragrance, demonstration gardens, a nature trail—and the George Washington Bicentennial Grove with its own redwood trail—complete the planting arrangements. The conservatory (John F. Kennedy Drive near Arguello Boulevard) is attractively Victorian and holds the usual collections of tropical plants as well as several large exhibitions throughout the year. The park itself is lush with rhododendrons, azaleas, dogwood, daffodils, camellias, iris, callas, dahlias, hydrangeas, and, in the fall, vast drifts of chrysanthemums. *A Japanese Tea Garden* is near the

San Diego Zoo

Strybing Arboretum

Hearst San Simeon State Historical Monument

arboretum, complete with peaches and plums and cherries, an arched gateway, a giant Buddha, moon-bridges, pools, and, of course, tea services. Allow plenty of time when strolling through the arboretum or the park; this is one of the half dozen American gardens that deserve several days to several weeks to enjoy properly. Arboretum and conservatory: weekdays, 8:00 A.M.–4:30 P.M.; Saturday, Sunday, and holidays, 10:00 A.M.–5:00 P.M. The park, in general, from sunrise to sunset.

SAN GABRIEL: *Fred A. Stewart, Inc., 1212 East Las Tunas, 91778.* One of the largest nurseries in the world devoted to orchid breeding and cut flowers. Thousands of orchids, many of them in bloom each month of the year, including prize cymbidiums, prize cattleyas, prize paphiopedilums, and more.Monday through Saturday, 8:00 A.M.–5 P.M. Sunday, 12:00 noon–5:00 P.M. Closed holidays.

SAN JOSE: *Japanese Friendship Garden, Kelley Park, Senter and Alma Streets.* Some parts of the garden have been copied from the Kor-a-kuen Gardens in Japan for their serenity and beauty. Daily.

Municipal Rose Gardens, Naglee and Dana Avenues. Bush roses on $5\frac{1}{2}$ acres of land, in bloom most of the year. Daily.

Rosicrucian Egyptian Museum and Buddhist Temple (both near Naglee and Park Avenues) have small but colorful gardens.

SAN MARCOS: *Cordon Bleu Farms, 418 Buena Creek Road, 92069.* A commercial nursery specializing in iris.

SAN MARINO: *Huntington Botanical Gardens, 1151 Oxford Road, 91908.* The gardens (85 acres) are part of the 207-acre estate of the Henry E. Huntington Library and Art Gallery. About 9,000 species and cultivars are contained within a well-landscaped area. By far one of of the most extensive cactus gardens covers a special 10-acre section and contains perhaps 25,000 plants. Agaves, aloes, cacti, mesembryanthemums, and other succulents are very well represented. The blooming period is largely during spring (February–April) and summer (May–July), but the South African plants are also colorful during the winter months. An Oriental garden is set within a small ravine. Palm collections and cycad collections are balanced with rhododendrons,

Japanese Tea Garden

azaleas, camellias, and flowering fruit trees. A Shakespeare garden, an herb garden, a rose garden, a cymbidium planting, and specimen trees (deodar cedars, araucarias, etc.) round out the botanic garden. Daily except Monday, 1:00 P.M.–4:30 P.M. Closed during October.

SAN MATEO: *Japanese Garden in Central Park.*

SAN SIMEON: *Hearst San Simeon State Historical Monument, 93452.* Formerly a home built by William Randolph Hearst to house his collections of antiques, and now a state monument with, among other things, 85 acres of pleasant gardens and mile-long pergola of flowering fruit trees. Only guided tours are available at a fixed price (about $3.00 for the garden tour). Tickets are available a day in advance or daily, both on a first-come basis. The best method is to make advance reservations by writing to the Hearst Reservation Office, Department of Parks and Recreation, P.O. Box 2390, Sacramento, California 95811. Five acres of the estate are formal gardens, with pools, fountains, and terraces. Within the arboretum area are acacia, coast live oak, eucalyptus, cypress, and other specimen trees. The rose

garden is pleasantly diversified, containing tree roses (50 cultivars) and bush roses as well as climbing roses. The plant list is not unusual, but it is surprisingly good, with the old familiar ornamentals: camellias, jasmine, fuchsias, succulents, and other subtropicals suitable for lavish display, perhaps as many as 300 varieties. Daily, 8:00 A.M.–3:30 P.M. Closed major holidays. Advance reservations are recommended.

SANTA BARBARA: *Santa Barbara Botanic Garden, 1212 Mission Canyon Road, 93105.* Gardenias, camellias, hibiscus, begonias, orchids, flowering fruit trees, and other plant varieties (about 1,000) on 65 acres, and an instruction greenhouse. The major collections are separated into an informal garden of California natives, with many wildflowers; and a desert plant section (a meadow of golden California poppies, wild strawberries, lupines, sea dahlias, bush poppies, Fremontia, and Douglas iris). Another section of the garden contains only unique plants from the Channel Islands; a boat trip to the islands is a must for naturalists visiting Santa Barbara if only to see the giant coreopsis in April. Throughout the botanic garden are native cypress, wild

Joshua Tree National Monument

lilac, chaparral, oaks, and firs. Nature trails. Daily, except rainy days, 8:00 A.M.–dusk. March and May are the preferred visiting months.

SANTA CRUZ: *Antonelli Brothers Begonia Garden, 2545 Capitola Road.* From June to November huge beds of tuberous begonias bloom under lath. A lathhouse with hanging basket begonias is unusually colorful. Daily, 8:30 A.M.–5:30 P.M.

Shaffer's Tropical Gardens, 1220 41st Avenue, 95060. A fine commercial collection of cymbidiums and phalaenopsis, both orchid groups containing many medal winners and their progeny. The cymbidiums peak in the spring, near St. Valentine's Day, extending through Mother's Day. Daily, during business hours.

SANTA ROSA: *Luther Burbank Memorial Gardens, 2050 Yulupa Street, 95401.* Burbank's home greenhouse and gardens, where he made many of his horticultural contributions. The gardens were renovated as a memorial as recently as 1960 and separated into a cactus and aloe garden. A series of formal gardens and a lathhouse contain many of the more notable Burbank introductions: the "paradox" walnut, prunus "Thundercloud," varieties of agapanthus, amaryllis, tritoma, and Shasta daisies. Daily.

SARATOGA: *Hakone Gardens* contain many plant and architectural memorabilia from the 1915 Japanese exhibit at the San Francisco Pan Pacific Exposition. Daily, 10:00 A.M.–sunset.

Villa Montalvo, Montalvo Road, 95070. The arboretum (175 acres) contains beautifully landscaped formal gardens; statuary and nature trails are an added pleasure. Tuesday through Sunday, 1:30 P.M.–4:30 P.M. Closed holidays.

SARATOGA: *Saratoga Horticultural Foundation, Inc., 20605 Verde Vista Lane, 95070.* A private foundation which opens its 6-acre plantings by appointment only, usually to qualified visitors.

SMITH RIVER: *Lily fields.* Not far from Fort Dick and Crescent City are great fields of Easter lilies grown for commercial markets. The sight of so many lilies and the fragrance is overwhelming.

SOUTH SAN FRANCISCO: *Acres of Orchids, Rod McLellan Company, 1450 El Camino Real, 94080.* The largest and best continuous display of orchids. The

Shaffer's Tropical Gardens

26

conservatory holds hundreds of plants in bloom during each month of the year. In the commercial collection there is a wide range of species, cultivars, and medal-award plants. Cattleyas, cymbidiums, and paphiopedilums are outstanding. Daily, during business hours. Groups may make arrangements with the advertising office.

SUN VALLEY: *Theodore Payne Foundation for Wildflowers and Native Plants, 10459 Tuxford Street.* An active foundation and membership which maintains a 22-acre wildflower and native plant garden. Free lectures and a seed distribution project to perpetuate California's wildflowers. Daily.

TIBURON: *Thomas Howell Botanical Garden.* A profusion of wildflowers in an area noted for them. From April 15 to November 15: daily, 12:00 A.M.–4:00 P.M.

VAN NUYS: *Busch Gardens, 16000 Roscoe Boulevard.* A sort of wonderland of lagoons, forests, gorges, lakes, and waterfalls, all appropriately planted. Daily. Fee.

WASCO: *Commercial rose fields; WASCO Festival of Roses.* Many of the major rose growers are represented in or near Wasco, among them Jackson and Perkins, Conklin, Montebello, and others. Over 2,000 acres of roses, producing half of the rose plants sold each year. Free bus tours of the rose fields are available during the festival period (September). Roses in bloom are a daily sight from May through October. For information and assistance about tours, visit the Wasco Festival of Roses office, *628 E Street, 93280*

WHITTIER: *Rose Hill Memorial Park, 3900 South Workman Mill Road.* A rose garden, with almost 400 varieties and a total of 4,000 bushes, and a Japanese garden. Daily, sunrise–sunset.

Many of the state and national parks in California function partly as arboretums or flowering plant reserves. Some of these parks are easily the equal of any man-made garden; others are frequently far superior to what man might accomplish. All redwood forest parks, for example, are ablaze with dogwood, azaleas, and rhododendrons in the spring, or are mystic cathedrals in the light and shadow of their fern undergrowths. Nearly always there are nature trails, and usually excellent guidebooks or plant catalogs for each park are available at the visitor centers.

Luther Burbank Memorial Gardens

Angeles National Park, Pasadena; Azalea State Reserve, Arcata; Big Basin Redwoods State Park, Pescadero; Cleveland National Forest, Pine Valley; Humboldt Redwoods State Park, Burlington; Inyo National Forest, Mammoth Lakes; Joshua Tree National Monument, Joshua Tree; Kruse State Rhododendron Reserve, Fort Ross; Muir Woods National Monument, Mill Valley; Sequoia and King's Canyon National Parks, Porterville; Shasta-Trinity National Forest, Trinity Lakes; Yosemite National Park, Yosemite Village.

Not to be overlooked are the California missions, most of which contain enchanting gardens and courtyards redolent of the past Spanish colonial period. More often than not, their use of native California plants provides gardeners with concepts and installations or arrangements that may be satisfactorily duplicated in whole by California gardeners, or in part elsewhere.

Mission Dolores, San Francisco; Mission La Purisima, Lompoc; Mission San Antonio de Padua, Jolon; Mission San Carlos Borromeo, Carmel; Mission San Fernando Rey de Espana, San Fernando; Mission San Gabriel, San Gabriel; Mission San Juan Capistrano, San Juan Capistrano; Mission San Luis Rey de Francia, San Luis Rey; Mission San Miguel, San Miguel; Mission Santa Barbara, Santa Barbara; Mission Santa Ines, Solvang.

Yosemite National Park

Acres of Orchids

Colorado

BOULDER: *Andrews Arboretum, Broadway and Marine Streets;* and three other major park displays: *Scott Carpenter Park, Martin Park, Central Park.*
University of Colorado. The museum (Henderson Building) on the campus has an excellent botanical collection. Monday through Saturday, 9:00 A.M.–5:00 P.M. Sunday and holidays, 2:00 P.M.–5:00 P.M.
DENVER: *Denver Botanic Gardens and the Boettcher Memorial Conservatory, 1005 York Street, 80206.* Although part of the arboretum is still under development (as is a Japanese Garden), there is plenty to see in the 20-acre planted area. It contains about 3,000 plants, of which some are natives of Colorado, as well as an herb garden, a waterfall and pool in the memorial garden, an easy-to-care-for garden, and backgrounds of juniper and conifers. Decorative use is made of many annuals. Collections of tropical plants (500) and cacti fill the conservatory. Botanic gardens: daily, during the daylight hours; closed Christmas. Conservatory: Monday through Friday, 9:00 A.M.–5:00 P.M.; Sunday, 10:00 A.M.–5:00 P.M.; closed Christmas.
The botanic gardens also operate a very large tract of land on *Mount Goliath* (about 50 miles from Denver on

Highway 5). The alpine flowering plants, June through August, are very much worth the drive. Check for dates with the information office at the botanic gardens.
Elitch Gardens, 4620 West 38th Avenue. Thirty acres of formal gardens placed within a larger recreation area. May through Labor Day: Daily, noon–midnight. Fee.
Washington Park, South Downing Street and East Louisiana Avenue. Colonial gardens, duplicates of those at Mount Vernon, Virginia. Daily, daylight hours.
GREELEY: *University of Northern Colorado, 11th Avenue, 80631.* On the 243-acre campus of the university are representatives of nearly all the indigenous plants of Colorado. Well arranged for viewing as well as appropriately placed in the landscaping. Winter can be spectacular, but the best plant time is spring through early summer. Daily during the school term.
PUEBLO: *Mineral Palace Park, Main Street.* A garden of roses (4,000) in bloom from about June through September. Daily, to sundown.
Miscellaneous areas: *Great Sand Dunes National Monument,* Alamosa. *Rocky Mountain National Park,* Estes. *Mesa Verde National Park,* Cortez. *Colorado National Monument,* Grand Junction. *Curecanti National Recreation Area,* Montrose.

Denver Botanical Gardens

Connecticut

Rose Garden, Elizabeth Park

BLOOMFIELD: *Connecticut General Life Insurance Company.* An industrial complex that utilized landscaping as an authentic adjunct to its building. Much of the 280 acres was left in its natural state, with only some thinning and grooming. The interior courts of the building make use of shrubs such as holly, azaleas, and roses, of pools and fountains, of bedding plants and, of spring bulbs. An informal garden has masses of chrysanthemums; and a walk is edged with flowering crabs, rhododendrons, azaleas, bayberry, mountain laurel, ferns, and viburnums. Daily, during business hours.

BRISTOL: *Bristol Chrysanthemum Nurseries, 73 Pinehurst Road, 06010.* Acres and acres of field-grown chrysanthemums, blooming from September through October, honored by the town with a Mum Festival in September. Daily, sunrise–sunset.

COS COB: *Montgomery Pinetum and the Greenwich Garden Center, Bible Street, 06807.* The Pinetum's collection of conifers is good, and there are seasonal woodland flower displays, as well as tulips, daffodils, and primulas. The garden center has a greenhouse. Daily, 8:00 A.M.–sunset.

COVENTRY: *Caprilands.* Extensive herb gardens.

DANBURY: *Historical Museum and Art Center.* A colonial garden in back of the museum.

DANIELSON: *Logee's Greenhouses, 55 North Street, 06239.* As complete a selection of begonias, geraniums, and rare plants as may be found in the east. Daily, during business hours.

EASTFORD: *Buell's Greenhouses, Weeks Road.* Extensive commercial collections of African violets, gloxinias, and other gesneriads. Daily during business hours.

EAST HADDAM: *Gillette Castle State Park, 06423.* The whimsey of actor William Gillette, now a Connecticut state park. The areas of formal gardens are actually inside the castle conservatory and just outside, along the patio. Lawns and native shrubs and trees are maintained in an informal setting. From Memorial Day to Columbus Day: daily, 11:00 A.M.–5:00 P.M.

FAIRFIELD: *Greenfield Hill.* A "village" unusually and thoroughly landscaped with a profusion of white and pink dogwood. Now designated as a historic site by the National Park Service. See it about the middle of May, avoiding weekends.

GREENWICH: *Audubon Center, 613 Riversville Road.* A

plant and wildlife sanctuary (430 acres) long noted for its self-guiding trails, flowering plants, and flowering shrubs. Tuesday through Saturday, 9:00 A.M.–5:00 P.M. Closed holidays.

HARTFORD: *Constitution Plaza*. A handsome and modern urban redevelopment, utilizing terraces, trees, and flowering plants to full advantage in the middle of the city.

Rose Garden, Elizabeth Park, Prospect Avenue and Asylum Avenue, 06103. The oldest municipal rose garden in the country. Nearly 1,000 species and cultivars are represented in the 14,000-plant collection including some of the original moss roses, ramblers, and similar old-time favorites as well as the latest tree roses. Blooms peak in mid-June. Daily, sunrise–sunset.

LITCHFIELD: *Litchfield Nature Center*. A wildflower garden within the 4,000-acre White Memorial Foundation nature area. Daily except Monday, 10:00 A.M.–4:30 P.M.

Tapping Reeve House, South Street. An exquisite old-fashioned garden, small but colorful.

White Flower Farms, 06759. The gardens cover nearly 2 acres and are about 20 years old; featuring perennials, bulbs, flowering shrubs, and trees. Commercially the farm specializes in rare plants. April through November: daily, 9:00 A.M.–5:30 P.M.

NEW CANAAN: *Olive W. Lee Memorial Garden, 89 Chichester Road*. A woodland garden sanctuary for native plants and endangered species, planted in drifts among ornamentals from round the world. Azaleas, rhododendrons, daffodils, primulas, ferns, hardy geraniums, hostas, phlox, violets, and even more demanding plants—shortia, arbutus, pyrola, double snow trilliums, and numerous others. About 1,000 species and cultivars (both native and ornamental) have been catalogued.

NEW HAVEN: *Biblical Garden, Yale University Divinity School*. A garden that has a large number of plants mentioned in the Bible. (Incidentally, the Marsh Botanical Garden of the university is no longer open to the public; it is now being used solely for research.)

Edgerton Park, Whitney Avenue. The former Brewster estate, now a city park, ideal for strolling in and observing the 150 types of shrubs established in the gardens. Daily, 10:00 A.M.–sunset.

Constitution Plaza

Pardee Rose Gardens, East Rock Park, Hamden, Amhryn Road and Park Road. Although primarily known for its roses, the park has displays of tulips, daffodils, gladioli, and large beds of annuals (marigold and stock). Among the shrubs and trees are such favorites as azaleas, dogwood, Japanese flame, and flowering fruit trees. The greenhouse exhibits in spring and fall, notably chrysanthemums. June through October: daily.

NEW LONDON: *Connecticut Arboretum, Connecticut College, Williams Street, 06320.* An arboretum of 370 acres, including several nature areas given over to woodlands, swamp, bogs, and a small tidal marsh. The woody plant collection (375 species) is in a semiwild setting of great charm, the paths radiating outward from the arboretum entrance. In spring, shadbush is followed by dogwood, hawthorn, and azalea. In mid-June the laurel walk is a pink glory. Beyond the lake are gums, maples, and oaks, which, in autumn, convert to fiery blazes of color, leaving the evergreens—hemlock, spruce, and holly—as green accents. The wildflower garden displays those plants native to the Northeast and is being constantly added to. A natural area, formerly thickets, has been thinned with herbicides to show off the mountain laurel, dogwood, high-bush berry, gray birch, and red cedar. The arboretum uses this area as a demonstration of the use of selective herbicides instead of nonselective defoliants. The flora of the arboretum has been catalogued and indexed (800 kinds of plants). Associated with the arboretum is the Thames Scientific Center (primarily educational) and the nearby Caroline Black Botanical Garden—a collection of ornamental shrubs and trees and an excellent iris garden. Daily, sunrise–sunset.

NORFOLK: *Campbell Falls State Park.* A natural waterfall, a brook, and a spring glade, the latter massively carpeted with daffodils. Daily.

Tapping Reeve House and Garden

NORWICH: *Mohegan Park Memorial Rose Garden, Rockwell Street and Judd Road.* Memorial pillars of roses, beds of rose bushes, a fountain, and a pagoda and terraces. The garden is part of a larger recreational area. Daily, sunrise–sunset.

STAMFORD: *Bartlett Arboretum, 151 Brookdale Road, 06903.* Now operated by the University of Connecticut. Among the 250 kinds of woody plants (2,000 specimens) grown on the 62 acres are rhododendrons and azaleas, conifers and dwarf conifers, and shrubs and trees known for their colorful leaves (yellow and purple). There is a bog walk, several demonstration gardens, and a wildflower walk (May). Daily, dawn–dusk.

STORRS: *Floricultural Display and Trial Gardens, University of Connecticut, Route 195, 06268.* The gardens are located on a 1½-acre grassy site on the campus and include about 340 feet of perennial borders. The major area is devoted to annuals (about 200 kinds) started each year from seed, either from all-American selections or from unusual types that might have some usefulness. There is a small collection of taxus, and a herb garden (75 species) is being developed. All plants are labeled, giving visitors a good chance to see and evaluate the newer introductions. Best months: from mid-July to mid-September. Daily, sunrise–sunset.

STRATFORD: *Boothe Memorial Park* has curiously Oriental-styled buildings, gardens, and floral displays.

WATERFORD: *Harkness Memorial State Park, 275 Great Neck Road.* Informal and formal gardens surrounding an Italianate mansion. From spring through fall there are always colorful flowers. Exotic plants, rare trees, and boxwood reputed to be over 200 years old complete the planting. Oriental statues are placed in the gardens, and nearby is a large greenhouse. From Memorial Day to Columbus Day: daily, 10:00 A.M.–sunset. Fee.

Harkness Memorial State Park

Delaware

DOVER: *John Dickinson Mansion, Kitts Hummock Road, 19901.* A restored, handsome colonial home with a formal English garden in which thousands of bulbs (varieties known in the 18th century) are planted. Tuesday through Saturday, 10:00 A.M.–5:00 P.M. Sunday 2:00 P.M.–5:00 P.M. Closed Easter, Thanksgiving, and Christmas.

GREENVILLE: *Eleutherian Mills.* The residence of E. I. du Pont, founder of the du Pont company. The mansion is surrounded by excellent gardens. Mr. du Pont's hobby was botany, and his estate was used for his experiments with North American flora. The grounds are open twice a year, from mid-April to mid-June and from October 1 to 31. Arrangements to visit the estate must be made through the Information Office, Hagley Museum, Greenville, Wilmington, Delaware, *19807.* Visitors are taken in a special bus from the museum. Tuesday through Saturday, 9:30 A.M.–5:00 P.M. Sunday, 1:00 P.M.–5:00 P.M.

NEWARK: *University of Delaware, 19711.* A campus arboretum of hollies in many varieties. Daily, during the school year.

ODESSA: *Corbit-Sharp House, Main Street, 19730.* Administered by the Winterthur Museum, the 18th-century home has a spacious formal garden of the period. Tiny evergreen hedges and brick walks border the flower and herb gardens that are constructed in geometric and heart designs. Two great sycamores, 200 years old, rise above the lawn and flowering shrubs. Tulips in the spring and chrysanthemums in the fall are extravagantly displayed. Tuesday through Saturday, 10:00 A.M.–5:00 P.M. Sunday, 2:00 P.M.–5:00 P.M. Closed New Year's Day, Independence Day, and December 24-25. Fee.

WILMINGTON: *Josephine Gardens, Brandywine Park, 18th and Market Streets.* Japanese cherry trees along a formal walkway and a fountain copied after one in the Villa Petruzzi, in Florence. Daily, 10:00 A.M.–4:00 P.M.

Crane Rose Garden, Kirkwood Rose Garden on 11th Street, and *North Brandywine Park.* Daily, sunrise–sunset.

Valley Gardens, Kirk Road. Many spring bulbs, magnolias, dogwood, flowering cherries, flowering crab, Japanese tree lilac, and golden-rain trees. Daily, 9:00 A.M.–sunset.

WINTERTHUR: *Winterthur Gardens, Route 52, 19735.*

Winterthur Gardens Pinetum

Above: *Corbett-Sharp House Garden*   Below: *Winterthur Gardens Museum*

Sixty acres of the former Henry du Pont estate, containing a magnificent woodland garden with azaleas, dogwood, and tulip trees; a quarry arranged to suit primulas and bog plants; heather, viburnum, and rhododendrons; ferns; and wildflowers. The pinetum along an allée includes such specimen trees as metasequoia, Japanese umbrella pine, flowering crab apple, summer magnolia, Japanese maple—all as fine as can be seen anywhere—and other trees not ordinarily found in collections. The Sundial Garden is formal. An enclosed garden has a reflecting pool and shrubs reminiscent of 18th-century France, with flowering plants in pots and small beds. April and May are spectacular with small bulbs in profusion, early rhododendrons and corylopsis, forsythia, bluebells, trout lilies, bloodroot, buddleias, and hostas. The famous Azalea Woods peak during the first half of May, along with dogwood, hybrid rhododendrons, violets, May apples, trillium, hybrid tree peonies, lilacs, beauty-bush, spiraeas. Autumn is lush with colored foliage from ripening fruits (blueberries) and frost-tinted leaves. The visiting days may vary a bit from year to year, and visitors would be wise to check in advance. Spring: mid-April through May; summer: May 30 through September 30; autumn: October 1 through 31. Daily except Monday, 10:00 A.M.–4:00 P.M. (Allow a minimum of 2½ hours to see the garden, and that is relatively fast.) Fee.

Josephine Gardens

Winterthur Gardens

District of Columbia

Bishop's Garden, St. Alban's Cathedral, Mount St. Alban, Wisconsin Avenue, 20016. Against a background of cedar and yew, Glastonbury thorn and old boxwood, this 54-acre garden has charm and distinction and contains a medieval herb garden (complete with herb cookbooks in the gift shop). The special gardens include: the Little Garden, the Garth Garden, the Hortulus Garden, a rose garden, woodland paths, and flower borders of annuals and perennials. Bulbs and chrysanthemums enrich spring and autumn seasons. Monday through Saturday, 8:30 A.M.–4:30 P.M.

Dumbarton Oaks, 1703 32nd Street, N.W., 20007. Within 12 acres there are perennial borders, terrace fountains, hedges of hornbeam, a pebble garden, and a rose garden. An espaliered magnolia is particularly interesting, as are the Japanese maples, deodar cedars, and other trees. Visitors most often come during mid-April and May, to see the herbaceous borders, or in October. But for those primarily interested in garden design and ornamentation any month is delightfully suitable. Daily, 2:00 P.M.–4:00 P.M. Closed from July 1 through Labor Day, and all holidays.

Dumbarton Oaks

Dumbarton Oaks

Dumbarton Oaks:
Opposite: *Pebble Garden*
Left: *Fountain Terrace*
Below: *North Garden*

Kenilworth Aquatic Garden, Anacostia Drive and Ponds Street, N.W., 20250. Collections of water plants, lilies and lotus, water poppy and water hyacinth, and many others, some of them fragrant. About 14 acres are given over to water lilies and lotus, which, on a hot day, should be viewed before noon, since many of the flowers close early because of the heat. The hardy day-blooming lilies (70 varieties among about 2,000 plants) bloom in June. The tropicals (including the night-blooming types) are in full bloom about the end of July. Native plants typical of ponds, marshes, and streams may be seen in natural settings. The progeny of several 2,000-year-old seeds, which were germinated in the garden, are on view near the greenhouses. Another lily worth visiting is the mammoth victoria; its six-foot fan-shaped leaves are capable of holding a man. Daily, 7:30 A.M.–sunset.

U.S. Botanic Garden Conservatory, Maryland Avenue and 1st Street, S.W., 20024. The conservatory has a small outdoor area for border plants and, inside, many of the customary greenhouse exotics, as well as a good collection of orchids and some palms. Seasonal displays utilize bulbs, azaleas, chrysanthemums, and poinsettias at appropriate times of the year. Daily, 9:00 A.M.–4:00 P.M.

U.S. National Arboretum, 28th Street and M Street, N.E., 20250. Many native trees and shrubs serve as a background for the extensive and extremely lovely planting (415 acres and 8,000 species and varieties of plants from all over the world). The Gotelli dwarf conifer collection is one of the finest in the world; the 1,500 specimens are established in areas surfaced with crushed bluestone. Dogwood, black walnut, and Spanish oak serve as plant foils in other areas. There is a naturalistic garden, a "Touch-and-See" nature trail, and a Fern Valley in a wooded ravine of great natural beauty. The Morrison Azalea Garden includes many of the Glenn Dale hybrids that were commercially introduced by the arboretum— and which must be seen, to be fully appreciated, around the first of May, give or take a week. From mid-March to mid-June some plants and shrubs are in bloom. Other interesting specialties: spring bulbs, camellias, rhododendrons, flowering quince and cherries and crab apple, excellent hollies. Staff hybridizers of the arboretum have selected and displayed new and superior forms of pyracantha, crape myrtle, viburnum, and

hibiscus. There is a sound children's program and a vegetable garden associated with it, as well as a youth-oriented garden program. Flower shows are staged on a seasonal—sometimes monthly—basis, and house-plant displays are noteworthy during October and November. The first major show is in late February, when 800 tubbed azaleas are exhibited. The Easter show consists of spring lilies of every kind. November is chrysanthemum time; and Christmas brings all kinds and colors of poinsettias (over 2,000 plants). And of course, orchids are on display at all times—brought from the arboretum's Popular Point Nursery. Ten plant societies hold their own exhibitions at the arboretum from April through mid-October. April through October: Weekdays, 8:00 A.M.–7:00 P.M. Saturday and Sunday, 10:00 A.M.–7:00 P.M. November through March: Weekdays, 8:00 A.M.–5:00 P.M. Saturday and Sunday 10:00 A.M.–5:00 P.M. Closed Christmas.

Other District of Columbia garden areas include:
The flowering cherry trees along the Tidal Basin and in East Potomac Park. In spring the flowering trees are an unforgettable national spectacular. The Chamber of Commerce has information about the flowering dates, which may change a bit from year to year and only last one week.
National Gallery of Art has several garden courts and fountains customarily planted with ferns and flowers.
Rock Creek Park. An area rich with dogwood, redbud, mountain laurel, and carpets of wildflowers in spring.
Shoreham Hotel Gardens, 2500 Calvert Street, N.W. Behind the hotel and open to visitors is the rose display and trial garden, surrounded by informal arrangements of azaleas, yews, and junipers.

Florida

BIG PINE: *Summerland Orchid Gardens, Summerland Key, U.S.1* A tropical garden of 90,000 orchid plants. Daily, 9:00 A.M.–5:00 P.M.

BONITA SPRINGS: *Everglades Wonder Gardens, Highway 41 South.* Collection of authentic Florida animals in an authentic Florida wilderness.

BOYNTON BEACH: *Alberts and Merkel Brothers, Inc., 2210 South Federal Highway.* A nursery of exotic foliage plants, tropical and subtropical flowers, and a good collection of orchids. Daily, during business hours.

CAPE CORAL: *Cape Coral Gardens.* Hanging gardens, lagoons, fountains, and reflecting pools in a tropical setting. About 1,000 varieties of hibiscus, 40,000 roses. Also a number of tourist attractions and entertainment. Daily. Fee.

CLEARWATER: *Eagle's Nest Gardens.* Exotic plants.
Kapok Tree Inn. Views of tropical gardens. Monday through Saturday, 5:00 P.M.–10:00 P.M. Sunday, 12:00 noon–9:00 P.M. Admission fee includes meal.

CORAL GABLES: *Garden of Our Lord, 110 Phoenetia Avenue, 33134.* Flowers, shrubs, and trees that are mentioned in the Bible or that are native to the Holy Land. An outdoor sanctuary. (An adjunct of the St. James Lutheran Evangelical Church.)
Gifford Arboretum, University of Miami, 33134. Two acres of native plants and shrubs. Daily.

CYPRESS GARDENS: *Florida Cypress Gardens, 33880.* The gardens are largely placed around Lake Eloise and are part of a larger tourist complex that is world-famous. Although most of the planting is winter-flowering, there are year-round displays. Azaleas, bougainvillea, cactus, roses, camellias, gardenias, some poinciana trees, and many old tropical favorites, as well as oddities, such as sausage trees and banyans. Daily, sunrise–sunset. Fee.

DANIA: *Flamingo Tropical Gardens.*

DAYTONA BEACH: *Bellevue Biblical Gardens, Bellevue Memorial, 1425 Bellevue Avenue, 32014.* A 1-acre garden whose Biblical plants are arranged in a chronological order as they appear in the Bible or during the life of Christ. Daily.

ESTERO: *Koreshan State Park.* Originally the garden was an orchard of tropical fruits, but the Koreshan brotherhood, established by Cyrus Tweed, filled it with hundreds of trees, shrubs, plants, and ground covers

Opposite: *Mountain Lake Sanctuary.* Below: *Cypress Gardens*

Everglades National Park

Thomas A. Edison Winter Home Botanical Gardens

from many countries of the subtropical and tropical world. Trees: poinciana, jacaranda, chocolate tree, sausage tree, monkey-puzzle tree, eucalyptus, and bamboo. Fruit trees: mangoes, lichees, avocado, guava, and other rare fruits. Daily.

FORT MYERS: *Flamingo Groves Botanic Garden, 3501 South Federal Highway, 33302.* Twelve acres of tropical fruit trees and flowering trees. Some shrubs and vines.

Thomas A. Edison Winter Home Botanical Gardens, McGregor Boulevard, 33901. A 13-acre waterfront park in which Edison planted a labyrinth of plants and shrubs collected from all parts of the tropical world. Among them are ornamental figs, a massive banyan, kapok, palms, sausage trees, and a dynamite tree, and, among the rarer exotics, plumerias and orchid trees. A recent gift to the garden was 4,000 meristem orchids. A Memorial Garden is hedged with bougainvillea. Orchid plants naturalized on trees are found along an avenue of mangoes. Most of Edison's plants ordinarily served some useful purpose; for example, from goldenrod he extracted a sort of rubber for automobile tires, and he used bamboo for the woody slivers in his electric light filaments.

Monday through Saturday, 9:00 A.M.–4:00 P.M. Sunday, 12:30 P.M.–4:30 P.M. Fee.

GAINESVILLE: *Willmot Memorial Gardens, University of Florida, 32601.* Although the gardens are primarily an outdoor laboratory for students in the university's Department of Ornamental Horticulture, they are equally useful to visiting gardeners. There are rare varieties of azaleas and camellias, a collection of junipers and specimen hollies, and an orchid greenhouse. Mid-January through March are the peak flowering seasons. Monday through Friday, 8:00 A.M.–5:00 P.M.

University of Florida Agricultural Experiment Station. Contains experimental plots and greenhouses for citrus, flowering shrubs, perennials, and annuals. The station is responsible for organized research that will lead to the improvement of Florida's widely varied agriculture, processing, and marketing. Daily.

HIALEAH: *Hialeah Park, East 4th Avenue and 25th Street.* A race track with tropical gardens. From mid-January to mid-March: daily, 10:30 A.M.–6:00 P.M.

HOMASSA SPRINGS: *Garden of the Springs.* A winding walk among tropical flowers and shrubs; an orchid

Koreshan State Park

display. There is a nature trail through an area of birds and animals. Daily, 8:30 A.M.–5:30 P.M. Fee.

HOMESTEAD: *Everglades National Park, 33030.* A tremendously large park (1,406,000 acres), not usually thought of as a garden in the strictly classical meaning. But it can be described as one of the greatest botanical gardens of native plants extant, because it involves ecological systems of importance to home gardeners, besides being extraordinarily beautiful. The main entrance is near Florida City. Daily. Free.

Orchid Jungle, 26715 Southwest 157th Avenue, 33030. A hummock forest of 23 acres packed with orchids on the ground and naturalized on the trees. A particularly beautiful massive oncidium practically monopolizes a tree near the lathhouse and greenhouse conservatories. Colorful with many interesting species of orchids. Daily, 8:30 A.M.–5:30 P.M. Closed Thanksgiving and Christmas. Fee.

Redlands Fruit and Spice Park, 24801 Southwest 187th Avenue, 33030. A collection of more than 30 varieties of economic shrubs and trees in a 20-acre park. Fruits, nuts, and primarily spices. Some rare trees, a poison plant grouping, plus a lipstick tree, a sandbox tree, a sausage tree, a candlefruit tree and an ylang-ylang tree. Usually some part of these plants is used for food or medicines, and the garden catalog lists a number of pleasant recipes. Weekdays, 8:00 A.M.–4:30 P.M. Saturday, Sunday, and holidays, 9:00 A.M.–5:00 P.M.

Subtropical Experiment Station (University of Florida), Route 1. Large collection of tropical fruits. This is one of the few places where such fruits can be successfully grown outdoors in the United States. Daily.

IMMOKALEE: *Corkscrew Swamp Sanctuary, Sanctuary Road (Route 846), 33934.* As with the Everglades National Park, this sanctuary is an extraordinary experience. This is Florida as it was before men trampled much of the state, disfiguring the land. Many plants rarely, if ever, seen elsewhere are here in profusion. A guidebook keyed to numbered markers is available for the mile-long boardwalk through the swamp. Daily, 9:00 A.M.–5:00 P.M. Closed major holidays. Fee.

JACKSONVILLE: *Oriental Gardens.*

KEY WEST: *Ernest Hemingway Home, 907 Whitehead Street, 33040.* The grounds are filled with trees and plants from many tropical sections of the world, particularly the Caribbean. Daily, 9:00 A.M.–5:30 P.M. Fee.

Martello Gallery and Museum, South Roosevelt Boulevard. An old fort with a botanical garden planted in the moat. Daily, 9:30 A.M.–5:00 P.M. Fee.

Peggy Mills Garden, 700 Simonton Street. Plants from tropical areas of the world. Patios and orchids, a very good collection. Daily, 9:00 A.M.–5:00 P.M. Fee.

LAKE PLACID: *Plantation Paradise.* Tropical gardens with pineapples. Many caladium-growing fields nearby. Daily, 9:00 A.M.–5:00 P.M. Closed during May.

LAKE WALES: *Masterpiece Gardens.* Five thousand flowering trees and plants are backgrounds for many art pieces. It is the site of the mosaic of Leonardo da Vinci's *Last Supper.* It contains a rose garden, a primeval forest, and a natural Florida jungle; also, birds and animals. Daily, 8:30 A.M.–5:30 P.M. Fee.

Mountain Lake Sanctuary. Designed by Frederick Olmsted for E. W. Bok, the 50-acre estate has hundreds of kinds of native Floridian plants. Many of the trees and shrubs are labeled. There is a beautiful reflection pool near the Bok Tower (carillon recitals), a tree fern grove and a live oak grove, and a nature reserve. Abundant azaleas, native ferns, cycads, osmanthus. Daily, 8:00 A.M.–5:30 P.M.

LEE COUNTY: The area around Fort Myers is the site of many chrysanthemum and gladioli nursery farms. There are 4,00 acres of gladioli (35,000 to 40,000 corms per acre). About 200 million chrysanthemum cuttings are rooted and shipped each year.

LARGO: *Suncoast Botanical Garden, 10410 125th Street, North, 33540.* Subtropical flowering trees and suitable Australian plants; a collection of bromeliads, citrus and eucalyptus trees, hibiscus, holly, magnolia—all on 60 acres (3,000 kinds of plants). Daily, sunrise–sunset.

MARINELAND: *Washington Oaks State Park, State Road A1A.* The most extensive collection of day lilies in Florida, enhanced by camellias, roses, and huge oaks and other native trees. The citrus grove is the oldest in Florida, first planted by the original Spanish owner. Daily.

MELBOURNE: *Florida Institute of Technology, Country Club Road, 32901.* A botanical palm garden (200 species). Daily, during the school term.

MIAMI: *Fairchild Tropical Garden, 10901 Old Cutler*

Vizcaya

Corkscrew Swamp Sanctuary

Fairchild Tropical Garden

Vizcaya

Road, *33156*. A major botanical garden and one of the largest in the country, beautifully landscaped with the world's largest collection of palms (500 species). Important collections of aroids, bromeliads, cycads, ferns, orchids. Most of the famous flowering trees of the tropics can be seen here. Special gardens: Cycad Circle, L. H. Bailey Palm Glade, Montgomery Pinetum, rain forest, rock garden, and rare plant conservatory. There are 2,500 varieties of plants contained within 83 acres. There is so much to see that it is almost imperative to make use of the garden's "tram" system. Daily, 10:00 A.M.–5:00 P.M. Closed Christmas. Fee.

Japanese Garden and Tea House, Watson Island, MacArthur Causeway, 33133. Complete with a circular garden, lagoons, and bridges, a quiet retreat in the classical Japanese style. Many of the hardy Japanese plants have been replaced with mild-climate plants. Circling the garden are 500 trees of 112 varieties. Daily, 9:00 A.M.–6:00 P.M.

Orchidglade, James and Scully, Inc., 2200 N.W. 33rd Avenue, 33142. As lovely a collection of orchids as can be found in North America.

U.S. Plant Introduction Station, 13601 Old Cutler Road, 33158. Two hundred acres of tropical and subtropical plants and shrubs and trees. The station specializes in the evaluation and research of fruits and ornamentals. Monday through Friday, 7:30 A.M.–4:00 P.M. Visitors are required to register.

Vizcaya, 3251 South Miami Avenue. An estate complete with an Italian palace, baroque terracing, and statues; and 10 acres of formal gardens, parterres, a plaza, a secret garden, a tea garden, a theater garden, and a water stairway. Daily, 10:00 A.M.–5:00 P.M. Closed Christmas. Fee.

MIAMI BEACH: *Miami Beach Garden Center and Conservatory, 3000 Garden Center Drive, 33139.* In the conservatory: good collections of orchids and bromeliads, ferns, and other exotics from Central and South America —approximately 5,000 plants (200 varieties), of which 1,500 are permanent. Also, a tropical rain forest with a waterfall and appropriate forest plants. Special displays are put on monthly by the local garden clubs. Along the parkways of Miami Beach, in themselves very colorful gardens, nearly 500,000 annuals are set out

Top: *Redland Fruit and Spice Park*.
Bottom, and opposite: *Ca'd'Zan*

49

yearly in season, foregrounds to an amazing landscaped collection of exotic foliage plants and flowering tropical trees—actually a sort of semiannual color explosion.

NAPLES: *Caribbean Gardens, Fleischman Boulevard and Goodlette Road, 33940.* The gardens were begun by Henry Nehrling and later commercialized by subsequent owners. Fifty acres of pine woods and cyprus hummocks contain Floridian botanicals and subtropical native plants. A greenhouse displays orchids, new ones daily; and a bromeliad house holds a good collection of these plants. The rest of the park, 150 acres, is given over to a zoo. Daily, 9:00 A.M.–5:00 P.M. Fee.

NORTH MIAMI BEACH: *Gardens and Cloisters of the Monastery of St. Bernard, 16711 West Dixie Highway.* A reconstructed Spanish Cistercian monastery (12th century) set in 20 acres of landscaped gardens. There are rare and striking tropical trees, and the patio is particularly colorful with brilliant flowers. Monday through Saturday, 10:00 A.M.–4:00 P.M. Sunday, 12:00 noon–4:00 P.M. Closed Good Friday, Thanksgiving, Christmas, and New Year's Day. Fee.

ORMOND BEACH: *War Memorial Art Gallery and Garden, 78 East Granada Street, 32074.* A 4-acre garden of tropical plants. Other exhibits include displays by local artists. Daily, 2:00 P.M.–5:00 P.M. Closed Christmas and during September.

Parrot Paradise, 298 Division Avenue. A 20-acre garden inhabited by rare birds. Daily, 9:00 A.M.–5:00 P.M. Fee.

PALATKA: *Ravine Gardens State Park, Twigg Street.* Home of the annual azalea festival in March, this is an 85-acre park whose ravines are massed wih azaleas (more than 105,000 of them), making a spectacular display in February. It also has ample camellias, dogwood, and large beds and drifts of annuals (300,000) for summer interest. September through June: daily, 8:00 A.M.–5:00 P.M. Fee.

PALM BEACH: *The Four Arts Garden, Four Arts Plaza, Royal Palm Way, 33480.* Subtropical plants in a decorative setting; also, a formal garden, a Chinese Garden, and the Cluett Memorial Gardens. A choice selection of plants. Daily.

Cluett Memorial Garden, Church of Bethesda-by-the-Sea, South Country Road. Extensive tropical landscaping.

POINT WASHINGTON: *Eden State Park.* Very lovely

Sunken Gardens

Caribbean Gardens

Highland Hammock State Park

gardens in 11 completely landscaped acres. Roses, day lilies, and similar ornamentals among moss-hung oaks. A reflection pool. Daily, 9:00 A.M.–5:00 P.M. Fee.

ST. PETERSBURG: *Sunken Garden, 1825 4th Street, North.* Thousands of azaleas, camellias, gardenias, hibiscus, bougainvillea, and other ornamentals; many annuals. There is an organ-pipe cactus of monumental proportions. All in all, over 5,000 varieties. Daily, 8:00 A.M.-dusk. Fee.

SANLANDO SPRINGS: *Sanlando Gardens.* One of the largest and most extensively planted gardens in Florida. Camellias and azaleas for winter and spring color; day lilies and other tropical plants in summer. Plant nursery. Daily, all year. Fee.

SARASOTA: *Ca' d' Zan, Ringling Museums and Gardens.* A Venetian palace placed in a 68-acre estate, which is filled with unusual ornamental features as backgrounds for two formal gardens (with roses in one); there is also an arboretum of rare plants. Weekdays, 9:00 A.M.–10:00 P.M. Saturday, 9:00 A.M.–5:00 P.M. Sunday, 1:00 A.M.–5:00 P.M. Fee.

Sarasota Jungle Gardens, 3701 Bayshore Road, 33580. A Biblical garden. Bromeliads, cacti, philodendrons, palms, crotons, and other subtropical plants and fruit trees. A tropical rain forest. Many varieties of brilliantly colored hibiscus. Bougainvillea in five colors. The 15 acres also contain a zoo and tropical birds. Daily, 8:00 A.M.–dusk. Fee.

ST. AUGUSTINE: *Gallegos House, 21st St. George Street.* A walled garden.

Salcedo House, 42 St. George Street. A restored garden of the Spanish period.

SEBRING: *Highlands Hammock State Park, 33870.* Native plants. An outstanding nature park with 3,800 acres of dense subtropical jungle; hardwoods, cabbage palms, orchids, bromeliads. Daily.

TALLAHASSEE: *Alfred B. Maclay Gardens State Park, Thomasville Road.* The finest collection of azaleas and camellias in the South—acres of them in massed plantings. Many native trees, including the rare Torreya. The park covers 308 acres. Open during the peak bloom period, from January 1 to April 30: Daylight hours. Fee.

Killearn Gardens State Park. This 306-acre estate contains woodlands, formal gardens, a camellia walk, and a

McKee Jungle Gardens

reflecting pool. Native trees, including Florida's state tree—sabal palm—and specimens of Torreya. Azaleas and mountain laurel form drifts of color near the flowering fruit trees. Daily, 9:00 A.M.–dusk.

TAMPA: *Busch Gardens, 3000 Busch Boulevard.* A park adjacent to the brewery buildings, lavish with seasonal displays of tropical ornamentals and annuals, winding paths, and sparkling lakes. The west garden has about 48 acres with 150,000 tropical trees and shrubs and 100,000 flowers. The balance of the estate, the east section (230 acres), well landscaped, is primarily for wild animals. Tuesday through Saturday, 10:00 A.M.–4:00 P.M. Sunday, 1:00 P.M.–4:00 P.M. Closed holidays.

VERO BEACH: *McKee Jungle Gardens, Route 1, 32960.* Orchids naturalized on trees, royal palms, sausage trees, giant bamboo (Burmese), tree ferns (Australian), and banyans. Also, many tropical birds and animals in a jungle setting: jungle trails and tropical pools of water lilies. An orchid display trail. Some 2,000 species and varieties of plants on 80 acres. Daily, 8:00 A.M.–5:00 P.M. Fee.

WEST PALM BEACH: *Dreher Park, Parker Avenue and West Lakewood Road.* A botanical garden is one of the features.

WINTER HAVEN: *Slocum Water Gardens, 1101 Cypress Garden Road, 33880.* Seven acres of land, of which 5 acres have lakes—155 ponds, pools, and tanks (some under glass). These contain mini-flowers to giants, from 8 inches to 12 inches in diameter. Many are fragrant or open only at night—a sort of "rainbow" of blues. Over 100 varieties of lilies, single and double lotus, and special bog plants are represented. Among the shallow water plants are the blue iris, arrowhead, cattail, canna, arum rush, parrot's-feather, and papyrus, as well as water lettuce, water hyacinths, and water ferns. Mid-March is a peak blooming period for the lilies. Daily.

WINTER PARK: *Kraft Memorial Azalea Gardens.*
Mead Botanical Garden, 930 Camellia Drive, 32789. Native tropical plants, shrubs, and flowers on 55 acres. Orchids, especially cattleyas, are a feature. Daily, 7:00–sunset.

Alfred B. Maclay Gardens State Park

Busch Gardens

Georgia

ATHENS: *Founders Memorial Garden, University of Georgia, School of Environmental Design, 325 Lumpkin Street, 30601.* A group of gardens justly honoring the first American garden club—the Ladies' Garden Club of Athens. The several garden areas are named the Boxwood Garden, the Perennial Garden, the Terrace Garden, and the Living-Memorial Arboretum. Also there are some excellent specimen trees within the $2\frac{1}{2}$-acre spread; for example, double flowering dogwood, dove wood, yellowwood, and others. The university's plant list contains a total of 150 different kinds of plants. Spring and summer are the best visiting periods. Daily, 7:00 A.M.–5:30 P.M.

University of Georgia Botanical Garden, Whitehall Road, 30601. Very young as such gardens go (1969), but its 275 acres have been well designed in a manner that will someday make it a rival of the best botanic gardens in the country. Eventually there will be a nature study area, a natural forest, a bog and swamp, ornamental groundcovers and ornamental shrubs, water plants, and many experimental plots, including a poisonous-medical plant section. At the present time there is a nature trail and many native plants from the Georgia Piedmont area. Daily, daylight hours.

ATLANTA: *Cator Woolford Memorial Garden, Cerebral Palsey Center.* A lovely show-place garden adjacent to the center.

Fernbank Science Center, 156 Heaton Park Drive, N.E., 30307. A natural forest with plants native to the area, located in a 65-acre area still relatively untouched by man. Rare plants such as Oconee-bells, resurrection fern, and others are featured. Trees include white oak, tulip poplar, red maple, mimosa. The center acts as a sort of bridge between man and his environment, using several of the sciences to complete the understanding of the physical world. Monday through Friday, 2:00 P.M.–5:00 P.M. Saturday, 10:00 A.M.–5:00 P.M. Sunday, 2:00 P.M.–5:00 P.M. Closed from November 15 to February 15.

Hurst Park. Huge displays of chrysanthemums in the fall. Summer annuals and magnolias; tulips for earlier blooming. Daily.

Piedmont Park, Piedmont Road, 30309. A formal garden of roses, a rose test plot, a conservatory, and a Bonsai

Opposite: *Fernbank Science Center.* Below: *American Camellia Society Arboretum*

Garden. Daily.

Redmond Thornton House, Atlanta Art Association. An eighteenth-century restoration complete with an authentic flower garden of that era and a kitchen and herb garden. A nice boxwood hedge is set in patterned arrangements.

The Swann House, Atlanta Historical Society, 3099 Andrews Drive, N.W. The society's spacious gardens (and the formal boxwood garden) at the rear of the house are pleasant to visit during spring and early summer. Monday through Friday, 10:00 A.M.–3:30 P.M. Sunday, 1:00 P.M.–3:30 P.M. Closed major holidays and during July.

Atlanta in April is a dogwood festival of considerable fame.

FORT VALLEY: *Massee Lane Camellia Gardens, Route 49, 31076.* These are the interesting, and famous, gardens of the American Camellia Society, one of the 'must-see' gardens for the rare camellias kept in the arboretum (more than 1,000 varieties on 7 acres of land). There is also a test plot and a greenhouse. Flowering is continuous from October to April, but usually peaks in February. Monday through Thursday, 8:30 A.M.–5:00 P.M. Friday and Sunday, 1:00 P.M.–5:00 P.M., only during the flowering season.

NEWMAN: *Dunaway Gardens.* An old-fashioned Southern garden set among an intricate network of natural rock, an arrangement devised to take advantage, by terracing, of the 20-acre rocky terrain. April through September: 9:00 A.M.–sundown.

PINE MOUNTAIN: *Ida Cason Calloway Gardens, Route 27, 31822.* A 2,500-acre recreation area and Southern beauty spot. A sanctuary for native trees and shrubs, lush with ornamentals; quince, crab apples, magnolias. There are 12 lakes and 18 miles of roads through woodlands and landscaped grounds; many "walking" trails. A greenhouse. There are seasonal displays of bedding plants—tuberous begonias, fuchsias, cyclamen—and a permanent display of unique botanicals. Part of the garden ($7\frac{1}{2}$ acres) has been turned into a vegetable garden. April to May flowers: azaleas, wildflowers, dogwood, mountain laurel, hydrangea, rhododendron. Summer is for roses, day lilies, perennials. September flowers: camellias and chrysanthemums. Daily, 8:00 A.M.–sunset. Fee.

Bonaventura Cemetery

SAVANNAH: *Bonaventura Cemetery, 330 Bonaventura Road.* A century-old planting of azaleas, wisteria, dogwood, camellias among moss-covered oaks. Early spring is best. Daily, 8:30 A.M.–6:30 P.M.

Juliette Gordon Low Birthplace, 142 Bull Street. A Regency home whose formal garden is as close as possible to the garden plan of 1870. Rose favorites of the 19th century, myrtle, climbing fig, lilac, verbena, hyacinth, etc. Monday, Thursday through Saturday, 10:00 A.M.–4:00 P.M. Sunday, 2:00 P.M.–4:00 P.M. Closed Thanksgiving, Christmas, and New Year's Day. Fee.

Owen-Thomas House, 124 Abercorn Street. The garden is small, only about 55 by 65 feet. But it contains only those plants known in 1820 or earlier. Tuesday through Saturday, 10:00 A.M.–5:00 P.M. Sunday and Monday 2:00 P.M.–5:00 P.M. Closed legal holidays. Fee.

U.S. Plant Introduction Station, 31405. Basic work is the testing and evaluation of new plants from all parts of the world. Emphasis is on chemurgic crops, but some ornamentals are evaluated as well. Collection of exotic bamboo (25 species of phyllostachys, commonly known as "running bamboo"). Daily, during working hours. Don't overlook the *squares of Savannah.* Walk down Bull

On preceding page
Clock-wise from top right:
New York Botanical Garden, New York, N.Y.
McCullough Mansion Garden, North Bennington, Vermont
Heritage Plantation of Sandwich, Sandwich, Massachusetts
Rockefeller Gardens, Seal Harbor, Maine
Watkins Iris Gardens, Concord, New Hampshire
Swiss Pines Gardens, Malvern, Pennsylvania
Winterthur Gardens, Winterthur, Delaware

Above: *Ida Carson Calloway Gardens*

Street, for example; some of the squares are mini-parks. Forsyth Park Square has 20 acres of landscaped ground, with a fountain, leafy green arcades of oaks, and wild color splashes of azaleas and camellias in season. Daily.

THOMASVILLE: *Rose test gardens, Thomasville Nurseries, 1840 Smith Avenue, 31792.* March and April are excellent months to visit this official test plot of the American Rose Society, which contains 2,500 bushes representing over 400 named varieties. From April 20 to October 20: Monday through Saturday, 8:00 A.M.–12:00 noon; 1:00 P.M.–6:00 P.M. Sunday, 2:00 P.M.– 5:00 P.M.

Garden tours of homes may be arranged through the local Chamber of Commerce any weekday; not on Sunday.

WACROSS: *Okefenokee Swamp Park; north entrance is on Route 177.* Together with the Everglades and Corkscrew parks, Okefenokee forms a triumvirate of botanical interest and delight, to gardeners as well. Gardeners who may be intrigued by the unusual and the rare or exciting will find this Georgia park site extremely satisfying and helpful in getting to know their habitats. The park is largely outside of the swamp itself, although boardwalks extend into it. Daily, 8:00 A.M.–sunset.

Forsyth Park

Hawaii

HAWAII ISLAND

HILO: *Hilo Nursery and Arboretum, 96720.* A state-operated arboretum on 190 acres, part of which is used to raise hardwoods for reforestation projects. The arboretum has 1,000 species of exotic trees and shrubs, such as palms, fruits, and rarer species. Monday through Friday, 7:45 A.M.–4:30 P.M. Closed holidays.

Liliuokalani Gardens, 25 Aupuni Street, 96720. A project of the County of Hawaii Department of Parks and Recreation.

Orchidarium Hawaii, Ltd., 524 Manono Street. The Orchidarium is a half-acre botanical garden used for orchid displays by many commercial nurserymen and hobbyists. Since Hilo is known as the "Orchid Capital" of the world, the Orchidarium is used to promote this concept and to stimulate orchid culture. Natural lava formations make ideal containers for the plants and act as excellent backgrounds for the exhibition plants. Plants from all over the world are always on display, and there is a monthly judging to introduce new and worthwhile species and hybrids. Daily, 9:00 A.M.–5:00 P.M. Fee.

KAUAI ISLAND

HANA: *Haleakola National Park.* A visit here is a "must see," if only just to see the Silverswords. These are plants, members of the sunflower family, that grow nowhere else in the world. Usually they are to be found only in the dry cinders of the crater above 7,000 feet. The silvery, dagger-shaped leaves and the flowers (yellow and reddish purple) on long stems (3 to 8 feet) are unusually beautiful. The Silverswords mature between 7 and 20 years, with 100 to 500 flowers per stem. After flowering, they die. July and August are the flowering months. Stop at the park headquarters for directions to the Silversword loop. Daily.

HANALEI: *Princeville Ranch, Highway 56, 96714.* Started as a nursery for the condominiums, it has been converted into a small park with over 150 varieties of plants.

KALAHEO: *Olu Pua Gardens, Highway 50, 96741.* Formerly a plantation manager's estate, the 12 acres are lush with 3,000 kinds of plants. Many of the plants are unique natives of Kauai; others are plants from many areas of the tropical world. Orchids, fruit trees, shrubs,

Olu Pua Gardens

Pacific Tropical Botanical Garden

Olu Pua Gardens

food plants, and bromeliads. Almost unlimited time is needed to wander through the 8 subgardens into which the plantation is divided. Jungle path (native plants and orchids); Hibiscus Garden; Oriental Garden; Palm Garden; Sunken Garden; Succulent Garden; Blue Garden; Kau Kau Garden (food). Daily, 8:30 A.M.–5:00 P.M.. Fee.

LAHAINA: *Lahaina Orchid Exhibit, Highway 30.* (Next to the Lahaina railroad station). A magnificent exhibit designed and constructed by six Kauai orchid growers. Over 300 varieties of orchids. Daily, 9:30 A.M.–4:30 P.M.

LAWAI: *Pacific Tropical Botanical Garden, 96756.* A young garden (1970) featuring native plants, medicinal plants (and their lore), economic plants, and a collection of hibiscus. A speciality is the propagation of endangered island plants and establishing them within the arboretum. Open by appointment only. Write to P. O. Box 758.

LIHUE: *Haleko Garden, Lihue Shopping Center, 96766.* A botanical garden on the mall surrounding the Haleko shops. The plants are identified. A Buddhist and Christian shrine adds interest.

NAWILIWILI: *Menehune Gardens, Highway 58.* A magnificent Hawaiian Garden made by people who know the area intimately. Although privately owned, visitors are welcomed and permitted to spend as much time as they wish on the estate. Lettered signs among the maze of plants identify the many species grown. Daily, 8:30 A.M.–4:30 P.M. Fee.

POIPU: *Plantation Gardens, 96705* (opposite the Sheraton Kauai Hotel). This garden was formerly known as Moir's and was featured in the book *Great Gardens of America* for its arrangements of cactus and tropical plants, ornamentation, and historic relics. It has one of the largest collections of African aloes; lava rock pools are filled with water lilies and lotus; it contains rare cacti, an extensive collection of frangipani, and lava rock arrangements much as the ancient Hawaiians left them. Tours are conducted by *tutus*—grandmothers—who intimately know the legends of Hawaii and the history of the gardens. Daily, 8:30 A.M.–4:30 P.M. Fee.

Roadside display, Lala Road, near the Community College. An unusual display of bonsai trees and shrubs.

Above: *Moanalua Gardens.* Opposite: *Alice Cooke Spaulding Gardens*

MAUI ISLAND

KULA: *Kula Botanical Garden, Upper Kula Road, 96790.*
Hawaiian herbs and hundreds of flowering plants and
shrubs set within a beautiful landscape of waterfalls and
gravel paths. Daily, 9:00 A.M.–4:00 P.M. Fee.
University of Hawaii Experimental Farm, Copp Road, 96790.
Terraces planted with many species of flowers and
shrubs; a rare collection of African cereus. Daily,
7:00 A.M.–4:00 P.M..
Another university experimental farm is located at
Makawao. A 34-acre tree farm of tropical fruits. Daily,
7:00 A.M.–3:30 P.M.
WAILUKU: *Heritage Gardens, Iao Valley, 96793.* Established as a tribute to the cultural and ethnic groups that
settled Maui. The pavilions and gardens are authentic
in every detail. The Japanese and Filipino gardens are
completed, the Chinese partly so. The Hawaiian, Early
American, and Portuguese areas are in the planning
state. Daily.

OAHU ISLAND

HONOLULU: *Alice Cooke Spaulding Gardens, 2411 Makiki
Heights Drive, 96822.* The gardens and the home of
Mrs. Spaulding are now part of the Academy of Fine
Arts complex, whose main buildings are at 900 South
Beretania Street. The gardens in themselves are notable
for the exquisite balance between Oriental and Occi-
dental landscaping and their horticultural plants. There
are several garden courts: the Oriental Court, which is
reminiscent of old Peking; the Hawaiian Garden, which
adjoins the Café Lanai; and the Terrace Gardens, the
Rabbit Garden, and the Orchid Garden—all of which
are excellent arrangements of orthodox plants and
exotic tropicals. The catalog lists 150 varieties of plants.
Tuesday through Sunday, 1:00 P.M.–4:30 P.M. Fee.
Bishop Museum. A living exhibition of plants useful to
Pacific people.
Byodo-In Temple and Gardens.
Harold L. Lyon Arboretum, 3860 Manoa Road, 96722. A

University of Hawaii Japanese Gardens

large arboretum (24 acres) primarily for the study of reforestation and tropical botanical research and instruction, operated by the University of Hawaii. It is open by appointment only to professionals in those fields or in related areas of pharmacology, medicine, and phytochemistry. It is best to make an application by letter well in advance of any contemplated visit. The arboretum is not open to the general public.

Honolulu Botanic Gardens is a complex of six city- and county-owned botanical sites on the island of Oahu.

Foster Botanic Gardens, 50 North Vineyard Boulevard, 96817. Aroids, orchids, and palms in profusion—2,600 species and varieties of plants on 17 acres and in a greenhouse display area. The oldest specimens in the gardens go back to 1850, when the gardens were privately owned. Gardeners should plan to spend the better part of a day here. Daily, 9:00 A.M.–4:30 P.M. Closed Christmas and New Year's Day.

Kawainui Aquatic Gardens, a fresh-water swamp at Kailua.

Koko Head Crater Botanic Garden. A 150-acre dry-land area in the eastern part of the island.

Loikalo Botanic Garden. A special Hawaiian ethnobotanical collection on 2 acres.

Sandy Beach Botanical Garden, adjacent to Koko Head Crater. 30 acres of tropical strand plants.

Wahiawa Botanic Garden, 1396 California Avenue, 96786.

About 30 acres of endemic plants, including palms, ornamental trees, aroids (1,500 species and varieties). Daily, 9:00 A.M.–4:00 P.M.

Waipahu Garden. Under design but not yet started. A 30-acre project to be devoted to Philippine plants.

Kapiolani Hibiscus Garden, 3620 Leahi Avenue. Two acres of hibiscus, consisting of 58 species and 350 varieties.

University of Hawaii, 2444 Dole Street, 96822. More than 560 kinds of plants and trees were used in landscaping the university campus, making it, for all practical purposes, a botanical garden. A campus guide to all of the plants is available. Tropicals are well represented, as are some subtropicals from similar areas within the continental United States. In the East-West Center complex there is a Japanese Garden with a three-level waterfall, pagoda, lanterns, colorful carp, and well-placed trees and shrubs. Daily during the school term.

Don't overlook these national parks, for their natural beauty, landscape areas, and gardens (both wild and somewhat cultivated):

HAWAII: *City of Refuge, Akaka Falls, Kilauea, Wailoa River.* MOLOKAI: *Palaau.* KAUAI: *Fern Grotto, Wailua River Reserve.* MAUI: *Iao Valley, Kaumahina, Waianapanapa.* OAHU: *Iolani Palace Gardens, Keaiwa Heiau. Diamond Head.*

Idaho

BOISE: *Ann Morrison Memorial Park, American Boulevard.* A fountain, a reflecting pool, and formal gardens reached by a tree-lined mall. The circular garden of roses is near the fountain and is enhanced by the colorful beds of annuals. Lighted at night. Daily, 8:00 A.M.–11:00 P.M. *Howard Platt Gardens, Union Pacific Depot grounds, 1633 South Capitol Boulevard.* The gardens overlook the city and are pleasant to visit in the evening. Daily. *Municipal Rose Garden, Julia Davis Park, US 30.* The park (about 45 acres) is next to the art museum, and peak bloom can be expected from June to September. Many trees. Daily, 8:00 A.M.–11:00 P.M.

CALDWELL: *Municipal Rose Garden.* A large experimental plot for testing and evaluating roses. Daily.

IDAHO CITY: *Rose Gardens, Luby Park.* There are 5,000 rose bushes in the garden.

LEWISTON: *Memorial Park.* Excellent flowering crabs backed up with dogwood, tulip trees, redbud, flowering plums, and evergreens. There is an official rose test garden with many hundreds of rose bushes to which at least 60 new varieties are added annually. May is the season for the flowering crab apples; somewhat later for roses. Daily.

MOSCOW: *Charles Huston Shattuck Arboretum, College of Forestry, University of Idaho.* The arboretum has 200 species of trees, largely natives of the northern Rocky Mountains, and appropriate woody shrubs. About 7 acres. Daily.

NAMPA: *Lakeview Park, US 30.* Some 70 acres of recreational facilities into which gardens are arranged.

POCATELLO: *Rotary Rose Garden, Ross Park.* All in all some 2,000 roses, among which are many varieties of teas, floribundas, climbers. June through October offers the best flowering period. Daily.

Lake Coeur d'Alene

Idaho is a difficult state, among several in the country, to visit solely for the purpose of seeing the city gardens and horticultural displays. There are just not that many of them, and none in the classical traditions of the great Eastern or Southern, or even Western, gardens. But the state is highly recommended in spring as having many of the best wildflowers spread over hundreds of thousands of acres in state and national parks. *The Crater of the Moon*

National Park, for instance, offers such a treat. A barren sort of land that is alive in spring with color from a wide variety of plants (more than 200 species), it also contains such shrubs as sagebrush, bitterbush, rabbitbush, mock orange, dwarf buckwheat, and monkey flowers. In this floral manner, Idaho manages to be as picturesque as, and perhaps even better than, many similar Western states.

Illinois

ARCOLA: *Rockome Gardens, Route 2, 61910.* Unusual arrangements of natural rocks in arches, borders, buildings, and fences, and other curious designs, all embedded in cement as an adjunct to flowering plants. Roses and annuals, pools and shaded walks, several formal gardens, a large informal planting, an herb garden, a mission cactus garden, and lily ponds. All of this is set in a sort of Amish wonderland. Early spring to late fall: daily. Fee.

AURORA: *Phillips Park, Parker Avenue and Hille Avenue.* A sunken garden and a tropical garden near a recreation area. April through October: daily, 10:00 A.M.–11:00 P.M. Fee.

CARBONDALE: *Southern Illinois University Outdoor Laboratory, 62901.* A university arboretum which, in addition to other plants, is an official holly arboretum.

CHICAGO: *Douglas Park, south of Ogden Avenue and east of Sacramento Boulevard.* Formal gardens of annuals and a water-lily basin. The annuals are placed in 26 beds; total planting, about 18,000. Of the 60 water lilies, 20 bloom at night. Daily, sunrise–sunset.

Garfield Park Conservatory, 300 North Central Park Boulevard, 60624. The conservatory, of great horticultural interest, is one of the finest in the world, comprising 4 acres of glass and 5,000 kinds of plants. Outdoors, on 16 acres of park land, there are formal bedding gardens, a Garden for the Blind, and two pools for water lilies. The conservatory collections are well chosen for their beauty and variety, and are very extensive. There are sections for palms (125 kinds); for ferns (175 kinds); aroids, cacti, and succulents (400 kinds); economic plants (192 species); and two display houses, each one capable of holding more than 25,000 plants, and featuring four major month-long displays each year—an azalea show in February, an Easter show, a chrysanthemum show in November, and a Christmas show. (The Lincoln Park Conservatory also duplicates these displays). Daily, between seasons, 9:00 A.M.–5:00 P.M.; during the conservatory displays, 9:00 A.M.–9:00 P.M.

Grant Park, between Randolph Street and 14th Boulevard. The Court of the Presidents is decorated with 20,000 annuals each spring and summer, and is a favorite subject for city photographers and as an outdoor lunching area for workers from the Chicago Loop. The Rose Garden,

Allerton House

Above: *Morton Arboretum.* Top: *Rockome Gardens*

a very large one, with 8,000 plants (260 varieties), is laid out in alternating panels of lawns and rosebeds. Daily.

Humboldt Park, west of Sacramento Boulevard, north of Division Street. A circular sunken garden of grass and colorful annuals set in alternate patterns. Daily.

Jackson Park Perennial Garden, 59th Street and Stony Island Avenue. A circle of lawns bordered by a dry wall garden; 15 beds and elaborate floral plantings from April to fall. Many spring bulbs, perennials, and annuals. An Oriental Garden. Daily.

Lincoln Park Conservatory, 2400 North Stockton Drive, 60614. The outdoor gardens (6 acres) contain a Grandmother's Garden—3 acres of old-time annuals and perennials (about 40,000 plants) and a rock garden (perennials, shrubs, trees). The conservatory (5 glass buildings, 3 acres of glass) is divided between a palm house, a fernery, a tropical house with rare orchids and excellent hybrids, and seasonal displays timed to coincide with those at the Garfield Park Conservatory. Daily, 9:00 A.M.–5:00 P.M.; during displays, 9:00 A.M.–9:00 P.M.

Parquette Park, Rose Garden and Trial Garden, 67th and Kedzie Avenue. If not the largest rose garden, it is very close to it: 40,000 roses bushes (80 varieties) and plenty of old-fashioned roses (500 plants, 85 varieties). The Trial Garden is largely for annuals and perennials. Nearby is a section for cacti, succulents, herbs, and some elegant topiary work. Daily, to sunset.

Rainbow Park, between 77th and 78th Streets and the lake front. A perennial garden featuring 8 large beds of Shirley poppies, dahlias, and other appropriate plants for a spring to fall display. Daily, to sunset.

Washington Park Formal Gardens, Cottage Grove Avenue and 55th Street. Huge plantings of popular bedding annuals in geometric arrangements. Also, such colored foliage plants as coleus, alternanthera, and others. Daily, to sunset.

(Note: All of the above parks are operated by the *Chicago Park District.* Information about the gardens and displays, the plants, peak seasons, and group tours can be secured from the headquarters Information Office, 426 East McFetridge Drive, Chicago 60605.)

DECATUR: *Scoville Gardens Park.* An Oriental Garden. June through August: daily except Monday.

Morton Arboretum

ELGIN: *Trout Park, Dundee Avenue.* A botanical garden.
EVANSTON: *Ladd Arboretum, McCormick Boulevard and Emerson Street.* An International Friendship Garden and a cherry-tree lane. Daily.

Merrick Park Rose Garden, Lake Street and Oak Street. Pleasantly landscaped gardens with roses as the feature. Daily.

Shakespeare Garden, Northwestern University Campus, Sheridan Road. Historically correct plants of the Shakespearean era in a beautifully designed setting. The garden, surrounded by a hawthorn hedge, contains many herbs, annuals, and perennials known to Shakespeare—and which can be grown in Illinois. Pleasant garden walks. Daily during the school terms.

FREEPORT: *Stephenson County Historical Museum, 1440 South Carroll Avenue.* An arboretum on part of the museum grounds. Friday through Sunday, 1:30 P.M.–5:00 P.M.

GLENCOE: *Chicago Botanical Garden, 775 Dundee Road, 60022.* Operated by the Chicago Horticultural Society (116 South Michigan Drive, Chicago 60603). There is still a good deal of work and planning before the garden officially opens. At this time the 300 acres (60 acres of lakes and 7 islands) have a home-landscaping center and a series of demonstration gardens suitable for Chicago homes. Monday through Friday. 8:00 A.M.– 4:30 P.M.

KANKAKEE: *Gladioli fields, Route 1.* One of the great commercial centers for growing cut gladioli flowers. Over 150,000 flower stalks are harvested between summer and fall.

LISLE: *Morton Arboretum, Route 53, 60532.* A good and very complete collection of woody plants, particularly their hybrids and cultivars capable of surviving the Illinois climate. It is justly famous for its flowering crab apples and lilacs (from April to mid-May flowering), as well as for its groundcovers and nature trails. An old-fashioned rose garden contains over 250 varieties of old favorites. The scheduled education program involves hedge and street trees for urban use, a prairie restoration project (25 acres and 140 species) and a landscape demonstration. Research greenhouse and laboratories undertake problems of growth and maintenance of ornamental plants. On the 1,500 acres there are 30 miles of "walking" trails and 4,800 identified trees, shrubs, and

67

plants. Since there are miles of woodlands, a car may be needed. May through October: daily, 8:00 A.M.–7:00 P.M. November through April: daily, 8:00 A.M.–5:00 P.M. Fee only for automobiles.

LOMBARD: *Lilacia Park.* A unique collection of lilacs (300 varieties) and tulips (100 varieties). Daily. Fee only during the special lilac or tulip shows.

MARION: *Schafle's Azalea Gardens, 503 East Boulevard.* An outstanding collection of azaleas on a private estate, now open to the public. Well landscaped with high shade trees (hollies, flowering crab apples, Japanese cherries), and backed with forsythia and japonica hedges. Flowering begins in mid-March with bulbs; azaleas in late April and May.

MONTICELLO: *Robert Allerton Park.* A private home and estate now owned and operated by the University of Illinois as an example of classical landscaping. A Sunken Garden, a Formal Garden, and a Lost Garden. Daily, after 10:00 A.M. except during hazardous weather in winter.

OAK PARK: *Oak Park Conservatory, Oak Park, 621 Garfield.*

PEORIA: *Glen Oak Park Conservatory and Rose Garden, Prospect Avenue and McClure Avenue.* The garden adjoins the conservatory and is formal in design and backed with a landscape of shrubbery. Some 2,000 rose bushes (80 varieties) surrounded with beds of annuals and perennials. Daily, all year.

ROCKFORD: *Sunken Gardens, Sinnissippi Park, 1300 North 2nd Street.* Flowering crab apples from May to early June; roses from June to October. Many beds of annuals and perennials bordered with hedges and trees. A lagoon and a greenhouse. Daily, 9:00 A.M.–4:00 P.M.

ST. CHARLES: *Grangemead Lodge.* A wildflower sanctuary.

SPRINGFIELD: *Abraham Lincoln Memorial Garden, 2301 East Lake Drive, 62707.* The garden covers 77 acres, featuring prairie flowers and meadow plants—wild anemones, hepatica, and other spring flowers of Lincoln's time—backed with redbud, shadbush, dogwood, crab apple, wild plums, and maples. The hickory forests have nature trails. The area planting is similar in type to that which Lincoln knew. Daily, to sunset.

Washington Park and the Thomas Rees Memorial Carillon,

Opposite: *Garfield Park Conservatory*. Above: *Lincoln Park*. Below: *Lincoln Park Rock Garden*

South MacArthur Boulevard and West Fayette Avenue. Surrounding the carillon—on which concerts are played in summer—are large trees and a lagoon; nearby there is a domed conservatory and a greenhouse for park floral displays. There are four seasonal gardens for continuous flowering: the informal Rose Garden (5,000 plants), the Dahlia Garden (1,000), the Chrysanthemum Garden (2,000 plants), and the Iris Garden. Daily.

WAUKEGAN: *Illinois Beach State Park.* The park contains 1,651 acres of sand ridges covered with scrubby black oak, rare Waukegan juniper, and many rare and unusual plants. June through September: prairie wild flowers—shooting star, prairie phlox, etc. Then prickly pears and sunflowers, asters and gentians in fall, a natural feature is the trailing juniper and bearberry.

All year, daily, except in hazardous weather.

WHEATON: *Cantigny War Memorial and Gardens, 15115 Winfield Road.*
An extensively landscaped group of flower gardens (10 acres) and a home-demonstration planting. Daily, summer, 9:00 A.M.–5:00 P.M.; winter, 10:00 A.M.–4:00 P.M.

WILMETTE: *Bahā'i Temple Gardens, 112 Linden.* Nine formal gardens surrounding a nine-sided temple and extending down to the lake shore. Tulips, hyacinths, and iris in spring; geraniums and annuals in May and June; roses from June through the summer. Background plantings of cydonia, flowering crab apples, and lilacs. Daily, 10:30 A.M.–4:30 P.M. From May to October, the gardens open at 10:00 A.M.

Indiana

EVANSVILLE: *University of Evansville, 1800 Lincoln Avenue.* Well landscaped. Daily during the school term.
FORT WAYNE: *Foster Park.* An excellent iris collection surrounded with peonies and lilacs.
Jaenicke Park, Greenwood Avenue. Ten landscaped and terraced acres; tulips and other bedding flowers.
Lakeside Rose Garden, 1500 Lake Avenue. Old and new favorites, 7,000 plants and 200 varieties. Also, a rose test garden. Daily, to 11:00 P.M.
Municipal Rose Garden.
HUNTINGTON: *Huntington College Botanical Garden and Arboretum, College Avenue, 46750.* Educational and research activities; 632 species and varieties on 40 acres of land. Trees, shrubs, medicinal plants, and laboratories. April through October: daily except Friday, 8:00 A.M.–5:00 P.M.
Memorial Park. A sunken garden.
INDIANAPOLIS: *Butler Botanical Garden, Butler University, 4600 Sunset Avenue, 46200.* Popularly known as the Holcomb Botanical Garden, or merely as the Holcomb Garden, in reference to John Irving Holcomb, a university benefactor. Twenty acres have been set aside

by the university for the study of living plants and the cultivation of rare species; some emphasis is placed on plant breeding. There are 600 trees in the wooded area, balanced by many flowering shrubs and plants. Daffodils (100,000) and crab apples; lilacs in variety; peonies, poppies, gladioli, rhododendron, and holly; annuals and perennials. Daily, sunrise–sunset.
Garfield Park, 2400 Shelby Street. A 128-acre park that has a sunken garden of annuals especially good during July and August. A conservatory with a permanent display of tropical, semitropical, and arid plants as well as three major displays each year: Easter display, November chrysanthemums, Christmas show and poinsettias. Daily, 7:00 A.M.–10:00 P.M.
George Washington Park, 3120 East 30th Street (near Garfield Park). A Japanese Garden.
Hillsdale Rose Garden, 7845 Johnson Road, 46250. Largest in the Midwest. Containing roses in 150 varieties—20,000 plants. A rose festival in early summer is attended by thousands of people.
LAFAYETTE: *Happy Hollow Rose Garden.*
Jerry E. Clegg Botanical Garden, 1854 North 400th Street,

Butler Botanical Garden

The Labyrinth

Butler Botanical Garden

East, 47905. A woodland arboretum in an area of 14 acres, with 300 kinds of plants catalogued. White oaks, dogwood, maples, and spring daffodils along the trails. The wildflower season is from mid-April to about mid-May, with plants such as Japanese anemone and amaryllis. Daily, 10:00 A.M.–sunset.

MICHIGAN CITY: *International Friendship Gardens, Pottawattomie Park, Route 12, 46360.* It features the gardens of many nations in both style and flowers. There is a continuous display of flowers from spring through summer—some 50,000 plants with representatives from 500 varieties. Tulips, roses, delphinium, phlox, and other bedding perennials. Special gardens: an English Garden, a Dutch Garden, a Polish Garden, and a Persian Rose Garden; also Italian, Indian, Asian, and German gardens—all of these nations are represented with plants that are most typical of each country. Many exhibition and festival dates. May through October: daily, 9:00 A.M.–sunset. Fee.

Don't miss *Dunes State Park* nearby on route 49N. Although this is not a classical garden in any sense of the word, it has a most unusual number of rare plants, including cacti, not found elsewhere, all growing on and around blazingly white sand dunes.

MUNCIE: *Christy Woods, Ball State University, Riverside Avenue and University Avenue, 47306.* About 100 kinds of native trees and shrubs and about 110 kinds of herbaceous plants in a woodland arboretum. Three-quarters of the area is wooded, the balance arranged in formal gardens, nurseries, greenhouses, and a bog area. Under cultivation are chrysanthemums, iris, peonies, and orchids. April and May are the best months for wildflowers and spring displays, October and November for chrysanthemums. Weekdays, 7:30 A.M.–5:00 P.M. Saturday, 8:00 A.M.–4:00 P.M. Sunday, 2:00 P.M.–4:00 P.M.

NEW HARMONY: *The Labyrinth.* Amur River privet hedges with puzzling paths and deadends, one path leading to a roofless church. Golden rain trees imported from the Orient (blossoming in mid-June). Daily, daylight hours.

Paul Tillich Park and Rappite gardens (near the Labyrinth). Contain only flowering plants known in the mid-nineteenth century.

Hillsdale Rose Garden

Garfield Park Conservatory

ORLEANS: *The Dogwood Capitol of Indiana.* So authorized by the state governor, where a great variety of dogwood has been planted.

RICHMOND: *E. G. Hill Memorial Rose Garden, Glen Miller Park, East Main Street.* About 73 varieties of roses, near a recreation area. Daily, 6:00 A.M.–11:00 P.M.

Hays Regional Arboretum, 801 Elks Road, 47374. A woodland arboretum with a nature education program—a sort of outdoor classroom. A beech-maple forest, tulip trees, ash, oaks, and other natives (147 species spread over 300 acres). A Fern Garden, a Children's Garden. From mid-March to mid-November: Tuesday through Saturday, 10:00 A.M.–4:00 P.M. Sunday, 12:00 noon–5:00 P.M. From mid-November to mid-March: daily, weather permitting, 1:00 P.M.–4:00 P.M.

SOUTH BEND: *Potawatomie Park, 1800 Mishawaka Avenue.* Two conservatories, with basic collections and several display periods. From June 1 to Labor Day: daily, 1:00 P.M.–8:00 P.M. Fee.

WABASH: *Honeywell Gardens, Route 15, 46992.* Children's and adult programs and cultural events. Formal gardens, a rose garden, a rock garden, and an evergreen garden. The arboretum has native Indiana trees, largely hardwoods, and a research area. Of the 25 acres open to the public, 9 are planted in gardens, the balance left as a wild garden or nature area. Rose Sunday in June is the highlight of the year, when many visitors come to see 1,000 roses in full bloom. May through November: Weekdays, 8:00 A.M.–7:00 P.M. Saturday and Sunday, 11:00 A.M.–7:00 P.M.

Butler Botanical Garden

Iowa

AMANA: *Old World Gardens.* Although the town is primarily known for its many artisans and craftsmen, it is one of the very few places left in the United States where Old World gardens may be found clustered about the quaint brick cottages.

AMES: *Horticultural Gardens, Iowa State University, 50010.* The gardens are essentially a teaching laboratory, but one with great interest to gardeners. About 2 acres are under cultivation, with plans to expand as necessary. Most of the annuals suited to the area are grown; and a few uncommon ones as well. The gardens are strongest in roses (about 500 varieties on exhibition); and a superb rose breeding program since 1900 and earlier. The university released seven new roses in 1972, and has been in the All-American Rose Selection Program since its inception. The gardens also have exceptional collections of peonies, iris, hemerocallis, and geraniums (having previously introduced 8 new geraniums); and a good group of heliotropes. The best time to visit is from early May until late September. Daily, sunrise to sunset.

ATLANTIC: *Frank Chapman Memorial Park.* A 5-acre wildflower preserve, charming in the spring.

BURLINGTON: *Crapo and Dankwardt Parks, Great River Road, 52601.* A portion of these parks is given over to formal gardens and an arboretum in which every tree native to the region may be seen. Daily, 5:00 A.M.–11:00 P.M.

CEDAR FALLS: *University of Northern Iowa Gardens, 50613.* Formerly the Iowa State Teachers College Gardens. Fifteen acres of native and cultivated trees, and a section for prairie wildflowers. A display greenhouse. Daily.

CLINTON: *Bickelhaupt Arboretum, 340 South 14th Street, 52732.* Another young arboretum in the developing stage. On the 10 acres are young trees such as Lombardy poplar, gingko, blobe locust, dawn redwood, crab apple, Kentucky coffee tree, cedar, and conifers. When completed, the arboretum will have 422 kinds of plants from 103 genera, exclusive of ground covers, some vines, and dwarf plants. Daily, sunrise–sunset.

DAVENPORT: *Municipal Rose Garden, Vander Veer Park, Lombard Street and Main Street.* A flower conservatory (several major exhibits each year) and a rose garden of

Arie den Boer Arboretum

Horticultural Gardens of Iowa State University

Vander Veer Park Conservatory

3,000 bushes (130 varieties). Daily.

DES MOINES: *Arie den Boer Arboretum, Fleur Drive and Locust Street.* One of the loveliest arboretums in the country, with more than 215 species and cultivars of flowering crab apples and a grand total of 2,000 trees. When they bloom, in early May, the sight of so much color is almost forbiddingly beautiful. The arboretum also has a rare-tree collection and special collections of hosta (180 kinds), many of them imported, and ground covers and peonies. Many other ornamental shrubs and flowering plants may be found in the larger park (Water Works Park) in which the arboretum is situated. The greenhouse displays cacti and other succulents. Within the main park, in addition to the ornamental plantings, there are fountains, pools, and lagoons with water lilies, lotus, and other aquatic plants. Both the arboretum and the park are owned and managed by the Des Moines Water Works, 1003 Locust Street, 50307.

Des Moines City Greenhouses, 2nd Street and College Street. There are special displays of chrysanthemums in November, and a spring show in March, besides the normal collections. Daily.

Ewing Park Lilac Arboretum, McKinley Road and Indianola Road. A 30-acre park with the finest collection of lilacs to be found in the Midwest. Also, flowering crabs, quaking aspens, and native shrubs (viburnum, dogwood, hawthorn, sumac, and other ornamentals).

Greenwood Park, 48th Street and Grand Avenue. Well known among gardeners for its many day lilies and roses (representing more varieties and cultivars than are usually found in such gardens). Many new roses are grown and evaluated each year for the Rose Society.

DUBUQUE: *Eagle Point Park, off Shiras Avenue.* A 162-acre recreational park with a sunken garden.

Grandview Park. Peonies in many colors and many varieties.

MARSHALLTOWN: *Iowa Soldiers Home, 13th Street and Summit Street.* Rose garden within the retirement home section. Daily tours from the headquarters building.

MUSCATINE: *Laura Musser Art Gallery and Museum, 1314 Mulberry Avenue.* A Japanese garden near the Edwardian mansion.

Muscatine Island Experimental Farm, Route 92 (Fruitland).

Kobes Gardens

Operated by the Iowa State University, it is an experimental vegetable farm with emphasis on crop-growing. Monday through Friday, 7:00 A.M.–6:00 P.M.

ORANGE CITY: *Kobes Gardens, 51041.* An extraordinary private garden open to the public since 1969. A melange of flowering plants and garden decorations, with fountains, pools, waterfalls, and an Oriental garden. It contains peonies, May trees, ornamental shrubs, rock gardens, roses, dahlias, tulips, and a section devoted to organic gardening. Also tons of ornamental rocks and some pioneer artifacts. From May 1 to mid-September: daily. Fee.

OSKALOOSA: *Edmonson Park.* Peonies.

PELLA: *The tulip festival* in early May is world-famous. It features Dutch costumes (with wooden shoes) and street-scrubbing, and thousands of tulips.

Fairhaven Park also has thousands of tulips and a sunken garden with beautiful beds of tulips.

PERRY: *Victor Fagan Wildflower Preserve. Highway 141.*

Two acres of wildflowers, trails. Spring: daily.

SHENANDOAH: *Earl May Seed and Nursery Company Trial Garden, North Elm Street, 51601.* A superb 76-acre display of flowering and vegetable plants, many on trial for the first time. A U.S. flag made of flowering plants is a specialty of the garden. Daily throughout the growing season, and an open house in July.

Henry Field Seed and Nursery Company, 407 Sycamore Street, 51601. A no less superb test garden and growing field. Open house in July.

The area around Shenandoah has several commercial flower farms and about 5,000 acres on which peonies, gladioli, and other flower crops are grown.

SIOUX CITY: *Grandview Park, 24th Street and Douglas Street.* Rose gardens with 3,000 plants, 300 varieties. And among other activities, concerts and civic gatherings. Daily.

Latham Park, 1915 South Lemon Street. Formal flower gardens of annuals and perennials; fountains. Daily.

Kansas

ARKANSA CITY: *Memorial Rose Garden.* Fifty beds of roses in many varieties.

BELLE PLAINE: *Bartlett Arboretum, 67156.* An excellent collection of flowers and grasses, shrubs and trees on 20 acres of land, particularly of those plants, woody and herbaceous, that will survive the Kansas climate. There are more cypress trees in the arboretum than in all of Kansas; plus Japanese table pine, English elm, pistachio, red maple, Japanese lilac, tree peony, sunburst locust, golden rain, mimosa, chinaberry—trees foreign to Kansas that may profitably be planted there. The arboretum features bulbs, roses, iris, flowering annuals, and perennials set inside mini-clipped hedges of privet, all of which makes it most unusual as an arboretum. There are also tiny lakes and a lagoon. Special features are a spring flower show in mid-April and a fall foliage spectacular as well as a display of chrysanthemums. Visits are best made during the early morning hours or early evening. From mid-April to November 30: daily, 9:00 A.M.–7:00 P.M.

COLDWATER: *Rich Rose Ranch, 67029.* About 475 varieties of roses may be seen among the 4,000 plants grown on 10 acres. There is a testing ground and an exhibition area for roses. A fall festival in early October is quite famous in the Midwest: in the sunken garden 3,000 dahlias are then in bloom. For variety and to back up the garden, the ranch uses magnolias, cypress, almond, catalpa, mulberry, and similar trees. May and June are good months to see the roses. Daily, dawn–dusk.

EMPORIA: *Peter Pan Park, a William White-Emporia Memorial Foundation garden.* An acre of tea roses and an acre of floribundas. Gardeners who are selective in their choices will like the types of roses here.

HAYS: *Fort Hays Kansas State College, 67601.* A Memorial Rose Garden of 300 varieties, all labeled, on the campus near Picken Hall. A young garden (1969) that is being added to and improved each year. Daily.

KANSAS CITY: *Municipal Rose Garden, Huron Park, Ann Avenue, between 6th Avenue and 7th Avenue.* A well-planned garden of 2,500 roses and a test garden. Daily.

LAWRENCE: *University of Kansas, 66044.* The campus is landscaped with a great variety of flowering crab trees that, in early May, attract thousands of visitors. The campus is located on top of Mount Oread, which

Below: *Meade Park Gardens.* Opposite: *Reinisch Rose Garden*

provides a unique view of the surrounding areas. Daily.
LEAWOOD: *Civic Park, 86th Street and Lee Boulevard.*
Roses.
MANHATTAN: *Eisenhower Museum Home, South East 4th Street.* Tulip beds, with 75,000 tulip flowers, and 1,000 rose bushes. Daily, 9:00 A.M.–5:00 P.M. Fee.
Municipal Rose Garden and Cico Park are both worth visiting. The latter park has a wheel-chair walk through a small arboretum.
University Gardens, Kansas State University, 17th Street and Anderson Street, 66502. On the campus is a group of gardens designed to display a specific object or a type of plant suitable for the Kansas climate. In one garden the pool and stone benches are features. In another native perennials are gathered. Another garden has roses; a fourth displays chrysanthemums. A fifth garden is given over to day lilies. The shrub collection has examples of most of the shrubs that grow well within the state boundaries. May through October: daily.
MILFORD: *Kansas Landscape Arboretum.* Established in 1970, the arboretum is operated by the Kansas State Horticultural Society whose address is c/o the Kansas State University in Manhattan (see above). Sections of the arboretum have been set aside for prairie wildflowers, for native trees (25 kinds), and for a grass preserve. The 193 acres of farmland and woodland were donated to the society by the U.S. Army Corps of Engineers. Spring is a good time to make a visit.
PRATT: *Municipal Rose Garden, 3rd Street and Thompson Street.* Two thousand roses contained within a city block. April to December: daily.
TOPEKA: *Gage Park Conservatory, 4320 West 10th Street.* During Christmas the jade plants and the annually flowering orchids come into bloom. And winter is a good time to see the tropical jungle collections since it is not crowded with the annual plants (40,000 of them) that are started here for later spring planting in the city parks. Monday through Friday, 8:00 A.M.–4:30 P.M. Sunday, 1:30 P.M.–4:00 P.M.
Gage Park Doran Rock Garden (adjoining the Rose Garden; see below). Two brooklets pass through the garden and are edged with typical water plants and a border of tulips. Surrounding this garden centerpiece are 30,000 plants and shrubs that are suitable to the Kansas

Fort Hays Kansas State College Memorial Garden

environment. Daily.
Gage Park Reinisch Rose Garden, Gage Boulevard and 8th Street. On 3 acres there are 7,000 rose bushes (330 varieties) grouped around a lily pool. The test garden is located between the rose garden and the rock garden, and is planted annually with many test roses from national growers. It is possible to see new roses here, among the several thousand that are planted, at least two years before they may be introduced. Daily.
Indian Hill Arboretum, Menninger Foundation, 6500 West 6th Street, 66601. A group of woody trees and shrubs oaks, pines, juniper, lilac, and thorns—that are used solely as a therapeutic aid for patients with emotional problems. Open only by invitation to qualified persons.
Meade Park Gardens and Arboretum, 124 North Fillmore Gardens, 66606. The peak display is in April and early May, when the lesser-known woody plants (400 kinds) that the garden is collecting come into bloom. Trees in the arboretum are limited to those that grow no taller than 30 feet. Near the arboretum are formal gardens and fountains, part of the landscaping for the Meade Mansion, which now serves as a garden center for the Topeka garden clubs. Arboretum and gardens: Daily, 6:00 A.M.–10:00 P.M. Center: Monday through Friday, 1:00 A.M.–4:00 P.M.
WICHITA: *Wichita Memorial Rose Garden, 3751 East Douglas Avenue.*

Kentucky

BARDSTOWN: *My Old Kentucky Home State Park.* Allegedly the home that Stephen Foster memorialized in song. The gardens, quite extensive, are filled with old-fashioned flowers. Iris and tulips in April and May; roses in June and throughout summer. Daily, 8:00 A.M.–5:00 P.M. Fee.

CLERMONT: *Bernheim Forest, Route 245 (Louisville-Bardstown highway), 40110.* The foundation responsible for Bernheim Forest cooperates with the University of Kentucky and the University of Louisville—as well as the area garden clubs—in both botanical and home research projects. Its arboretum, 250 acres in a 10,000-acre preserve, has hedge displays, a Quiet Garden, wildflowers, and a nature trail. The horticultural collections occupy about 15 acres: azaleas, rhododendrons, viburnums, crab apples, dogwood, holly (a number of varieties on Holly Hill), nut trees, and redbud, among others; and good beds of kerria and brooms. A special garden is set aside for plants with compact habits (dwarf euonymus); and another garden for those plants with specific needs, either for sun or for shade (the Sun and Shade Trail). In time a children's garden will be added, as well as a synoptic garden and a fragrance garden. A nature center and museum helps to explain the work and the purpose of the arboretum. There are miles of roads (about an hour's drive), but considerably more time should be spent in the gardens. From mid-March to mid-November: daily, 9:00 A.M.–sunset.

FLOYDSBURG: *Duncan Memorial Cemetery, Crestwood.* A natural planting of native trees and shrubs. And a very good rose garden and perennial garden.

FRANKFORT: *Liberty Hall, Main Street and Wilkinson Street.* An 18th-century garden, beautifully restored, especially noted for the collection of old roses and the boxwood hedges along the walks and around the gardens. Daily, 10:00 A.M.–5:00 P.M. Fee.

State Capitol. The floral clock, a planter set over a pool, is appealing to gardeners searching for oddities. Spring and autumn and winter have different floral displays: from pansies and begonias set against a background of alternanthera to special Christmas decorations.

GOLDEN POND: *Tennessee Valley Environmental Education Center, 42231.* A 5,000-acre wooded area (Land Between the Lakes) set aside by the Tennessee Valley

Bernheim Forest Landscape Arboretum

Authority as an interpretive area. It features nature trails, displays, an educational farm, youth programs, and special outdoor classes for the handicapped. In no sense a garden, it does serve as a sort of arboretum of native plants (it does have a planning arboretum) and in large part as a demonstration reforestation project.

HAZARD: *Bobby Davis Memorial Park*. A small park beautifully landscaped with native shrubs and trees, good flower beds, and an excellent rose garden—a more than charming tribute to Perry County youths who were killed in World War II.

LEXINGTON: *Ashland, East Main Street and Sycamore Road*. The home of Henry Clay, with a pleasant formal garden. A recent introduction is the herb garden and the vegetable garden, both set in a pattern of parterres. Visitors have been encouraged to taste and sample the herbs, particularly the rarely grown hyssop and lamb's ears, or artemisia—the herb that allegedly restores hair. Daily except Monday, 9:30 A.M.–4:30 P.M. Fee.

Christ Church, Market Street. Interesting shrubs and flowers in a cloister garden.

Hunt-Morgan House, 201 North Mill Street. A small city garden that has considerable merit as an example of the gardens that used to be. Tuesday through Saturday, 10:00 A.M.–4:00 P.M. Sunday, 2:00 P.M.–5:00 P.M. Fee.

Lexington Cemetery, 833 Main Street, 40508. A wide variety of many unusual plants and flowers. Four acres of gardens: an annual garden that is pleasant in summer; a rose garden blooming from spring to fall; beds of dahlias and chrysanthemums for November; a sunken garden and pools. Other plant materials include hardy water lilies, lotus, iris, tuberous begonias, and many spring-flowering trees (dogwood, cherry, peach, redbud, crab apple). Daily, 8:00 A.M.–5:00 P.M.

LOUISVILLE: *Cave Hill Cemetery, 701 Baxter Avenue*. Rare trees, shrubs, and plants. Daily, 8:00 A.M.–4:30 P.M.

Farmington, 3033 Bardstown Road. Restored period gardens, using plants and shrubs that were common before 1820, and a kitchen garden of the same period. Tuesday through Saturday, 10:00 A.M.–5:00 P.M. Sunday, 2:00 P.M.–5:00 P.M. Closed Christmas and New Year's Day.

General Electric Appliance Park. About 50 acres landscaped with 1,100 shrubs and trees. Much of the look and the

Tennessee Valley Environmental Education Center

The Lincoln Cemetery

The Lexington Cemetery

Bernheim Forest Landscape Arboretum

feel of the natural area has been kept. There is one service greenhouse. Daily, 8:00 A.M.–5:00 P.M.

MAMMOTH CAVE: *Mammoth Cave National Park, 42259.* Few people, among them most gardeners, are aware of the surface charm of the park. It is a sort of natural arboretum of wildflowers not often seen elsewhere which in spring make converts of the most adamant traditional gardeners. Nature trails lead through dozens of patches of wild orchids, daisies, day-lily drifts, crested iris, primroses, wild roses, and violets. More than 150 species and varieties are listed in the park's plant guide. Flowering begins in April and lasts through August, peaking usually in June and July. Daily, summer, 7:30 A.M.–4:00 P.M.; winter, 8:00 A.M.–4:00 P.M. Fee.

PINEVILLE: *Pine Mountain State Resort Park, 40977.* The mountain laurel festival, which usually occurs during the last weekend in May, has become the occasion for an annual spring pilgrimage for thousands of Kentucky gardeners and out-of-state visitors.

Louisiana

BATON ROUGE: *Cohn Arboretum, Foster Road.* Donated to the city in 1965, it is a young arboretum but well stocked. On the 16 acres over 300 varieties of native plants, trees, and shrubs have been identified and labeled. Others have been added, or will be as they are secured. An experimental area is planned for growing special plants, or plants with special requirements. Wide walkways edged with flowers, ponds for water lilies, a greenhouse for tropicals and for propagation. In season there is a liberal display of annuals. Daily except Friday, winter, 9:00 A.M.–6:00 P.M.; summer, 10:00 A.M.–7:00 P.M.
Louisiana State University Gardens, Essen Lane, 70803. The university's Burden Research Center maintains two ornamental sections open to the public: the trial garden for roses and the trial garden for annuals. The campus itself is landscaped with hibiscus and beds of daffodils, gladioli, and chrysanthemums. Weekdays, 7:30 A.M.–5:00 P.M. Saturday and Sunday, 7:30 A.M.–dusk.
FRANKLIN: *Oaklawn Manor.* An antebellum home surrounded by a large grove of live oaks; gardens. Daily, 8:30 A.M.–4:30 P.M. Fee.

Opposite and below: *Rip Van Winkle Gardens*

JEFFERSON ISLAND: *Rip Van Winkle Gardens, 70545.* Originally a Spanish grant, then a refuge for the pirate Jean Lafitte, finally a home for the actor Joseph Jefferson. The gardens are now open to the public through courtesy of the Bayliss Foundation. The 25 acres have been landscaped and planted for year-round interest, a feat possible only in such areas of the Americas as this. The gardens are English in formality and varied in design, actually a series of gardens within gardens, carefully planned and joined by beautiful forest paths. There are azaleas in the wooded areas, an old-fashioned camellia garden and a rose garden, a magnolia garden with interesting hybrids, an Alhambra Garden with fountains, bamboos, an Oriental Garden, tropical glens, an iris pool, an old and new camellia garden, and woodland gardens with trails and wildflowers set side by side with tropical exotics. Old sugar kettles are used as prominent ornaments; wisteria clambers on trees; huge beds of annuals are brilliant with color; daffodils and narcissi are naturalized. Native trees are varied and interesting. There is no single best time to visit the gardens; the choice is dictated by caprice or by

Ira S. Nelson Horticultural Center

Laurens Henry Cohn Memorial Arboretum

a specific gardening interest. Daily, 9:00 A.M.–5:00 P.M. Fee.

LAFAYETTE: *Ira S. Nelson Horticultural Center, University of Southwestern Louisiana, 70501.* New varieties of roses in abundance, a spectacular collection of amaryllis, and annuals. The center operates on the campus, which is itself a sort of in-use arboretum of camellias, azaleas, spring bulbs, magnolias, pines, cypress, and giant oaks. On the campus also is a Louisiana swamp—Cypress Lake—with many swamp plants; eventually the center will plant it with at least one example of every kind and variety of Louisiana swamp plants. Near the lake is a collection of Louisiana iris. Other plants, rare and exotic, from Mexico, Central America, and South America, are growing in the conservatory or one of the 4 greenhouses. About 120 orchid species, 80 kinds of bromeliads, and a very large collection of tropical foliage plants. The amaryllis collection is more than excellent, as is the heliconia collection. The center also maintains an All-American annuals test garden and a rose test garden. Daily during the school sessions.

LORANGER: *Southwestern College Experimental Gardens.*

Many tropical plants are grown and displayed in the greenhouse. Collections of chrysanthemums, hibiscus, amaryllis, camellias, azaleas, dahlias—all in many varieties. Visiting hours are by appointment only on application to the Department of Horticulture.

Zemurray Gardens. Well-established azaleas, camellias, dogwood, bulbs (in 10,000 lots), wildflowers—all in all, more than 25,000 plants, ornamental trees, and shrubs. The gardens are part of an 11,000-acre tract of natural and man-made lakes and ponds. Forests of pine, gum, and oaks surround the gardens; and statues are placed inside for ornamental interest. A lake surrounded by azaleas and an azalea bowl are two major attractions during February and March. Paths and trails are made for leisurely viewing and walking. Among its collections the estate has a very good planting of Louisiana iris. Greenhouses are used for displays of tropicals and for foliage plants. A spillway from the lake adds the sound of running water to otherwise quiet surroundings. Daily.

MADISONVILLE: *Fairview State Park.*

MANY: *Hodges Gardens, Route 171 (Many-Leesville High-*

Hodges Gardens

way), 71449. Although they include independent gardens for seasonal displays, the gardens are more famous for their year-round beauty and interest. On 4,700 acres—only part of which is devoted to ornamentals—there are camellias, azaleas, jasmine. Old and new varieties of roses cover 7 acres. There are chrysanthemums, Louisiana iris, and day- and night-blooming water lilies, as well as spring bulbs and wildflowers, hibiscus always in bloom, and a profusion of annuals and perennials. Wisteria and redbud edge the forest trails. Day lilies and pink honeysuckle vie for attention. An abandoned quarry has been adorned with plants blooming in year-round succession. Walks for every season and waterfalls and pools make walking a delight. Oaks and crape myrtle, magnolias and similar ornamental trees are interesting parts of the preserve, as are also the native trees and the pines that have been collected from all over the world. Four greenhouses have been set aside for orchids, ferns, bromeliads, anthuriums, gesneriads, cycads, cacti and euphorbias. Daily, 8:00 A.M.–sundown. Fee.
MARKSVILLE: *Marksville Prehistoric Indian Park.*
MONROE: *Louisiana Purchase Gardens and Zoo, Tichelli Road, 71201.* Primarily a 140-acre tourist resort, but with excellently landscaped gardens and moss-laden trees, over 5,000 plants. Daily, 8:00 A.M.–sundown. Fee.
NEWELLTON: *Louisiana Dutch Gardens, Great River Road.* Spring flowers, particularly tulips, a rose garden, and summer-flower gardens. Daily, 8:00 A.M.–5:00 P.M. Closed Christmas. Fee.
NEW IBERIA: *Avery Island Jungle Gardens, Avery Island Road.* The name "jungle" is still appropriate for this area, once densely overgrown with climbing fig and wisteria, although 200 acres have been cleared for the gardens. The collection of camellias is famous for its variety (1,000 kinds). The azaleas are equally famous for their profusion; there are acres and acres of them. Louisiana iris and enormous water lilies exist nearly side by side. Waterfalls and wildflowers. Many rare plants, including the wasi orange and flaming scarlet African daisies. Plants from every quarter of the globe: Chinese wisteria and 60-foot-tall clumps of Chinese timber bamboo; an unusual evergreen survivor from the coal age; finger bananas, papayas, and soap trees; Indian crape myrtle and Oriental holly. Slopes of xanthosoma and aralias.

87

A Chinese garden with a Buddha temple and a lagoon. Sunken gardens and palm-lined drives. It is the kind of garden that is good for all seasons and for all hours of the day. Daily, spring and summer, 8:00 A.M.–5:30 P.M.; autumn and winter, 8:00 A.M.–5:00 P.M. Fee.

The Shadows-on-the-Teche, 117 East Main Street. The scene of many movies about the Old South. The mansion grounds are lush with live oaks and cedars. A formal garden is enclosed within clipped bamboo hedges. Brick walks, ancient camellias, and garden statues. Daily, 9:00 A.M.–4:30 P.M. Closed Christmas. Fee.

NEW ORLEANS: *Conservatory, Audubon Park, St. Charles Avenue.* Seasonal displays as well as the main collection of tropical plants. Monday to Friday, summer 9:00 A.M.–5:30 P.M.; winter, 9:00 A.M.–5:00 P.M. Saturday and Sunday, all year, 9:00 A.M.–7:00 P.M. Closed major holidays and during Mardi Gras.

Long-Vue Gardens, 7 Bamboo Road, 70124. There are five gardens currently established on the 8-acre tract, all of them relatively new. The main garden is Spanish—inspired by the Generalife at Granada, a cool and green water garden. There is a walled garden, with fragrant roses, jasmine, and sweet olives, and containing a loggia—all surrounded by seasonal flowers. The other, and more intimate, gardens feature a *pigeonnier*, a lily pond, a "yellow" garden whose flowers are golden yellow throughout the year, and a woodland garden of native plants and wildflowers. A nursery with greenhouses and a potting shed may also be seen. Daily except Monday, 1:00 P.M.–5:00 P.M. Closed legal holidays and during July and August. Fee.

Rose Garden, City Park, Esplanade. In addition to the roses there are many azaleas, gardenias, and camellias.

RUSTON: *Louisiana Polytechnic Institute Arboretum, Tech. Station.* Three acres of trees and shrubs. Daily, sunrise–sunset.

ST. FRANCISVILLE: *Afton Villa, Route 61.* An eight-room pioneer home completely enclosed in a French Gothic mansion; and one of the finest Southern gardens. A formal garden and a sunken garden—complete with azaleas, camellias, gardenias, and lilies—are set out in the antebellum tradition.

Catalpa. A Victorian cottage set in a 30-acre garden in which nearly every variety of plant, shrub, and tree

Hodges Gardens

The Shadows-on-the-Teche

native to Louisiana may be seen. Daily, 9:00 A.M.–5:00 P.M. Closed during December and January. There may be a fee.

The Myrtles Plantation, West Feliciana Parish, Route 61. The plantation house is set among live-oak trees heavily festooned with Spanish moss, which gives it a feeling of serenity and quiet. The informal gardens are not large, but they, too, impart a feeling of serenity, a quality that is all too often lacking in modern home gardens. Bordering the gardens, the front gallery is of iron lace 112 feet long. Tours daily, 9:00 A.M.–5:00 P.M.

Oakley, Route 965. There is a large planting of Louisiana iris around the lake; elsewhere native trees and shrubs and a nature trail honor Audubon, who lived here as a tutor to Eliza Pirrie. The estate is now a national park. Daily 9:00 A.M.–5:00 P.M. Fee.

Rosedown Plantation and Gardens, Route 10, 70775. The restored mansion and the 2,800-acre estate is one of the most attractive in the South. The antebellum gardens are elaborate and have been designed to follow as closely as possible the earlier originals. Authentic plant materials have been used throughout, and the look of the 17th-century styling has been maintained. Old camellias—many of them original—now form a sort of natural arboretum of both rare and beautiful plants. Century-old azaleas and hip gardenias still exist; as well as shrubs, equally old and some enormous in size: sweet olive, crape myrtle, deutzia, and mock orange. Caladiums

and similar foliage plants border the walks. The trees, many of which are specimens, include oak and magnolia and sawara cypress; an oak allée is edged with hydrangeas and gardenias. There is a kitchen garden and a medicinal plant garden. March through August: Daily, 9:00 A.M.–5:00 P.M. September through February: Daily, 10:00 A.M.–4:00 P.M. Fee.

SHREVEPORT: *R. S. Barnwell Memorial Garden and Art Center, 501 River Parkway, 71101.* The botanical garden is at the foot of Milam Street and on the bank of the Red River. A magnolia arboretum is in the planning stage. Weekdays, 9:00 A.M.–4:00 P.M. Saturday and Sunday, 1:00 P.M.–5:00 P.M.

VILLE PLATTE: *Louisiana State Arboretum, Chicot State Park.* A woodland arboretum of 301 acres, complete with nature trails and native plants, trees, and shrubs. Loblolly pine, redbud, wild azalea, pawpaw, tulip trees, dogwood, many oaks, witch hazel, black gum, hickory, spicebush, sourwood; native iris, jack-in-the-pulpit, buckeye, decumaria, switch cane, wisteria—and many, many other plants and trees. Daily, sunrise–sunset.

Don't overlook *Louisiana's floral trails*. While much of the nation is blanketed with cold, Louisianans are delighting in early spring blooms. *Dogwood Trail*, Plain Dealing: late March. *Redbud Festival*, Vivian: March. *Azalea Trail*, Lafayette: February and March. *Floral Trail*, New Orleans: Friday after Easter. The *Garden District*, and the *Vieux Carrée*, New Orleans.

Maine

AUGUSTA: *Togus Veterans' Hospital*. A memorial lilac hedge; gardens and a greenhouse. Daily, spring and summer. Visitors should check in with the Veterans' Hospital information desk before entering the garden.

BAR HARBOR: *Sonogee, Eden Street*. An Italianate villa with formal gardens; large beds of roses, dahlias, and begonias. May and June: daily, 9:00 A.M.–5:00 P.M. July and August: daily 9:00 A.M.–8:00 P.M. Fee.

Wild Gardens of Acadia, Acadia National Park, Sieur de Mont Spring, 04609. An area around the nature center that has been given over to wildflowers, a sort of sampling of the many that will be found in the park itself—an inducement, as it were, to walk the trails of the national park and find these plants growing in their natural environment. The botanical garden at the center is subdivided into 12 sections, some for viewing birds, but most for locating and recognizing flowering plants. Hardwoods: hazel nut, American hop hornbeam, pagoda dogwood, ferns, and black chokeberry. Roadside plants: the edible berries, field juniper, eyebright, and others. Meadows and beach sections, the latter with the rare arctic beachhead iris. The dry heath: rhodora, blueberry, huckleberry, corydalis, and partridgeberry. A moist area for miniature dogwood, lily of the valley, purple fringed orchis, and the startling cardinal flower. The other areas are divided into shrubs (viburnum, shadbush, etc.); conifers, among which may also be found lady's-slipper, jack-in-the-pulpit, clintonia, and even mountain laurel; and a marsh where showy lady's-slipper, northern calla, sundews, and the more delicate orchids may be found. Late spring and early summer are the best times to visit the gardens although they, as well as the park, are open through September. Daily, 8:00 A.M.–8:00 P.M.

CAMDEN: *Merry Gardens, Simonton Road, 04843*. Commercial greenhouse growers (really more of a mail-order business) that specialize in house plants (800 varieties). Herbs and geraniums, begonias, succulents, cacti, ferns, ivies, African violets. There is an outdoor summerhouse, and many perennials and rock garden plants suitable to the climate of Maine. Monday through Friday, 8:00 A.M.–5:00 P.M. Saturday 8:00 A.M.–12 noon.

DEER ISLE: *Ames Pond*. Hardy water lilies. July and August: daily.

KENNEBUNK: *Franciscan Monastery and Gardens, 04046*.

Originally a Roman Catholic installation, the monastery was taken over by a Lithuanian Franciscan group and developed into a shrine, of which there are a number in addition to grottoes and chapels. The monastery grounds are bordered with massive evergreens, mountain laurel, flowering shrubs, and many hardy perennials. A pleasant woodland path leads to the seashore and boat dock. Daily.

KITTERY POINT: *The Lady Pepperell House and Garden, 03904*. A rather famous and interesting house, since Lady Pepperell's husband was the only American ever to be made a baronet. There is a rose arbor and roses, and an old-fashioned, pleasant garden. From mid-June to mid-October: Tuesday through Saturday. Fee.

NORTHEAST HARBOR: *Asticou Azalea Gardens, 04662*. A filled-land garden project, indicating what can be accomplished with very little assistance by man. There are herbaceous gardens as well as the better-known azalea gardens; and a botanical terrace with a great variety of flowering plants collected from all over the world, a pond, and a Japanese dry garden inspired by Ryoan-ji at Kyoto. Daily, all year.

Thuya Gardens, Seal Harbor Road, 04662. Azaleas in an Oriental setting. Herbaceous perennials and native Maine plants set in a formal English garden. June through October: daily 7:00 A.M.–sunset.

ORONO: *Fay Hyland Botanical Plantation, University of Maine, 04473*. Largely the native plants of Maine, established on nearly 5 acres of land. There are over 200 species and varieties. Miss Hyland was a famous botanist of the Northeast who did much to popularize the plants indigenous to the area, identifying them and helping to recognize their cultural values and requirements. Daily, daylight hours.

PORTLAND: *Henry Wadsworth Longfellow House, 487 Congress Street*. A restored garden, very much like the original and rather extensive for the Northeast climate. From mid-June to mid-September: Monday through Friday, 9:30 A.M.–4:30 P.M. Saturday, 9:30 A.M.–noon. Fee.

The Rose Circle, Derring Oaks Park, State Street. A group of 800 roses (70 varieties), many of them new introductions. Most of them are either hybrid teas or hybrid perpetuals, grandifloras or floribundas. Two circles, both enclosed

Asticou Azalea Gardens

by a hedge and entered by 6 paths, are made up with 18 beds of roses. Daily.

ROCKLAND: *Ureneff Begonia Gardens, 169 Camden Street, 04841.* A sunken garden in a wild, woodsy setting with a brook running through the center. Both standard and hanging basket tuberous begonias are featured, many of the latter being hung from the oak and ash trees around the garden. Earlier in the season there is a profusion of wildflowers; and there is always a profusion of ferns. From July 1 to September 21: daily, to 5:00 P.M.

SEAL HARBOR: *Rockefeller Garden.* Formal, herbaceous borders enclosed by a wall topped with Chinese tiles. Chinese sculpture, a moon gate, and reflecting pool. Open only on Wednesday, 10:00 A.M.–4:00 P.M. July 15 to August 30.

SOUTH BERWICK: *Hamilton House and Garden.* Extensive gardens and terraces.

SPRINGVILLE: *Harvey Butler Rhododendron Sanctuary.* A 30-acre stand of rhododendrons in early July; and a fine display of painted trillium in May. There are two of these gardens in Maine; the other is at Woolwich. Both are operated and managed by the New England Wild Flower Preservation Society, Hemenway Road, Framingham, Massachusetts, 01701 (which see). Visitors interested in such gardens should write to the society for information about visiting hours, special features, plant lists, and fees if any. In both Maine gardens guests may see such flowering plants as buttercups, devil's paintbrush, blue vetch, chicory (introduced from Europe and naturalized), fireweed and mullein, evening primroses, the rare and very special Indian pipe; plus wild roses, steeplebush, meadowsweet, the famous blue iris of Maine, black-eyed Susan, beach pea, and several hundred others.

VINALHAVEN: *Ambrust Hill Reservation, Atlantic Avenue.* A well-laid-out reservation for wildflowers, with easily accessible paths. The season is short, the flowers colorful, and they bloom early. May through July: daily, sunrise-sunset.

WOOLWICH: *Robert P. Tristram Coffin Wild Flower Reservation.* A tract of 185 acres on the shores of Merry-meeting Bay, where the fern population is extremely good. See Springville, Maine, and Framingham, Massachusetts, New England Wild Flower Society.

Sherwood Gardens

Maryland

ANNAPOLIS: *Hammond-Harwood House and Gardens, 19 Maryland Avenue.*

Paca Mansion and Gardens. 186 Prince George Street. A replica of the original gardens designed for Governor Paca in 1765. Only plant materials known at that time, or indigenous to the Middle Atlantic states, have been used. Part of the gardens' parterre designs emerged when bulldozers cleaned off the debris of later years. There are now five terraces of parterres and a wild garden.

BALTIMORE: *Baltimore Museum of Art, Wyman Park, Art Museum Drive.* Rose and perennial gardens.

Cylburn Park, 4915 Greenspring Avenue, 21209. Other than wildflowers, which are sensational, the 176-acre park has an herb garden, beds of annuals and ornamental grasses, a formal garden, and a greenhouse. Also, collections of magnolia, Japanese maple, and boxwood. There is a variety of trails; and an arboretum based on systematic plant groups is being developed. A greenhouse provides a workshop area for the garden center now housed in the park mansion. Daily, dawn-dusk.

Druid Hill Park Rose Garden, Gwynn Falls Parkway. A good grouping of roses outdoors; and indoors, in the conservatory and display greenhouses, a tropical plant collection. Daily, 11:00 A.M.–4:00 P.M.

Sherwood Gardens, 204 East Highfield Road. On a 7-acre private estate, more than 100,000 tulips, to which new varieties are added yearly; they are spectacularly colorful from the last week of April to the middle of May. Azaleas (5,000) and a large collection of boxwood are two other features. The evergreen garden has many species and cultivars from other countries, including an excellent selection of flowering cherries blooming during the first two weeks of May. Daily, during daylight hours.

BELTSVILLE: *U.S. Department of Agriculture Experimental Gardens, US 1, 20705.* Chrysanthemums, lilies, roses, and gladioli are worked on in the field-growing areas. Winter and summer plants are grown under glass. One of the primary concerns of the station is the management and growth of flowers in greenhouses. Also, much of the station research is with plant diseases and disease-control methods. Write the Visitor Staff for available dates.

DICKERSON: *Sugar Loaf Mountain.* The mountain has been registered as a national landmark because of its

Brookside Botanical Gardens

geological interest and its striking beauty. It is controlled by Stronghold, Inc., a charitable corporation whose basic purpose is to bring back the native chestnut as a timber tree (and as a decorative or food tree) by developing a resistance to the blight that has destroyed so many chestnut trees and forests. All means of research are being used—chemical, physiological, hybridizing, and other systems. Currently there is a walking trail and an auto trail. Planned for the near future are a wildflower garden, a forest demonstration area, and a nature center. Daily, 9:00 A.M.–sunset.

GAITHERSBURG: *Seneca State Park, Clopper Road.* A large tract devoted to many species and cultivars of peonies (250 different kinds). The more than 30,000 plants are best seen during the last week of May and the first week of June. Daily, weather permitting, 9:00 A.M.–7:00 P.M.

GALENA: *Shorewood Gardens.*

HAGERSTOWN: *Fort Frederick State Park.* A reforestation project is creating an arboretum as a demonstration of the forest trees suitable to western Maryland. Twenty-seven different species were originally planted in 1-acre blocks some 40 years ago, and have proved to be hardy. Daily.

LILY PONS: *Three Springs Fisherie, 21717.* Despite the name, the firm has one of the largest collections of water plants: from "viviparous" mini-water lilies to giants, from hardy to tropical, from day-blooming to night-blooming; yellow and white, hardy reds, fantastic blues, and magenta. Other water plants include lotus, water iris, pickerel rush, and oversized arrowheads. The gardens are on the edge of the Monocacy River. April through August: Monday through Saturday, 9:00 A.M.–3:00 P.M. Sunday, 1:00 P.M.–3:00 P.M. Closed Easter, Thanksgiving, Christmas, and New Year's Day

NEW GERMANY: *Savage River State Forest, Garrett County.* A rhododendron display equivalent to any in the country, either tamed or free. A hardwood forest with a good representation of native trees, including wild cherry, tulip poplar, birch, maple, and others. Daily.

SOUTH RIVER: *London Town Publick House and Gardens.* The last standing brick building from the original London Town era (1744–50). Now in the process of

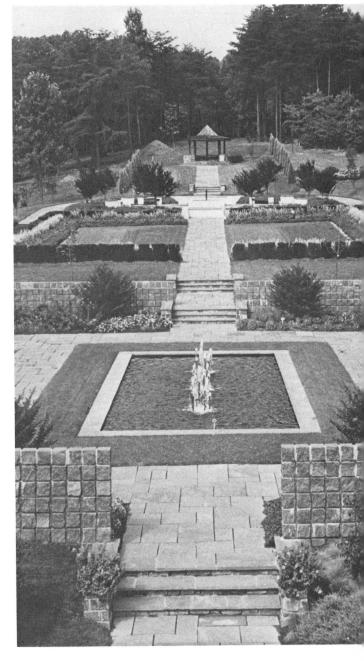

Opposite, above, and below: *Brookside Botanical Gardens*

restoration, it will include a series of gardens on the 10 acres of natural woods gardens (arboretum). Completed or in the process of completion: a marsh garden, a winter garden, a wildflower garden, and more formal plantings of ornamental plants. Daily, 10:00 A.M.–4:00 P.M. Fee.

TOWSON: *Hampton Mansion, Hampton Lane*. A restored formal parterre terrace garden. It is very close to the original design. Small clipped hedges of boxwood enclose the parterre. An herb garden in the form of a wheel is next to the kitchen wing. Monday through Saturday, 11:00 A.M.–5:00 P.M. Sunday, 1:00 P.M.–5:00 P.M. Fee.

WHEATON: *Brookside Botanical Gardens, Wheaton Regional Park, 1500 Glenallen Avenue, 20902*. The largest public garden in Maryland and certainly one of the loveliest in the country. Acres of gardens (25) in a variety of forms from very formal to the casual beauty of Azalea Walk, where rhododendrons and dogwood vie for attention with the azaleas. There is a good holly collection and an equally good planting of flowering crab apples and flowering cherries. The formal garden—400 feet long—is symmetrically arranged with colorful plants, clipped hedges, brick and flagstone walks, and pools and fountain. Ornamental grasses, a feature of the gardens, add a touch of green, blue, and yellow as

well as varied textures. The rose garden selections are those most suitable to the area and include a preview of the new all-America winners. The fragrance garden, new this year, will contain plants of unusual smells, textures, and tastes, with a braille guide for each. The demonstration garden features the best annuals of the year. The Gude collection, when completed, will have specimen trees and shrubs, some quite rare. Three greenhouses, all open for visits, are near the gardens; two of them maintain continuous displays of tropical plants—largely ferns and gesneriads—in addition to seasonal shows. Christmas, of course, is highlighted with poinsettias and other traditional plants—cyclamen, kalanchoe, and Jerusalem cherry. At Easter there is a radiant display of lilies against backgrounds of azaleas and hydrangeas. November is lush with chrysanthemums, both standards and flowing cascades, outdoors and in the conservatory. The propagation greenhouse is open to those who would like to see modern methods of plant propagation and plants in various stages of growth. Tuesday through Saturday, 9:00 A.M.–5:00 P.M. Sunday, 1:00 P.M.–6:00 P.M. Closed Christmas.

Don't overlook the many *homes and gardens tours* in spring. Write to Maryland Home and Garden Pilgrimage, Room 223, Belvedere Hotel, Baltimore, 21202.

Massachusetts

AMHERST: *Rhododendron Gardens, Amherst College, Route 116.* Established in 1912, the garden is still used for special events as well as for educational purposes. Now supplemented with azaleas and mountain laurel, the flowering display lasts from May to mid-June. Daily during the school term.

ASHLEY FALLS: *Bartholomew's Cobble, Route 7.* On 20 acres of land, a curious geological fault, is a natural rock garden, complete with more than 500 species of flowers and ferns. It is one of the loveliest natural gardens in the country.

BARNSTABLE: *St. Mary's Church Garden, Main Street.* A small garden of very great charm and significance. Spring flowers. Daily.

BOSTON: *Boston Public Garden, Boston Common.* Established in 1893, the public garden still has tulips in spring and seasonal displays; it also contains formal gardens and rare trees (labeled). Daily, sunrise–sunset.

Fenway Park Rose Garden, Park Drive. Primarily a group of hybrid teas and climbers. There is also a similar display at Franklin Park in Jamaica Plain. Daily, various hours during winter and summer.

Isabella Stuart Gardner Museum, 280 The Fenway. A Venetian palazzo museum whose inner court is one of the great beauties of the country and of considerable horticultural interest. In this court are rare plants from the museum's greenhouse. An outdoor garden is filled with tulips and roses in season and with flowering fruits, evergreens, and unusual ground covers. Chrysanthemums in many varieties and shapes close the flowering season. May through October; Tuesday, Thursday, and Saturday, 10:00 A.M.– 4:00 P.M. Sunday, 2:00 P.M.–5:00 P.M. Monday, Wednesday, and Friday, organized tours.

CAMBRIDGE: *Mount Auburn Cemetery, 580 Mount Auburn Street, 02134.* The oldest "garden" cemetery in the states; and an arboretum with 1,000 labeled trees, many of them excellent specimens and some of them over 100 years old. Dogwood, crab apple, flowering cherries; beeches, maples, oaks, all three in variety. Kentucky coffee tree, bald cypress; and, more rare, cork tree, umbrella pine, Turkish hazelnut, saw-toothed oak. Daily, summer, 8:00 A.M.–7:00 P.M.; winter, 8:00 A.M.–sunset.

Ware Collection of Glass Flowers, Harvard Botanical Museum,

Opposite, and above: *Arnold Arboretum*

Garden in the Woods

Oxford Street. An internationally famous collection of hand-shaped glass flowers, intricate and accurate in appearance, size, and color, even to minute details too small to see. They are the products of the workshop of Leopold and Rudolph Blaschka, in Germany, from 1886 until 1936. They are not only great works of art, but each specimen is also one of a kind. There are 847 species of plants illustrated in the glass collection, plus separate models of enlarged floral parts. Monday through Saturday, 9:00 A.M.–4:30 P.M. Sunday, 1:30 P.M.–4:30 P.M. Closed Independence Day and Christmas.

CHELMSFORD: *Bartlett Park, Acton Road (Route 27)*. An arboretum operated and maintained by the Conservation Commission, with all specimen plants labeled and established in their natural habitat. Daily.

DANVERS: *Glen Magna Mansion, Route 1*. Pleasant gardens and the McIntyre Tea House. May through October; daily, 10:00 A.M.–4:00 P.M. Fee.

DIGHTON: *Bristol County Agricultural School, Segreganset*. An annual chrysanthemum festival that attracts many gardeners and visitors to the school. November.

EAST FALLMOUTH: *Ashumet Holly Reservation and Wildlife Sanctuary, Ashumet Road, 02536*. Old holly favorites are grown here; and new varieties tested for the Holly Society.

FRAMINGHAM: *Garden in the Woods, Hemenway Road, 01701*. Managed by the New England Wild Flower Preservation Society, the 42-acre botanical garden has 4,000 species and varieties of native North American plants. It is probably the most extensive collection in the country. There are two extravagantly beautiful features: a field of 10,000 cardinal flowers and a bank of 2,000 lady's-slippers. The special collection of variants and albinos is unique. Although both the cultivation of plants and education loom large in the society's purposes, greater stress is placed on education (through classes and workshops) as a method of conservation—the preservation of native plants for the future. The best months for the flowering plants are May and June. From April 1 to November 1: daily, 8:30 A.M.–5:00 P.M. Fee.

The Society also operates eight other botanical preserves: two in Maine (Springfield and Woolwich), two in Massachusetts (Weston and Winchendon), three in

Above and opposite: *Botanical Garden of Smith College*

New Hampshire (Groton, Bradford, and Plainfield), and one in Vermont (Peacham).

HANCOCK: *Hancock Shaker Village*. Vegetable gardens of the early 18th and 19th centuries. From June 1 to mid-October: Daily, 9:30 A.M.–5:00 P.M. Fee.

IPSWICH: *Arthur Shurcliff Memorial Garden, Whipple House*. A pleasantly restored 17th-century garden with clamshell walks and formal flower beds. The plants are authentic replicas of those originally used in the garden, even to some old roses that are actual descendants of the plants of that period. In some ways the research of old documents, to discover what plants were in use, was as intriguing as the plants themselves. From April 1 to November 1: Tuesday through Friday, 10:00 A.M.–5:00 P.M. Sunday, 1:00 P.M.–5:00 P.M. Fee.

JAMAICA PLAIN: *Arnold Arboretum, The Arborway, 02130*. With considerable justification, the arboretum is one of the oldest and certainly one of the most famous in the country. It is a living collection of history, research, and plant adventures. Founded in 1872 and managed by several famous plantsmen (C. S. Sargent and E. H. Wilson among others), the 265-acre arboretum

has introduced about 500 plants to American gardens, increased its collection of trees and shrubs to 6,000 kinds; and maintained special collections of dwarf conifers (some 200 years old and 2 feet high), bonsai, and shrubs. Among the arboretum's specimen trees are weeping hemlock, golden larch, and a katsura tree. The large collections include honeysuckle, viburnum, mock orange, rhododendrons, azaleas, flowering crab apples, and lilacs. When the flowering crabs and lilacs bloom, it is a display of grandeur that should not be missed. Somewhat later the flowering cherries and magnolias and mountain laurel are magnificent. The best times to see these shrubs in flower is from late April to mid-June; but there is really no one best time to visit the arboretum, since every month of the year has interesting features and happenings. The arboretum maintains several research greenhouses and a medicinal garden for the College of Pharmacology. The world-wide search for new plants and excellent variations still goes on, as does a world-wide program of education. One of the arboretum trails, the Chinese Walk, has many of the original plants brought back by E. H. (Chinese) Wilson; it is

a favorite walk of plant historians, who can see the factual achievements of a plant explorer. Daily, sunrise–sunset. There is a fee for automobiles, for which permission must be obtained from the administration office.

Franklin Park. A rose and herb garden.

LENOX: *Tanglewood Music Center.* Fine old pine trees and hemlock hedges in an attractively arranged music center.

NEW BEDFORD: *Buttonwood Park and Botanical Garden, Rockdale Ave.* Daily, 7:30 A.M.–dusk.

NORTHAMPTON: *Botanical Garden, Smith College, College Lane, 01060.* In actual fact, the 300-acre college campus is the botanical garden, and it has been designated as an arboretum, so planned that the trees and shrubs are grouped in plant families (276 shrubs and trees in 45 families). The garden and the arboretum have grown as the college developed and now have 3,600 species and varieties in many plant categories, constituting an excellent, integrated teaching aid for the students. A series of beds for herbaceous perennials is also classified—a bed to each perennial family—so that taxonomy students may clearly see the distinctions between plant families. The rock garden is one of the oldest in the country and has no peer for beauty. The alpine plants are a "must see" during the second and the third weeks of May. There is a pond for water plants and a marsh in preparation, as well as an area for shade plants and one for cacti. The greenhouses (actually, a range with a large display area) are filled with tropical water plants, orchids, begonias, ferns, palms, bamboo, figs, crotons, aroids, bromeliads, nepenthe—even acacias and sarracenias. They, too, along with the propagating house, are a working laboratory for Smith students. Behind Capen Hall are the rose collections, herbs of botanical interest, annuals, and a perennial border. Displays in spring and fall: spring bulbs in early March and chrysanthemums (including cascade mums) in the first week of November, many of them hybrids produced by previous Smith classes. However, nearly any month in any season has both interest and beauty, although the period from March through June is the high point of the growing season. Arboretum: daily, sunrise–sunset. Greenhouses: daily, 8:00 A.M.–5:00 P.M.;

Heritage Plantation of Sandwich

closed Christmas.

QUINCY: *Adams National Historic Site, John Quincy Adams House, 135 Adams Street.* Interesting old formal gardens of the period. From mid-April to mid-November: daily, 9:00 A.M.–5:00 P.M. Fee.

SALEM: *Essex Institute, 132 Essex Street.* A China trade garden, and herb garden, and boxwood-bordered beds in the flower garden, May through November: Tuesday through Saturday, 9:00 A.M.–5:00 P.M.

First Church of Salem, 316 Essex Street. An exciting garden, if only because it may be the oldest garden in continuous use. The garden, which has undergone many changes, has a history that goes back 300 years. It is now more functional, attuned to church use, yet without having lost its period flavor. An interesting Colonial garden of shrubs and perennial borders, with a restored wisteria arbor and granite paving blocks for walks. Daily, all year.

SANDWICH: *Heritage Plantation of Sandwich, Grove Street and Pine Street, 02563.* A 76-acre garden estate with landscaped grounds and 12 nature trails. Here is the largest collection of Dexter hybrid rhododendrons

(35,000)—he lived and worked as a hybridizer on the estate—which is being added to as new Dexter hybrids are located. A collection of shrubs and trees (1,000) suitable to the climate of the Cape. Other attractions, primarily early Americana from the Lily estate, have been added to broaden the scope of interest for tourists. The best months for visiting gardeners are May, June, and July. From May 1 to mid-October: daily, 10:00 A.M.–5:00 P.M. Fee.

SHELBURNE FALLS: *The Bridge of Flowers, Route 2, 01370.* A truly spectacular garden on a bridge over the Deerfield River, probably the only one of its kind in the world. Originally an abandoned trolley span, the bridge now has a complete watering system, and beds, and boxes filled with plants; it is lighted by night during the flowering season, from spring to fall. Annuals and perennials in variety, small shrubs, and other seasonal displays make the bridge a pleasant walkway. The view of the bridge from the river banks is almost as enchanting as the bridge itself. April through November: daily, until 10:30 P.M.

STOCKBRIDGE: *Berkshire Garden Center, 01266.* An

Adams National Historic Site

Bridge of Flowers

interesting garden of 15 acres containing an herb garden (90 varieties), a rose garden (unusual varieties), a rock garden, perennial borders, and a collection of day lilies. A lathhouse has been built for tuberous begonias, a greenhouse for cacti and other specimens. Nearby is a test garden for ornamental grasses. From a previous tenant the garden center inherited an orchard and a vineyard. The garden: April through November, daily, sunrise–sunset. The center: Monday through Friday, 9:00 A.M.–5:00 P.M.; Saturday, 10:00 A.M.–5:00 P.M.

Naumkeag, Prospect Street, 01262. The former home of Mabel Choate, who willed the house and gardens to the Trustees of Reservations. The gardens are formal, with promenades and groves of unusual trees. The landscaping is done in the older European interpretations of Chinese and Japanese gardens. From May to Labor Day: daily except Monday, 10:00 A.M.–6:00 P.M. Fee.

WALTHAM: *Field Station of the University of Massachusetts, 240 Beaver Street.* Perennials in great variety. Trial gardens for annuals and perennials; greenhouses. From June 1 to mid-September: daily.

Lyman Estate, The Vale, Lyman Street. A kitchen garden,

and grapes growing in the greenhouse. Visits must be arranged through the Preservation of North East Antiquities, 141 Cambridge Street, Boston 02114.

WELLESLEY: *Walter Hunnewell Pinetum, 845 Washington Street, 02181.* Although the estate is privately owned, visiting is permitted in the gardens and the pinetum. The pinetum was begun in 1882; many of the original trees have survived, and the conifer collection is the oldest in the country. It contains the false cypress, green-weeping hemlock, Alberta spruce, white fir, Hatfield yew (a pinetum introduction). The rhododendron collection is the most notable private one in the Northeast; flowering begins in May. The orchids (greenhouse) flower in March. An Italian topiary garden is both versatile and distinctively shaped. Very little topiary is seen any more. Arboretum: daily, during the daylight hours. Greenhouse: daily, 9:00 A.M.–5:00 P.M.

Wellesley College Botanic Garden and Arboretum, Central and Washington Streets, 02181. There are many deciduous and evergreen trees on about 24 acres of the campus and a small garden used primarily by students for their class-work. The Margaret C. Ferguson Greenhouses are well

Stanley Park of Westfield

arranged and well planted. Daily, during school terms, 8:00 A.M.–4:30 P.M; but make arrangements first with the college administration office or the information office.

WESTFIELD: *The Stanley Park of Westfield, Kensington Avenue and Granville Road, 01085.* The park, originally established by the Stanley Home Products Company, is now operated by a charitable corporation for the benefit of all people. Complete with a carillon and a Wurlitzer organ (concerts during the summer), the 120-acre area has many trails and well-established gardens. A 2,500-bush formal rose garden, a rose testing garden for new all-America selections. A 5-acre arboretum of native trees, fountains and ponds with hardy water lilies, and acres of lawn excellently landscaped with rhododendrons and mountain laurel along the borders. Many walks flanked with wildflowers lead to the annual and perennial beds, noted for their delphiniums, lilies, iris, and spring bulbs. The flowers are good from spring to fall. Daily, 8:00 A.M.–sunset (sometimes later when there are evening concerts).

WESTON: *The Case Estates, Arnold Arboretum, 135 Wellesley Street, 02193.* A 112-acre nursery and trial ground for the Arnold Arboretum in Jamaica Plain. There is a tree and shrub nursery for the production of stock, either replacements for the arboretum or new items, some of which are released to commercial nurseries for introduction to American gardens. The garden maintains excellent collections of hosta, rhododendrons,

holly, and Oriental crab apples; also day lilies, daffodils, and lilies. It also has an experimental plot for ground covers and—particularly pertinent to gardeners—a low-maintenance garden of perennials. Testing goes on continuously in the garden, and plants and trees are checked particularly for hardiness. From mid-April to September 30: Daily, 9:00 A.M.–6:00 P.M.

Hubbard Trail. A 22-acre suburban tract owned by the Weston Trail and Forest Association. And operated by New England Wild Flower Preserve Society as a natural garden. April and May are the best months.

WILMINGTON: *Kartuz Greenhouses, 92 Chestnut Street, 01887.* Growers of gesneriads, begonias, dwarf geraniums, hoyas, succulents, and other exotics. As one horticulturist commented: "A visit to these greenhouses is almost a major course in growing house plants or conservatory stock." Daily, year round, including Saturday.

Don't overlook these state parks:

Borderland State Park, Sharon. Formerly the Oakes Ames estate.

Bradley W. Palmer State Park, Topsfield. Many lily ponds and masses of mountain laurel, rhododendrons, and rare trees.

Phelon Hill and Granville State Forest, Granville. Dramatic displays of mountain laurel.

Pittsfield State Forest. Masses of wild azaleas in the spring. *Swan State Forest*, Monterey. Exotic trees in a forest setting. *Moore State Park*, Paxton.

Michigan

ADRIAN: *Hidden Lake Gardens.* Miscellaneous bulbs, iris, and a rock garden.

ANN ARBOR: *Matthaei Botanical Gardens, University of Michigan, 1800 Dixboro Road, 48105.* More than 3,000 kinds of plants on 60 cultivated acres; 270 acres remain as a natural garden. Attractively landscaped grounds surround the gardens. The rose garden and the medicinal gardens are important; and the wood-fern collection, especially the hybrids, is the best in the country. The display conservatory has tropical plants, cacti, and similar greenhouse subjects. The research greenhouse, with its bromeliads, ferns, and orchids, is open on request. Trails have been cut through the natural area, leading to a pine plantation, a hickory forest, a lowland forest, a marsh, and a prairie. The university has two other plant stations nearby, the Horner woods and the Radrick bog and forest. Daily, 9:00 A.M.–5:00 P.M.

Nichols Arboretum, University of Michigan, Geddes Avenue, 48104. These gardens, just off the campus of the university, are used more as a park by students than as an arboretum. Daily, sunrise–sunset.

BATTLE CREEK: *Irving Park.* Tulips and annuals.

Leila Arboretum. Flowering crab trees.

BENTON HARBOR: *House of David, Route 139.* Throughout the park there are fine gardens, a rock garden of considerable merit, and a fountain around which annuals bloom in summer. Also a greenhouse. Daily.

BLOOMFIELD HILLS: *Cranbrook House, 360 Lone Pine Road.* Fountains, cascades, and many sculptures enliven the gardens, which are planned for continuous color, spring through fall. In the spring there are tulips and daffodils, spring bulbs in profusion, bleeding hearts, arabis, and alyssum. Then iris and peonies, followed by delphinium, day lilies, lilies, and daisies. Hibiscus, phlox, and annuals for midsummer. Dahlias for a pre-fall interest. Landscaped with flowering shrubs: dogwood for spring, lilacs in considerable variety, and many fine ornamentals. April through October: Monday through Saturday, 2:00 P.M.–5:00 P.M. Sunday 2:00 P.M.–6:00 P.M. Fee.

DEARBORN: *Ford Arboretum, Ford Motor Company, The American Road, 48121.* A landscape of trees and shrubs, each clearly labeled, that are native to the state of

Anna Scripps Whitcomb Conservatory

Ford Arboretum

Beal-Garfield Botanic Gardens

Michigan. Nearly 1,000 trees, most nearing maturity, and more being added yearly. Redbud, wild crab apple, wild plum, Juneberry, and other favorites on 14 acres of land just north-west of the central office building. Daily.

Greenfield Village. A town more noted for its Americana, it has an English Cotswold garden and the Clara B. Ford Garden. A Henry Ford Museum. Daily. Fee.

DETROIT: *Anna Scripps Whitcomb Conservatory and the Henry A. Johnson Memorial Gardens, Belle Isle Park, 48207.* The horticultural complex covers 15 acres. A formal garden of annuals flanked by gardens of perennials and dahlias, a water garden, and a promenade lined with seasonal floral displays. The conservatory has a permanent collection of cacti and ferns, palms and orchids (5,500 plants with a year-round succession of bloom), and other tropical plants (300 species and 60 plant families). It is also used for five displays during the year: Easter (lilies, tulips, narcissus, rhododendrons, azaleas); Mother's Day (hydrangeas, marguerites, perlargoniums); summer (coleus, caladiums, fuchsias, gloxinias); Christmas (poinsettias, begonias); winter

(cyclamen, cinerarias, primroses, camellias). Major collections include fuchsias, chrysanthemums, and rhododendrons. Daily, summer, 9:00 A.M.–7:00 P.M.; the rest of the year, 9:00 A.M.–5:00 P.M.

Oak Park. Iris, dahlias, native plants, and rock plants.

Zoological Gardens, 8450 West Ten Mile Road, Royal Oak. In addition to the animals to be found here, the park's planting is both numerous and good. There are many tulips throughout the spring months; the collection of shrubs and trees is well chosen; the rock garden is excellently situated; and 2 acres of dahlias in the fall provide a considerable splash of color. The annuals are also plentiful and usually interesting. From mid-May to November 30: daily, 10:00 A.M.–5:00 P.M.

EAST LANSING: *Beal-Garfield Botanic Gardens, Michigan State University, 48823.* The gardens have been incorporated into the existing 2,000-acre campus, making the campus an arboretum; and it is used as such by the students. There are 7,000 species and varieties of woody plants along the 60 miles of walks. The actual botanical garden is a 5-acre plot bordering on the Red Cedar River. The 5,000 species are arranged in four groups, or

Beal-Garfield Botanic Gardens

categories: systematic (botanical relationships), economic (useful to men), ecological (useful to communities), and landscape (ornamental; including an excellent collection of rhododendrons and azaleas).

The Horticultural Gardens, Michigan State University. The gardens, also on the campus, are used for demonstration purposes as well as for testing plant performance under the central Michigan climatic conditions. On a bit more than 2 acres, the gardens have been arranged formally and color-related to provide pleasing combinations. Plants and flowering periods have been integrated to show examples of satisfactory planting schemes. Rose Gardens: floribundas and hybrid teas from the All-American selections, usually shown and tested before they are offered for sale by commercial firms. Combination Garden: perennials, biennials, annuals, and bulbs arranged to demonstrate both sequence and color. Perennial Garden: plants that will provide continuous bloom throughout the season. Annual Garden: nonhardy plants started yearly; different color schemes are planned each year. Bulb Garden: hardy and nonhardy bulbs, and special-interest plants of lilies, amaryllis, tuberous begonias, and chrysanthemums. Water Garden: hardy and tropical water lilies. Seasonal highlights occur about the middle of each month, from mid-April to mid-September. Daily, at all times.

FLINT: *Sunken Gardens, Municipal Center.* Against a background of redbud, tree wisteria, fragrant viburnum, yews, and pine, the sunken garden features a succession of tulips, geraniums, salvias, and other plants. Daily.

HOLLAND: *Tulip-Time Festival.* A four-day celebration of tulips, which are on display everywhere and, especially, on the nearby tulip farms. Mid-May: daily.

KALAMAZOO: *Crane Park.* Formal gardens of roses and many spring bulbs. Both informal and natural garden areas. Daily.

LANSING: *Cooley Gardens, Potter Park.* Roses.

MACKINAC ISLAND: *Grand Hotel Gardens.* Formal borders of perennials and annuals.

NILES: *Fernwood, Inc., 1720 Range Line Road, 49120.* Primarily a nature center, Fernwood has a boxwood garden, an herb garden, a very good rock and perennial garden, and lilacs and flowering crab apples. The major portion of the arboretum area (180 acres) emphasizes

Hidden Lake Gardens

natural planting. Native trees, ferns, wildflowers, and bog plants, all revealed by a series of walks and trails. The purpose of the center is threefold: natural science and environmental education; horticulture and gardening; related arts and crafts. Most programs are calculated to involve all three aims. There is a consistent effort to continue planning for, and planting, ornamentals such as roses, flowering trees, and evergreens. From April 1 to October 31: daily except Monday, 9:00 A.M.–5:00 P.M.

TIPTON: *Hidden Lake Gardens, Route 50, 49282.* Managed by the Michigan State University, the gardens have a wide variety of trees, shrubs, and flowers on 407 landscaped acres (out of a total of 600) in the Irish Hills section of Tipton. In both natural and man-made environments, the arboretum offers a choice collection of plants: flowering crab, cherry, hawthorn, juniper, lilac, magnolia, maple, mountain ash, oak, spruce, willow, yew, and rhododendrons and azaleas. Some 150 genera and 1,800 species are represented. There is a dwarf shrub garden and an ornamental shrub garden used for demonstration purposes, as well as an All-American annual and perennial garden and a primrose collection. The conservatory complex (8,000 feet of glass) has a tropical dome for both economic and ornamental plants; the arid dome has a similar division of plants; and the temperate dome is used largely for displaying unusual house plants, seasonal flowers, and choice woody plants. The balance of the complex is left as a natural area, with walking trails and 6 miles of roads. There is no special month for viewing, since the variety of plant materials provides a continuous spectacle; but April and May and, later, October, have interesting floral and foliage peaks. Weekdays, 8:00 A.M.–sunset. Saturday, Sunday, holidays, 9:00 A.M.–sunset. Conservatories: weekdays, 8:00 A.M.–7:00 P.M. Saturday, Sunday, and holidays: 9:00 A.M.–7:00 P.M. Fee only for automobiles.

Don't overlook *Isle Royale National Park*, Houghton, *49931.* Unique in its isolation in Lake Superior—yet not too difficult to reach—the park provides a superior hunting ground for gardener-naturalists. Here the deciduous and nondeciduous trees meet and wildflowers abound—but the season is short. Easily found is Indian pipe; and just as easily located are 30 kinds of terrestrial orchids, trilliums, bunchberries, even raspberries and blueberries, and hundreds more. June through October: daily, by boat or plane.

Minnesota

AUSTIN: *The Hormel Foundation Arboretum.* The facilities and research program of the Foundation have been taken over by the park department of Austin. The Foundation's collection of evergreens and woody plants (90 species) will be maintained, as will the tree demonstration project, but they will become part of a nature center (240 acres) that is being planned. Visitors should check with the park department on the status of the development.

CHASKA: *University of Minnesota Landscape Arboretum, Route 1, 55318.* On 558 acres, a large part of which is still woodland, the arboretum grows 3,000 kinds of plants and supports 3 miles of road, 6 miles of trails. Much of the land reached by trail is either open field, or prairie, or marsh and bog and ponds. Because of this and the nature of the planting, spring (wildflowers and a maple syrup demonstration) and fall (foliage color) are usually the best visiting periods. Within the actual garden area special attention is given to ground covers, hedges and vines, and formal gardens of annuals. The special plant collections include azaleas, clematis, flowering crabs, hostas, lilacs, peonies, and ornamental grasses. A section is given to old-fashioned roses and to shrub roses, both of great charm and significance. The primary objective of the arboretum is to locate ornamental plants, shrubs, and trees that are ideally suited to Minnesota gardens, or which by breeding and selection may become so. It is essentially a program of investigation, evaluation, and education, not the least of which is answering many phone calls and letters from Minnesota gardeners in search of information. Daily.

MINNEAPOLIS: *Eloise Butler Wild Flower Garden, Glenwood Parkway.* An old garden in terms of existence (founded in 1907) and a persistently beautiful one. On its 13 acres are more than 1,000 flowering plants in woodlands, bogs, and prairies. A Violet Path winds among an area of lady's-slippers, ferns, azaleas, and rhododendrons. The West Path contains trilliums and hepatica. The path through the bog march is heavy with

Como Park

University of Minnesota Landscape Arboretum

Above: *Lake Harriet Garden Center.* Below: *Lyndale Park*

Como Park Conservatory

ginger and wild calla. Other walks feature lupines and penstemons. The variety is abundant and represents some of the best native plants of Minnesota and the Northern regions. From April 1 to November 10: daily, 8:00 A.M.–6:00 P.M.

Garden Center and Rose Garden, Lake Harriet Park, West 42nd Street and King's Highway. The center provides examples of plants that can be used for home landscaping. In the center's garden area there are places for iris, day lilies, annuals, perennials, and evergreens. All roses suitable to Minnesota are grown—from shrub roses to tea roses and tree roses; as well as vines such as clematis and tuberous plants such as dahlias and peonies. Daily.

Greenhouse of the College of Pharmacy, University of Minnesota Campus. Medicinal plants are grown, observed, and studied—or displayed. Daily during school terms.

Kenwood Parkway Gardens, Kenwood Parkway. Each year the city park department sets out displays of new varieties of annuals and perennials among the shrubs and trees; nearly all of the native woody plants of Minnesota can be viewed along the parkway.

Lake Minnetonka Gardens.

Lyndale Park, West 42nd Street. A rose garden, a rock garden, and a bog garden. The rose garden has more than 5,000 plants and a wide variety of hybrids.

The city center of Minneapolis has been transformed into a mall, a garden of trees and shrubs, and flowers in season, with very limited access by automobile—a new experience in urban planning.

ST. PAUL: *Como Park Conservatory, 1224 North Lexington Parkway, 55103.* The conservatory (3 acres of glass plus 7 other growing houses nearby) is used for seasonal shows as well as for the display of its permanent collection of tropical plants (150 kinds). A fern house, a sunken garden, lily pools, palms, economic plants, and others, from acacia to zingiber. Display: a spring show (March–April); a summer show which previews home garden plantings and stresses annuals; a fall show of chrysanthemums—with many of the plants taken from stock that goes back to 1915, and a winter display (around December). "Gates Ajar," a special feature of the conservatory, combines a sort of wheel of life, an anchor, and gates—all composed with flowering plants. Daily, winter, 10:00 A.M.–4:00 P.M.; summer, 10:00 A.M.–8:00 P.M. Near the conservatory is the McKnight Formal Garden.

WHITE BEAR LAKE: *Manatou Island Gardens.*

Mississippi

BAY ST. LOUIS: *Darwood on the Jourdan, Kiln Road.* Fifty acres of woodland and formal gardens. A fountain and pools decorated with dwarf azaleas and tropical foliage plants. The larger garden is excellently landscaped with magnolia, holly, pine, and oak, with drifts of azaleas, camellias, crape myrtle, and mimosa; naturalized bulb planting. Daily. Fee.

Holly Bluff on the Jourdan, Kiln Road. About 3,700 acres of natural and landscaped areas, with informal trails along the river and lagoon and through a pine forest. Haws, maples, oaks, pines, gums, and bays; holly (Southern as well as Asiatic); golden rain trees, hibiscus, and similar tropical plants. Three hundred varieties of camellias, some quite rare. Fire thorn, lilies, azaleas, dogwood, redbud. Daily. Fee.

BELZONI: *Wister Henry Gardens.* Roses in quantity; chrysanthemums. A garden house and a lake. Daily. Fee.

BILOXI. *Beauvoir, 200 West Beach Boulevard.* The last home of Jefferson Davis, President of the Confederate States of America. An informal garden of camellias and azaleas.

Longfellow House and Gardens, Pascagoula Beach Drive.

Veterans' Administration Center, Harrison Avenue. Native plants of Mississippi placed along the winding roads of the center. A sunken garden of azaleas and other colorful subtropicals. Daily, 7:00 A.M.–5:00 P.M.; but first check in with the central office.

COLUMBUS: *Antebellum homes.* In addition to the home-and-garden pilgrimage held each year in the first week of April, ten homes and gardens are open the year round only by appointment through the local Chamber of Commerce (tel. 601-328-4491), 318 Seventh Avenue North, 39701. There is a nominal fee to see such historic homes as White Arches, Amzi Love, Themerlaine, Waverly, and Wisteria Place—all privately owned and lived in. Some of the gardens are as original and as historic as the homes.

GLOSTER: *Gloster Arboretum, 39638.* All of the magnolia species native to the United States may be seen here, as well as the Oriental species. The collection of azaleas consists of those species native to the Southeast and, especially, Mississippi. Other collections range from redbud to maples, with a good sampling of berries and ornamental plants, such as Louisiana iris, violets, ferns,

Opposite: *Mynelle Gardens.* Below: *The Elms*

day lilies, and hyacinths. Saturday and Sunday, after-
noons.
HOLLY SPRINGS: For information about the town's
antebellum home-and-garden pilgrimage, write to the
Holly Springs Garden Club, 38635.
JACKSON: *Mynelle Gardens, 4738 Clinton Boulevard.* The
gardens were started in 1920 and built slowly until, in
1957, the city officials convinced Mynelle Hayward to
open them as a civic duty because they constitute a
botanical garden of considerable merit. The gardens
have a very wide variety of plants, 100 kinds of trees,
thousands of azaleas, camellias, gardenias, other flowering shrubs and perennials, and naturalized spring bulbs.
Day lilies are a favorite hybridizing project of the garden
and more than 20,000 special plants are kept on hand
at all times. There are $1\frac{1}{2}$-miles of flower-bordered
walks, edged with many old favorites and plants with
exotic fragrances. A lake and a lagoon where Louisiana
iris thrive, along with Japanese iris and masses of other
water and bog plants, are part of the tract. A Japanese
garden is placed on an island, and a stand of giant
Japanese bamboo is not too far away. The old-fashioned
roses in the rose collection are direct descendants of
roses that originated in the period between 1696 and
1894. There is nearly always considerable bloom in the
garden, but there are peaks from March through May
and again in June, when day lilies, iris, and hydrangea
flower. In the late summer the tropical plants such as
crape myrtle and ginger begin to bloom. The fall
chrysanthemums last until Christmas. Daily, dawn–
dusk. Fee.
LUCEDALE: *Palestinian Gardens.* The Holy Land has
been re-created in miniature on 40 acres of land. Though
small, most of the buildings may be walked through.
The "tour" covers 400 miles of Bible scenes, accurately
scaled. Scenic paths lead through flowering shrubs and
trees and over small bridges that connect the many
"towns." Flowers are everywhere. There is a Dead Sea
and a Sea of Galilee, each also appropriately scaled
down. Nearby a garden is set aside for weddings. Daily.
Fee.
NATCHEZ: *The Natchez Pilgrimage.* This annual event
usually takes place from the first weekend in March
through the first weekend in April, and it is one of the

Above: *White Arches*. Below: *Gloster Arboretum*

D'Evereux

Natchez Trace Parkway

Waverly Plantation

great events of the South. Thirty private homes in the city are opened during this period for visitors to see the enchanting interiors and exteriors. To visit all of these homes requires three days and a considerable amount of time. The tour includes such historic homes as Linden and Melrose, Cherokee and The Elms, Greenleaves, Rosalie, D'Evereux, and Longwood, with its galleries and cupola. They are all period pieces, inside and out, often with formal or informal gardens that are a gardener's dream and a collector's delight. For information about the tour, write to the Natchez Pilgrimage, P.O. Box 347, Natchez, Miss. 39120. Fourteen of these antebellum homes are open during the year on a limited basis, usually on certain weekdays. Arrangements to visit them may be made at Stanton Hall, 401 High Street, where directions and information are available. Fee.

OXFORD: *Elmore Gardens.* The gardens specialize in roses—many varieties, from quite old to the latest all-American selections. Appointments to see the gardens may be made at the Oxford-Lafayette Chamber of Commerce in the center of the town (tel. 601-224-4651).

PASS CHRISTIAN: *Wildflower Gardens, Menge Avenue.*

An 11-acre woodland in which most of Mississippi's native plants, trees, and shrubs are preserved.

TUPELO: *Natchez Trace Parkway.* Travelers who take this parkway through Mississippi are always pleased by the varied and lovely scenery along the historic route, yet somehow often fail to see the natural gardens along the way. There are nine of them between Tupelo and the southern terminus, none of them too large to visit in an hour or so of rest from driving. Among them they present aspects of Mississippi as it must have been a hundred years or more ago. Information about the gardens is available at the Trace headquarters visitor center at Tupelo. Two of the most attractive are the Cypress Swamp and the Rock Spring Trail. One is a typical bald-cypress swamp untouched by man, the other a typical hardwood forest of frontier times. Both are filled with wildflowers during spring and early summer.

VICKSBURG: *Cedar Grove.* An antebellum mansion, and gardens extending down to the river.

McRaven. The lovely gardens surrounding McRaven have century-old live oaks, boxwood, magnolias, a bay

Natchez Trace Parkway

magnolia, camellias, and other Deep South traditional plants that antedate the Civil War. From mid-February to mid-November: Monday to Saturday, 9:00 A.M.–4:30 P.M. Sunday, 2:00 P.M.–4.30 P.M.

WAYNESBORO: *The Waynesboro Nursery, Mount Zion.* The largest grower of pine trees in the world in the heart of the pine belt: 36 million seedlings growing on a 160-acre plot. It is a source for reforestation projects and for other uses. The methods used in securing and germinating pine seeds are most unusual; seeds are extracted from pine cones by forced hot air. Of the 522 million young pines produced in the past, it is estimated that, planted in a double row 6 feet apart, they would reach to the moon, with enough seedlings left over to plant 2,000 acres. Monday through Friday.

Pilgrimage Week. In the springtime, around April and May, 15 cities in Mississippi have home-and-garden tours. It is the one time of the year when beautiful old homes and gardens are open to the public, usually for some charitable or civic purpose. The fees charged are not excessive, for the returns in gardening pleasures and the opportunity of living for a little while in an atmosphere of serenity and beauty are well worth the price. For information about these tours, write to the Mississippi Travel Department, Agricultural and Industrial Board, 1504 State Office Building, Jackson, Miss. 39205.

Missouri

CAPE GIRARDEAU: *Rose display garden, Parkview Drive and Perry Avenue.* The latest All-American selections are maintained in this garden next to the campus of Southeastern Missouri State College. The project also has some of the older classical roses, furnishes information about subirrigation of gardens, mulches, and foliar feeding, and gives out other useful garden advice. April through November: daily.
Ten-Mile Garden, Highway 61.
CENTRALIA: *The Chance Gardens, Singleton Street.* More than 450 varieties of roses are on view here at all times during the flowering season. Also, an Oriental garden with a torii gate; and stone, wood and flowers arranged in an Oriental mood. Lilies and lotus. The gardens are illuminated at night. May through October: daily.
GRAY SUMMIT: *Missouri Botanical Garden Arboretum on Routes 44 and 100.* An adjunct of the Missouri Botanical Garden in St. Louis. Here are the native trees and shrubs of the Ozarks, flowering plants, and many foot trails on 1,800 acres of plateau land. Naturalized daffodils turn the area into fields of gold and sharp green. March through May is the most colorful period. April and May: daily.
INDEPENDENCE: *Glendale Rose Garden.* Formal beds of more than 5,000 roses.
KANSAS CITY: *Lennington Gardens, 7007 Manchester Avenue.* The specialty is day lilies; many, many varieties.
Missouri Garden Center, 51st Street and Wornall.
KIRKSVILLE: *State Teachers College.* Beds of iris and daffodils flanked by flowering crab apples and magnolias.
LEE'S SUMMIT: *Unity School of Christianity, Route 50.* Formal gardens in which the roses are outstanding. A lily pool and a fountain. Daily.
NEOSHO: *The Flower-Box City.* Neosho has undertaken a city beautification program by installing 3,500 plant boxes—boxes of all kinds, made from wood hammered from metal, cemented with bricks—all for the purpose of containing flowering plants in the spring and evergreens in the fall. The small city is literally engulfed with geraniums, petunias, verbena, coleus, begonias, even caladiums—anything, in short, that will live and thrive in plant boxes placed all over the city's sidewalks and streets.
ST. ALBANS: *St. Albans Gardens.* A peony display in

The Jewel Box Conservatory

The Missouri Botanical Garden Conservatory

spring; roses somewhat later. A formal garden and a wildflower garden.

ST. JOSEPH: *Krug Park, 11th Street and King's Park Road.* A lagoon, a reflecting pool with water lilies, flower borders of annuals. in a magnificently landscaped park, with a wide variety of trees and shrubs that are in themselves well worth the visit. Daily.

ST. LOUIS: *The Jewel Box, 1501 Oakland Avenue (Forest Park).* So called because the conservatory, built in rising tiers of glass rectangles, gleams and sparkles like a jewel when it is illuminated at night. It is one of the most original greenhouse structures in design and certainly the loveliest in the country. There are seasonal flowers in an amazingly attractive contemporary setting, and monthly shows. There is no time of the year without floral color and drama. Inside the conservatory is a series of aerial walkways from which the planting may be viewed, and on which plants also are placed. The interior is filled with palms and ficus, and hung with ivies and philodendrons, among which the seasonal displays are placed. Outside, pools of water lilies lead to the entrance; around them are the formal gardens.

Among the 104 beds of roses, over 30 varieties may be seen; 25,000 perennials form a floral clock. From April 27 to October 26: daily, 12:00 noon–9:00 P.M. From October 27 to April 26: daily, 9:00 A.M.–6:00 P.M. *Forest Park* is also the site of the city's 18 greenhouses, in which plants for the Jewel Box are grown, as well as flowering stock for the city parks (250,000 plants). In St. Louis County, 23,000 shrubs and trees are maintained at the city nursery for park and street replenishment.

Missouri Botanical Garden, 2315 Tower Grove Avenue, 63110. Still called Shaw's Garden for its founder who retired at the age of forty to take up botany in this then frontier city, the botanical garden is best known for its climatron. The climatron is a half-acre conservatory dome in which four separate climates are maintained through the use use of a series of hot-air pipes and other equipment. A very innovative building, held in place by a geodesic framework, it was initiated by Dr. Fritz Went. Its two-level interior contains a hibiscus garden and a waterfall, pools of water lilies, a mist forest, and a world-famous collection of aroids, cacti and other succulents, orchids, and tropical flowers. On the upper level there is a group of economic plants and a rain forest that can be seen from a circular ramp beneath the dome. The display house puts on four seasonal shows: Thanksgiving (chrysanthemums), Christmas (poinsettias), early spring (orchids), spring (lilies). The Linnaean House, a handsome old brick-and-glass structure that remains from the original group of greenhouses, holds the camellia display. Outdoors, in the general garden of 75 acres, are water-lily pools for, among others, the giant victoria regia lily, plus an old-fashioned garden, two rose gardens, and a new herb garden. The gardens, as a whole, have more than 5,000 kinds of plants— sufficient for weeks and even months of pleasant study or contemplation. Also part of the outdoor areas is a Linnaean Garden, which visually dramatizes a succession of bloom, an Italian Garden with formal beds laid out geometrically, and an Economic Garden. Some of the gardens are used for testing new plant materials, checking their adaptability to the St. Louis area. Climatron: Monday through Saturday, 9:00 A.M.–5:00 P.M.; Sunday, 9:00 A.M.–6:00 P.M.; holidays, 9:00 A.M.–7:00 P.M. Public greenhouse: daily, 9:00 A.M.–5:00 P.M., except when

The Jewel Box Conservatory

Loose Park Garden

special displays are scheduled. Gardens (Tower Grove Park): April through November, daily, 9:00 A.M.–5:00 P.M.; December through March, daily, 10:00 A.M.–4:00 P.M.

National Headquarters of the National Council of Garden Clubs, 4401 Magnolia Avenue, 63110. A major project of the National Council to initiate garden centers throughout the country has improved and enlivened garden activities and stimulated a civic awareness and community service. As a result of its special interest and know-how, many cities now have garden centers, educational activities, and libraries, and some very good gardens indeed. The headquarters building is unusually attractive. Monday through Friday, 9:00 A.M.–4:00 P.M.

SPRINGFIELD: *Phelps Grove Park.* An interesting collection of roses, dahlias, and annuals.

STOVER: *Water lily and lotus gardens.*

WEST KANSAS CITY: *Loose Park Garden.* Municipal Rose Garden.

Missouri Botanical Garden

Montana

BILLINGS: *Pioneer Park, 3rd Street West.* A small rose bed, annuals, and a planting of trees hardy in Montana.

BUTTE: *Columbia Gardens, Route 10-S.* Owned and operated by Anaconda Company, the gardens are primarily recreational. The short spring and summer seasons in Montana are not conducive to gardening on a grand scale, although much can be done with evergreens and trees. Asters, geraniums, petunias, and snapdragons are the basic flowers in the Columbia Gardens; each is arranged in beds that are decorative in shape—harps, hearts, or butterflies, for example. April through October: daily, 8:00 A.M.–11:00 P.M.

GLACIER NATIONAL PARK: *Glacier Park Lodge Garden.* A display of annuals and perennials (the delphiniums and lupines are good). A greenhouse for cut flowers. From June 1 to mid-September: daily.

GREAT FALLS: *Gibson Park.* A rock garden and several flower beds.

Memorial Gardens. About a block by a block-and-a-half of flower beds, hedges, and peonies. Some native trees.

KALISPELL: *Woodland Park.* A rose garden.

MISSOULA: *Sunset Park.* A memorial rose garden and a rose testing field. About 2,000 roses are grown, some for testing. Flowering continues from June through most of October. Daily.

MOCCASIN: *Moccasin Experiment Station, Montana State University (Bozeman).* The plants maintained in the experimental plots are grown primarily to determine the hardiness of various ornamentals in relation to the rigorous climate. There are two rock gardens, some miscellaneous planting areas, and a wildflower garden.

WOODSIDE: *A wildflower preserve* next to Highway 93.

Nebraska

Nevada

KEARNEY: *Harmon Park, 30th Street and 5th Avenue.*
LINCOLN: *Antelope Park, 27th Street and D Street*. Several hundred varieties of roses, many annuals and perennials, and a sunken garden. May through October: daily, sunrise–sunset.
Pioneer Park and Nature Center, 3300 South Coddington. A playground for children and gardens for adults.
NEBRASKA CITY: *Arbor Lodge State Park Arboretum, 2nd Avenue.* The lodge and the arboretum were part of the estate of J. Sterling Morton, Secretary of Agriculture under Grover Cleveland, who became the founder of Arbor Day. It is a curious fact of history that such a memorial holiday devoted to planting trees should emerge from a state almost barren of trees. And toward this purpose the arboretum was initially undertaken, to search for appropriate trees that would persist under the climatic conditions of Nebraska. The arboretum now lists 280 species of trees, including some rare chestnuts, ginkgos, and tulip trees, most of which were planted by Secretary Morton, and a 1½-acre stand of pine trees. There are formal gardens and a well-cared-for rose garden. From April 15 to October 31: daily, 1:00 P.M.– 5:00 P.M. Fee.
NORTH PLATTE: *University of Nebraska North Platte Experiment Station.* Experimental plantings of field-grown chrysanthemums, penstemons, and other perennials. Also woody plants such as mock orange, lilac, rose, cotoneaster, viburnum, honeysuckle, and mountain ash. All in all, approximately 600 species and varieties of flowering plants and shrubs, ground covers, ornamental vegetables, small fruits, and dwarf trees are being selectively bred to withstand the Nebraskan climate. Chrysanthemums have already achieved this purpose; and carnations are in an intermediate stage. The high quality of the station's plant products, as seen in the testing blocks and fields, makes any visit more than worthwhile. There is an annual open house in late September; otherwise visits may be made at convenient times of the day between 8:00 A.M. and 4:00 P.M., and should be confirmed at the central administration office.
OMAHA: *Mount Vernon Municipal Gardens.* A reproduction of the George Washington Gardens at Mount Vernon, Virginia.

Nevadians are proud of their state, believing that great public gardens are an affront to their extraordinary domain. They have, as one gardening correspondent suggested, "plenty of space and sagebrush and no air pollution (well, hardly any)."
This belief partly rises out of the difficulties that gardeners encounter in the state; an unusually dry climate, very little rain, and often indifferent soil. And in part, unquestionably, as the result of so much available natural beauty. When the few inches of annual rain comes the plains and mountains of Nevada become for a few weeks a massive carpet of flowers. For the arid plants of Nevada must grow, flower, and seed themselves in a matter of weeks, rather than months. But those weeks are dazzling with poppies and asters, wild heliotrope and mallow, verbena and desert-gold, and the dozens of other annuals and perennials. And the always omni-present sagebrush and desert mahogany, the Joshua trees and yuccas, and many intriguing cacti.
Contrary to expectations, though, Las Vegas does have its Squire Park where roses are grown. And many garden club members maintain very lovely gardens of cacti and other succulents; even, in some cases, beds of annuals and perennials. And some hotels have a somewhat semi-tropical garden area where colorful annuals may be used; and which, of course, tend to disappear rapidly in the heat of summer.
So plants and flowers are, actually, where the discerning garden traveler finds them (there are few trees in Nevada except in the Lake Tahoe region).
Nonetheless, there are garden clubs in the larger cities whose members are well-educated in desert gardening and wildflower trails, and where and when to see them. Equally knowledgeable is the Nevada Department of Economic Development (whose address is listed in the appendix). The department maintains brochures about the state parks and information about the floral season. As one Nevada official replied to a query: "Each of our parks (state) has its own unique vegetation; and depending upon the year and season may present spectacular displays in all zones from the low or hot desert type in the Valley of Fire to the alpine forests at Lake Tahoe-Nevada State Park." And when the rainfall, the temperature, and the season is right—Nevada glows.

Alpine Gardens

New Hampshire

CONCORD: *Watkens Iris Gardens, Fiske Road*. Beautiful varieties of iris, frequently the result of the gardens' own hybridizing program. Peak bloom from June 1 to 15.

CORNISH: *Saint-Gaudens National Historical Site*. The studio, home, and garden of the sculptor Augustus Saint-Gaudens. From May 25 to October 15: daily, 8:30 A.M.–5:00 P.M. Fee.

DURHAM: *Lilac Arboretum, University of New Hampshire, Main Street*. In addition to the plants in the arboretum, there is a good collection of lilacs on the landscaped campus. The arboretum specializes in the hybridizing and development of its lilacs; and also conducts field tests of vegetables and perennials that may be beneficially grown by New Hampshire gardeners. Greenhouses. Daily, 8:00 A.M.–5:00 P.M.

EXETER: *Exeter Wild Flower Gardens*.

FITZWILLIAM: *Rhododendron State Park*. A famous 16-acre stand of wild *Rhododendron maximum*, flowering between July 1 and 15. From June 24 to Labor Day: daily. Fee.

GOFFSTOWN: *Flowerland Farms, Route 13*. Displays of iris and phlox and other perennials. Rock garden plants. May through November: daily.

HAMPTON FALLS: *Little Gate to the City of Gladness, Kensington Road, South*. Originally an ice house, the 10-by-18-foot chapel was created and consecrated in 1932. Daily from May to July, visitors stop to enjoy the quietness of the wild gardens, the phlox and the wild herbs. Water lilies may be found along the riverbank.

LITTLE HARBOR: *Wentworth-Coolidge Mansion, Little Harbor Road*. There are no formal gardens, but garden historians will be interested in the lilacs surrounding the house, which are direct descendants of the lilacs brought to this country before 1700. Flowering is usually during late May. From Memorial Day to October 12: daily, 10:00 A.M.–5:00 P.M. Fee.

LYNDEBORO: *Curtis Dogwood State Forest*.

MEREDITH: *Huntress Farm Gardens*. Although noted for their bearded iris (best seen in mid-June), the gardens also display day lilies and Oriental poppies lovely enough to gladden a collector. June through October: daily.

MOUNT WASHINGTON: *Mount Washington Arctic*

Fitzwilliam State Park

Gardens. Five species of arctic flora (normally seen only in the Arctic) and some species unique to the area have been growing above the timberline of Mount Washington since the Ice Age. In June these plants literally burst into bloom on the alpine meadows. Other alpine flowers of the Presidential Range of mountains come into bloom about this time also. Reached via toll road or cog railway.

NORTH WOODSTOCK: *Lost River Reservation*. A 900-acre area of strange rock formations, a disappearing river, and 300 varieties of native plants easily observed along the trail. From mid-May to mid-October. Daily. Fee.

PORTSMOUTH: *Governor John Langdon Mansion Memorial, 143 Pleasant Street*. The gardens are typical of the 18th-century Colonial style: a wildflower garden and an enclosed formal garden. June through October: Tuesday through Saturday, 10:00 A.M.–4:00 P.M. Closed holidays. Fee.

Moffatt-Ladd House, 154 Market Street. A late-18th-century home whose 1-acre terraced garden has grass steps, peonies, roses, herbs, perennials, and annuals, all arrranged as an old-fashioned garden. From May 24 to October 15: Monday through Friday, 10:00 A.M.–5:00 P.M. Closed holidays. Fee.

Prescott Park, Marcy Street. A large formal garden and fountain among other objects of historic interest.

Strawbery Banke, Hancock Street. A 10-acre historic site where Portsmouth began in 1630. Thirty of the old buildings in the area have been saved and restored. Others will be added, with landscaping, a tree farm, a shrub nursery, an orchard, and plantings of lilac and willow. A monumental project that, when completed, will be interesting to all historians and gardeners. From May 1 to mid-October: Fee.

RINDGE: *Garden of Remembrance, Cathedral of the Pines, Cathedral Road*. A memorial to the war dead, now proclaimed a national shrine. The gardens circling the cathedral knoll are informally planted with rhododendrons, azaleas, lilacs, flowering quince, and beds of annuals and perennials. From May 1 to November 1: daily.

RYE BEACH: *Fuller Gardens, Little Boar's Head*. A beautiful garden during the short New England summer. Roses and tuberous-rooted begonias. Daily during the flowering period. Fee.

Note: Beginning in mid-September, color foliage reports are made on this fall spectacular. These reports may be had, upon request, from the Foliage Editor, Office of Vacation Travel, P.O. Box 856, Concord, N. H. 03301.

Wentworth-Coolidge Mansion

New Jersey

ALPINE: *Greenbrook Sanctuary, Palisades Interstate Park, Route 9W*. A small and exquisite cross-section of wildflowers, trees, and shrubs that are native to the lower New York and central New Jersey areas. Daily.

BRIDGETON: *Bridgeton City Park*. Rhododendrons and azaleas.

COLUMBIA: *Delaware Water Gap National Recreation Area, 07832*. Roads and trails along the river and among the hills from Portland, Pennsylvania, to Port Jervis, New York, provide spectacularly close viewing of wild rhododendrons and how they grow. Curiously, rhododendrons are one of the first plants to move into areas despoiled by men and then abandoned; dogwood and cherry are among the second-growth forests. The purpose here, as in other natural areas, is not so much to observe the loveliness of nature as it is to study how plants grow when left to themselves; for all garden plants, too, were once wildings, and unless their backgrounds are known, they cannot be duplicated or improved. Daily, the year round; but best in mid-May and June.

CONVENT STATION: *Shakespeare Garden, St. Elizabeth's College.*

EAST HANOVER: *Hanover Park Arboretum, Mount Pleasant Avenue, 07936*. Eight acres of a garden-type arboretum.

EAST MILLSTONE: *Colonial Park Rose Garden, Mattler's Road.*

ELIZABETH: *Boxwood Hall, 1073 East Jersey Street*. Home of Elias Boudinot, with a garden of the period. Tuesday through Saturday, 10:00 A.M.–12:00 noon; 1:00 P.M.–5:00 P.M. Sunday, 2:00 P.M.–5:00 P.M. Closed Thanksgiving Day, Christmas, and New Year's Day. Fee.

The Henry S. Chatfield Memorial Garden, Warinanco Park, Linden Avenue and Acme Street. Tulips and other spring bulbs, Japanese cherries, an azalea garden, a rock garden, and about 20 formal beds. Annuals for summer display; chrysanthemums and other perennials for fall. The park, year round; spring and fall are the best seasons for the gardens. Daily.

GLADSTONE: *Willowwood Arboretum, Hacklebarney Road, 07934*. An educational and research arboretum that is open to the public by appointment only. On 130 acres there are 2,000 species and varieties of shrubs and trees,

Delaware Water Gap National Recreation Area

Above: *Frelinghuysen Arboretum*. Opposite: *Rutgers Display Garden*

and several small gardens: formal, herb, Japanese, and wildflower. The collections of ornamentals include dogwood, holly, lilac, and ferns; the trees include willows, maples, and, particularly, conifers. Before visiting the arboretum, write to the Director for available dates.

GLEN RIDGE: *The gardens of Dr. Cynthia Westcott, 96 Essex Avenue.*

HOLMDEL: *Holmdel Arboretum, Holmdel Park, Longstreet Road, 07733.* Nurserymen in the area contributed 260 kinds of shrubs and trees to this project of the Shade Tree Commission of Monmouth County. Primarily ornamental plantings: crab apples, cherries, magnolias, and evergreens such as cedars and conifers (including dwarf varieties). Ground covers and spring bulbs. Spring is the most interesting season, from mid-April to May. Daily, 8:00 A.M.–dusk.

LAKEWOOD: *Georgian Court College, Lake Drive and Lakewood Avenue, 08701.* The 200-acre campus has fountains, statues, a Japanese garden and an Italian garden—all part of the former Gould estate. Daily; but visit the administration office first for information and directions.

LINWOOD: *Fischer Greenhouses, Oak Avenue.* Some of the finest African violets, especially within the Rhapsody series, gloxinias and other gesneriads; mini-growing plants, a good selection of hybridizing stock, and many foliage plants. The display house is particularly beautiful from spring to fall, with flowering saintpaulias, columneas, and episcias. Daily, 8:00 A.M.–5:00 P.M.

MONTCLAIR: *Rose Garden and Garden Center, Brookdale Park, 60 South Fullerton Avenue.*

MORRISTOWN: *Frelinghuysen Arboretum, 30 Whippany Road, 07960.* Formerly the estate of Matilda Frelinghuysen and now owned and operated by the Morris County Park System. There are old cedars, oaks, and boxwood that have been growing there for nearly a hundred years. The park system has added a center for horticulture and education, has planted azaleas, rhododendrons, flowering crabs and flowering cherries, Japanese maples, and a pinetum, and has naturalized many spring bulbs. To be added to the 135 acres: native azaleas and a rose garden. Daily, 9:00 A.M.–5:00 P.M.

Great Swamp Outdoor Education Center, Pleasant Plains Road. Some directions suggest Bernardsville or Basking Ridge as towns nearer to the Great Swamp; but Morristown provides an easier directional route. The swamp is a 15,000-year-old masterpiece of nature that so far has been preserved intact. Actually the "swamp" is a mixture of marshland, meadowland, dry woodland, and brush-covered swampland. It is this mixture that makes the Great Swamp a unique natural garden unmatched elsewhere in the Northeast. Plants vary in size from the miniature duckweed to towering red oaks. And there is an abundance of beech, maple, poplar, oak, birch, tulip tree, many kinds of shrubs and innumerable flowering plants, such as the pink lady's-slippers, ferns, skunk cabbage, marsh marigolds, and iris, and an excellent stand of mountain laurel. Spring, especially June, is a perfect time to visit the area, although to many visitors the autumn-flowering witch hazel will be lovely. Daily, sunrise–sunset.

Schuyler-Hamilton House, 5 Olyphant Place. Now DAR headquarters. The gardens are interestingly Colonial. Tuesday and Sunday, 2:00 P.M.–5:00 P.M.

Wick House Herb Garden, Jockey Hollow State Park.

MOUNTAINSIDE: *Watchung Reservation, Coles Avenue, Route 22.* A museum nursery and walking trails that pass through groves of birch, cedar, maple, pine, and and many dogwoods. Wildflowers and ferns beneath the shade trees. Daily.

MOUNT HOLLY: *John Woolman Memorial, 99 Branch Street, 08060.* A Colonial, period-piece garden. Daily, 9:00 A.M.–4:00 P.M.

NEWARK: *Branch Brook Park, Lake Street, The Ballantine Gate.* An extraordinary collection of flowering cherries; over 2,000 of them planted in drifts that, in spring, are as colorful and exciting as the Washington, D.C., trees—even though less well known. In the hilly, wooded section there is a good stand of native trees. Another section of the park features dogwood and rhododendrons; and in the fall there are chrysanthemum displays. Daily, sunrise–sunset.

NEW BRUNSWICK: *Rutgers Display Gardens, Ryders Lane, 08903.* A great holly orchard (125 varieties, which should be seen in November) and three trial grounds for other hollies, including 100 varieties of Japanese holly

Prospect Gardens

(spineless). A rhododendron and azalea garden that is spectacular from late April to mid-June. Small ornamental trees and shade-tree gardens, a nursery stock garden to grow plant materials for educational and research purposes, a shrub garden, a garden for yews, and another for evergreens. An annual garden, including the most recent All-America selections, plots for hedges and vines, and a dogwood trial garden. In addition, there are two experimental plots, a lathhouse, and a laboratory. The display gardens provide gardeners in the area an opportunity to see and to evaluate plants that are suitable and available for the New Jersey area. The nearby Helyar Woods has nature trails through an old oak forest and a swamp. May through September: Daily, 8:30 A.M.–dusk. October through April: Daily, 8:30 A.M.–4:30 P.M.

The Pine Barrens. A land abundantly covered with pitch pine and oaks, streams and lakes, blueberry and cranberry farms, cedar swamps and sunny bogs. The wildflower gardens at Oswego Lake are pleasant. And for the gardener-botanist there are pitcher plants and Venus's-flytraps, introduced into the area from the barrens of North Carolina.

PLAINFIELD: *Cedar Brook Park, Park Avenue.* There is a Shakespeare garden filled with plants and vines of the 16th century—hawthorn and old roses, ivy and herbs, perennials—plants mentioned in Shakespeare's plays and sonnets, all labeled with the chapter and verse in which they appear. There is also a spring display of daffodils, an iris garden, a peony garden that includes most of the major types and kinds of peonies, and a wildflower preserve. Daily, dawn–dusk.

POWERVILLE: *Emily Hammond Wild Flower Trail, Tourne Park.* One of the most beautiful plantings of wildflowers in the country. Daily.

PRINCETON: *Morven, 55 Stockton Street.* Built in 1701, now the official residence of the Governor of New Jersey. The garden is quiet and distinguished, using catalpas and sycamores, yet preserving the look of an 18th-century Colonial landscape. Tuesday, 2:00 P.M.–4:00 P.M. Next to it are the *Prospect Gardens*, old English in design; a "half wheel," with the "spokes" as paths, flanked by flower borders. Color in the garden is planned for continuity, spring to fall: spring bulbs of tulips, hyacinths,

Skylands of New Jersey

daffodils; June—foxgloves, delphiniums, Canterbury bells, and peonies; summer, annuals; and fall, chrysanthemums. Actually, the entire campus of the university is an arboretum of a kind that has been used as a landscape, a background and foreground to the university's buildings.

RINGWOOD: *Ringwood Manor, Ringwood State Park, Route 23 (Ringwood Avenue)*. An old manor house set on 95 acres of shrubs and trees and formal gardens ornamented with French and Italian statues. Since acquiring the property, and an additional 600 acres, the state has renewed the plantings, made some improvements, and established a wildlife sanctuary and a natural area. May through October: daily. Fee.

Skylands of New Jersey is also within the limits of Ringwood State Park, not too far from Ringwood Manor. It was formerly the 1,200-acre estate of Clarence McKenzie Lewis, who built the beautiful English castle. His great hobby was horticulture, and over a period of 28 years he collected plants from all parts of the world, so that now there is something for every visiting gardener in the 250-acre cultivated gardens. The formal gardens

were designed as a series of terraces, opening a view toward the distant hills, and divided into lesser gardens. A Cupid Garden, a Lilac Garden, etc. There are magnolia-lined walks, a half-mile of flowering cherries, greenhouses, a moraine garden, a 5-acre wildflower garden, a pinetum, and a collection of azaleas and rhododendrons. Recently the state of New Jersey has added 10,000 Holland tulips and made plans to expand several of the plant collections; it also plans to build a lecture hall for slide shows, flower displays, and horticultural conferences. May through October: daily. Fee.

SADDLE RIVER: *Tricker Water Gardens*.

SANDY HOOK: *Sandy Hook State Park*. Nearly 800 acres on the barrier penninsula that has the largest natural holly forest found along the Atlantic seacoast. Daily. Fee.

SEASIDE HEIGHTS: *Island Beach*. Dunes and cedars as a background for wildflowers in the spring. A major lesson in planting arid gardens, as well as in ecology. The botanical preserve has been undisturbed by man since 1650. Many of the shrubs and trees have been stunted as a result of the weather and soil. Daily. Fee.

SHORT HILLS: *Cora Heartshorn Arboretum, The Stone*

House, 324 Forest Drive South, 07078. An educational, cultural, and recreational facility with responsibilities toward maintaining the arboretum. About 17 acres with many fine specimens of hardwood and deciduous trees (55 varieties); flowering trees and evergreens; many ericaceous shrubs: holly, mountain laurel, rhododendrons, azaleas, blueberries; and hundreds of kinds of wildflowers and ferns. Museum: from late September to mid-June, Tuesday and Thursday, 3:00 P.M.–5:00 P.M.; Saturday, 10:00 A.M.–12:00 noon. Arboretum and trails: daily, all year.

SOMERVILLE: *Duke Gardens Foundation, Route 206-S, 08876.* Privately owned by the Doris Duke Estate. There are natural woodlands, lawns, and a series of display greenhouses on about 8½ acres. The artistry and beauty of the special gardens, a sort of never-never land under glass, is known world-wide. Of the eleven gardens kept permanently on display, there are Colonial, Chinese, Edwardian, English, French, Indo-Persian, Italian, Japanese, Tropical Jungle, American Desert. The plant materials are numerous and varied, often exotic. There are camellias and succulents, gardenias and cacti,

orchids and tree ferns, jacarandas and boxwood; not that these combinations of plants are found together, but they may be as close as one greenhouse to the next. Also, the gardens provide for seasonal displays using bulbs, poinsettias, and chrysanthemums. A recent innovation has been the opening of the gardens for night tours when the greenhouses are illuminated. Query the Director of the gardens for dates and times. September through May: daily, 1:00 P.M.–5:00 P.M. Closed Christmas and New Year's Day. Fee. To be certain of seeing the gardens, it is wise to make advance reservations.

SOUTH ORANGE: *Gotelli Arboretum, 66 Crest Drive.* A private arboretum established on 2 acres, and with more dwarf plants than are ordinarily seen in most collections. The arboretum also has conifers and evergreens, outstanding azaleas and rhododendrons, and excellent tree peonies. Daily, year round.

SUMMIT: *Lager and Hurell Greenhouses.* One of the most notable collections of orchid species in the country. Daily, during business hours.

TRENTON: *William Trent House, 539 South Warren Street.*

University of New Mexico

The house, set in the center of a pink-and-white hawthorn hedge, has four small area gardens on each side; each of the gardens is devoted to a special planting feature. The beds are designed in the manner of English knot gardens and contain many of the older perennials—iris, old roses, phlox, aquilegia. There is also a rose garden and an herb garden. The visiting hours are various; usually, daily, about 10:00 A.M.–5:00 P.M.; Sunday, 2:00 P.M.–4:00 P.M.

UPPER MONTCLAIR: *Presby Memorial Iris Garden, Upper Mountain Avenue*. A complete range of iris types as well as historically significant clones; and more often than not newly named hybrids and varieties—all dated and named. Siberian and Japanese iris find a place along the border of the brook. Beds of tall bearded iris are edged with mini-dwarfs. The historical bed of iris displays types from antiquity to modern times. Indeed, the garden has iris of all kinds, heights, breeds, and colors. A very distinguished garden that especially should be seen from about May to mid-June. Daily, year round.

WAYNE: *Terhune Memorial Park, Route 202*. The elegant and scenic gardens of the former estate of Albert Payson Terhune. Daily, 9:00 A.M.–11:00 P.M.

WILDWOOD: *Bert Hoover Arboretum, Bennet and Park Boulevards*. The arboretum is privately owned, and permission must be obtained by writing to P.O. Box 121, Wildwood, N. J.

WOODBRIDGE: *Bible Gardens, Beth Israel Memorial Park, Route 1*. Here may be seen many of the shrubs, trees, and herbs that sheltered the Israelites and provided them with food and medicines. The four gardens each illustrate significant passages from the Bible. Garden of the Promised Land: stones and pebbles from Israel, acacias and vines. Garden of Moses: a monolithic sculpture surrounded with examples of bulrushes and similar plants of Mosaic literature. Garden of Jerusalem: cedars, olives, and figs reminiscent of peace. Garden of Kings: tamarisk, mulberry, and pomegranates (which supplied much of the decorative motives and ornamentation of the Temple). Daily except Saturday, 9:00 A.M.–4:30 P.M. Closed major legal holidays and Jewish holidays.

New Mexico

ALAMOGORDO: *Garden Center, 10th Street and Orange Street.* An experimental garden of plants that will survive in this area of New Mexico, trees, shrubs, and flowers. Also a Memorial Rose Garden.

White Sands National Monument, Route 70, 88310. A curious plant adaptation to the shifting sands. As the plants are threatened with burial their stems grow longer, sometimes as much as 40 feet. And as the sands recede, the plants may be left high on pillars of the gypsum sand.

ALBUQUERQUE: *Native Plant Trial Gardens.*

Sandia Peak Botanical Gardens, at the foot of the aerial tramway. There are over 900 different species and varieties of native shrubs and trees, cacti, and wildflowers that are usually found in the zone between 5,000 and 7,000 feet in New Mexico. Daily, from 9:00 A.M.

University of New Mexico Campus, Central Avenue. A rose garden and a garden of native flowering plants, shrubs, and trees. The biology department has an interesting small greenhouse. The 700-acre campus is unusually attractive, with familiar and some unfamiliar plants and combinations. Flowering crab apples and catalpas, hawthorn and honey locust, even honeysuckle, side by

side with arid desert vegetation—a most interesting combination. The president's house has a magnificent desert planting of cottonwood, locust, and juniper, with beds of tulips, daisies, and perennials. Daily.

CARLSBAD: *Zoological/Botanical State Park of the Southwest, 88220.* Part of the 600 acres is given over to collections of desert plants. The several elevations in the park provide two distinct zones of plant life, Lower and Upper Sonora, each with its indigenous planting. The cactus collection is very extensive, including species from Central and South America. Daily.

At nearby *Carlsbad Caverns* the surface areas have a plant check list of 600 species, although no attempt has been made to establish them in easily seen colonies. The list includes the usual junipers, yuccas, agaves; and the unusual: stream Helleborines (orchids), native crotons, and many others, some not usually observed by gardeners.

CLOVIS: *Hill Crest Park, Sycamore Street and 10th Street.* A beautiful sunken garden near Swan Lake and the Zoo.

COLUMBUS: *Pancho Villa State Park.* Created to commemorate the last hostile action between Mexico

University of New Mexico

and the United States, it contains mementos of General Pershing's Camp Furlong and a good desert botanical garden. Specimens of the spinny ocotillo, yucca, mesquite, purple cholla, staghorn cholla, polkadot plant, and bunny ear plant. Opuntias and barrel cacti abound, as do many other species. The stone-lined paths break up the gardens into easily observed sections. Daily.

DEMING: *City of Rocks State Park, Route 680, 88030.* In addition to its fantastic rock formations the 680-acre park has a desert arboretum of cacti and other native desert plants. An interesting aspect is seeing how plants, not in the collection, have gained a foothold within this area of volcanic tuffs. Daily.

GLORIETA: *The Glorieta Baptist Assembly Gardens.* Unique and extensive garden for the area, with a variety of plants.

LAS CRUCES: *A. R. Leding Cactus Garden, University Park, New Mexico State University.* Most of the cacti,

agaves, and shrubs are natives of the area that can be seen to better advantage within the bounds of the garden. Major blooming occurs in May. Daily, 8:00 A.M.–5:00 P.M.

LOS LUNAS: *Cactus Garden, Bosque Mobile Village, Route 47.* Visitors are taken on conducted tours of the garden each Monday during June, from 10:00 A.M. to 3:00 P.M. The garden is private.

PORTALES: *Eastern New Mexico University Campus Gardens, Route 70.* Contact the campus Office of Public Affairs.

RATON: *Memorial Rose Garden, Library Park.*

ROSWELL: *Municipal Rose Garden, Main Street and 11th Street.* Museum and Art Center grounds.

SANTA FE: Beautiful patios may be seen at the *Art Museum,* the *Old Governor's Palace,* and the *State Capitol,* which, incidentally, is landscaped with annuals and perennials.

Sandia Peak Botanic Garden

New York

ALBERTSON: *Fanny Dwight Clark Memorial Gardens, 193 I. U. Willets Road, 11507.* A branch of the Brooklyn Botanic Garden of New York (which see). The gardens have 12 acres, 3 lakes, several hundred trees, and a garden that is being developed. Visitors should phone the Brooklyn Botanic Garden (tel. 212-622-4433) before making a trip to the gardens.

BERGEN: *Bergen Plant Swamp Sanctuary, Swamp Road.* A 1,000-acre swampland filled with native azaleas, sugar maple, black haw, and many other native trees that have been introduced to culture. There are many kinds of orchids as well as the lovely lady's-slipper in several colors, the rose pogonia, and the blue iris. Daily.

BUFFALO: *Buffalo Botanic Garden, South Park Avenue and McKinley Drive.* Sixteen display greenhouses in an area of 115 acres. On continuous exhibition are 4,000 species and varieties of tropical and economic plants. Daily, 8:00 A.M.–4:00 P.M.

Delaware Park, Elmwood Avenue. A 415-acre project with a large formal rose garden.

Humboldt Park, Fillmore Street and Best Street. An acre and a half of roses (3,000 bushes and 250 varieties); and the Niagara Frontier Rose Trial Garden.

CENTERPORT: *Vanderbilt Museum, Little Neck Road.* Mosaic walks of colored pebbles, a courtyard, and 180 linden trees; a glassed-in terrace, a fountain and pool, and a boxwood garden on 43 landscaped acres. May through November: daily except Monday, 10:00 A.M.–4:00 P.M.

CLINTON: *The Root Glen Foundation, Inc., 107 College Hill Road, 13323.* Ten acres of alpine plants, peonies (the Saunder hybrids), and shade trees. Daily, dawn–dusk.

COOPERSTOWN: *Fenimore House, Route 80,* A medicinal herb garden of 24 beds, each devoted to a single group of herbs; all beds are edged with hyssop. Most of the herbs grown were selected from 18th-century herbals and medicinal books.

CROSS RIVER: *Meyer Arboretum, Ward Pound Ridge Reservation.* The arboretum has selected and placed in the tract of woodlands (175 acres) other native plants of the area. Children and adult programs. Daily except Monday, 9:00 A.M.–sunset. Closed during winter. Also located within the reservation is the Luquer-Marble Memorial Wildflower Garden, a 6-acre tract that has

Fort Tryon Park

Above: *George Landis Arboretum*. Opposite: *Inisfree Garden*

100 different kinds of wildflowers. Early spring is the best time to see the flowers. Daily except Monday, 9:00 A.M.–sunset. Closed during winter.

Ward Pound Ridge Reservation, 10518. The Reservation includes both the arboretum and the wildflower garden (see above), and in itself has 4,500 acres of woodland trails. Open all year.

CROTON-ON-HUDSON: *Van Cortlandt Manor. Albany Post Road.* The most famous part of the manor's gardens is the "Long Walk," first planted in 1749 and recently restored. Crocus and daffodils, tulips and violets give way, along the walk, to dianthus, phlox, and iris. And these in turn are replaced by a continuous spectacle of old roses, peonies, and all of the perennials so long and so often favored by Colonial gardeners. Near the walk is an herb garden. Daily, 9:00 A.M.–5:00 P.M. Fee.

ELIZABETHTOWN: *Colonial Garden, Church Street.* An effort on the part of the Essex County Historical Society to reproduce an authentic early American garden. Many of the flowers are typical of those grown, both annuals and perennials, by the colonists, and the garden

fencing and other ornaments have been reproduced from known mansion gardens. The garden has an authenticity not always found in such restorations. June through September: daily. Fee.

ESPERANCE: *George Landis Arboretum, 12066.* A collection of Oriental and United States conifers, malus, viburnum, cotoneaster, and native plants; horticultural plantings that include spring bulbs, a garden of roses, and a garden of iris; collection of Bonsai—all in all, 2,500 plant varieties on 100 acres of land, half of which is a native stand of trees. The best time to visit the garden is between mid-April and the end of May. From April 1 to November 15: daily.

FARMINGDALE: *Gardens of the State University Agricultural and Technical Institute, Melville Road.* The Department of Horticulture is involved with many plant tests, perennial and annual All-American selections, the Eastern Dahlia Trial Grounds, a demonstration rose garden, and a research laboratory for ornamentals. Monday through Friday, 8:00 A.M.–5:00 P.M., Saturday, 8:00 A.M.–noon.

GARRISON: *Boscobel Restoration, Route 9D, 10524.* The

Morris Dyckman mansion relocated on 36 acres of landscaped grounds, with a boxwood garden, an herb garden, a rose garden, and an English garden. Also an orangerie, most unusual in the United States, and a good collection of orchids in the greenhouse. Spring is a good season to visit the gardens; the house, anytime. There is a Sound and Light program on Wednesday and Saturday evenings. April through October; daily 9:30 A.M.–5:00 P.M. November through March: daily, 9:30 A.M.–4:00 P.M. Fee.

GENEVA: *Legg Dahlia Gardens, Hastings Road, 14456.* Three acres of dahlias (over 500 varieties), in bloom from August through October. Daily, sunrise–sunset.

HOLLEY: *Fancher Arboretum, State University at Brockport, Lynch Road, 14470.* A university experiment that has reconstructed the natural forest tree communities on a 50-acre tract. All of the native trees of New York are represented, such as hop hornbeam, shagbark, oak, and others. Garden interest is primarily in those trees that are grown for fall foliage interest (mid-October).

HYDE PARK: *Vanderbilt Mansion National Historic Site, Route 9D, 12538.* The arboretum on the Vanderbilt estate was begun in 1828—some 70 years before the mansion was built—and some of the trees still survive: gingkos, sugar maples, Kentucky coffee trees, and others. There is an Italian garden that is quite lovely in its layout and display of greenery. Gardens: daily, 9:00 A.M.–dusk. Mansion: daily, 9:00 A.M.–5:00 P.M. Closed Monday from Labor Day to June 15. The grounds are free.

ITHACA: *The Cornell Plantations, Cornell University, 100 Judd Falls Road, 14850.* The several collections include lilacs, nut trees, rhododendrons, tree peonies, viburnums, and hostas. Many spring flowers. The Mary Rockwell Azalea Garden, a wildflower garden, hedges, and a synoptic shrub garden. The woodland and field arboretum occupies an area of 1,500 acres, and plans have been made to landscape a large portion of it. On the college campus are the *Minn's Gardens* near Bailey Hall, a rock garden, and a rose test garden. The university's Veterinary College has the *W. C. Muenscher Poisonous Plants Garden,* which contains historic and dangerous and useful medicinal plants. Daily.

LOCUST VALLEY: *Bailey Arboretum, Bayville Road,*

Mohonk Show Gardens

11560. The Bailey Arboretum was originally part of the Frank Bailey Estate. Over 600 kinds of trees have been planted on the 42-acre estate since 1916, including such rareties as the dawn redwood, a dwarf Nikko fir, the fragrant snowbell, and the katsura tree. In addition, there are tree peonies, boxwood, and viburnums, which make up a large part of the shrub collection. A working greenhouse is on the premises. From March 1 to November 15: daily, 10:00 A.M.–5:00 P.M.

LYNDONVILLE: *Robin Hill Arboretum, Platten Road, 14098.* Trees and shrubs. Daily, sunrise–sunset.

MILLBROOK: *Innisfree Garden, Tyrrell Road, 12545.* Terrace gardens around the mansion have been described as architectural gardens. They are the expression of the late Walter Beck's concepts of Oriental and Western influences on the gardening arts. The gardens are essentially of a natural design, using man-made streams, waterways, and terraces. Many specimen trees, rhododendron, and mountain laurel. May through October: Tuesday through Friday, 10:00 A.M–4:00 P.M. Saturday and Sunday, 11:00 A.M.–5:00 P.M. A fee is charged only on weekends.

MONTICELLO: *Shofu-den Garden.* A replica of a Japanese palace garden. Extensive and beautiful grounds.

NEWARK: *The National Rose Garden,* a division of Lilac Time, has been sold for a shopping center project. Some roses will be maintained on or near the mall.

Sarah Coventry Gardens, Route 88. Formal gardens and a bird sanctuary in a 187-acre park. Fountains are lighted during the evening hours. Daily, to 10:30 P.M.

NEWBURGH: *Thomas C. Desmond Arboretum, 94 Broadway, 12550.* More than 800 species and varieties of trees, shrubs, and vines, both native and foreign, on 50 acres, as well as white-flowering and Piedmont rhododendrons. Monday through Friday, 10:00 A.M.–4:00 P.M. It is advisable to make reservations several days ahead.

NEW PALTZ: *Mohonk Show Gardens, Mohonk Mountain House, Mohonk Lake, 12561.* The gardens are part of the grounds of the hotel and are free to guests; a fee is charged for those visiting the gardens only. The preserve has 7,500 acres of woodlands, nature trails, and a well-marked wildflower path. The gardens (on 15 acres) have old-fashioned roses, large annual and perennial borders, a rock garden, a planted dry wall and some

Brooklyn Botanic Garden

field-grown plants. There are flowering crab apples, Japanese maples, tree lilacs, and beeches. A greenhouse is used for propagations and displays. Spring and summer are excellent visiting seasons. Daily, sunrise–sunset.

NEW YORK: For a city of concrete and steel, New York has more gardens within its city boundaries than any other comparable city in the country. Some are near the city boundaries, but most are in the heart of the town or near the centers of each borough.

Abby Aldrich Rockefeller Sculpture Garden, Museum of Modern Art, 11 West 53rd Street. A delightful combination of trees, shrubs, pools, fountains, and statuary. Weeping beeches, Lombardy poplars, hornbeams, andromeda, ivy, and seasonal flowers—and ample benches and sitting places. Daily, to 6:00 P.M. Fee.

Bartow-Pell Mansion and Gardens, Shore Road, Pelham Bay Park, 10464. A stately manor house with terraced gardens leading to a pool. Extremely pleasant to visit in the spring. Tuesday, Friday, and Sunday, 1:00 P.M.–5:00 P.M. Fee.

Brooklyn Botanic Garden, 1000 Washington Avenue, Brooklyn, 11225. Fifty acres in the heart of Brooklyn that are

magnificently arranged and landscaped, and are kept meticulously. The Japanese cherries and the Kanzan cherries are extravagantly beautiful in April, especially along the cherry esplanade. Also spectacular are the azaleas and rhododendrons in the formal garden or in the nearby rhododendron glen. Other gardens: a Garden of Fragrance, the Crawford Rose Garden (particularly recommended), a Japanese hill-and-pond garden, a Ryoanji Garden with a portion of a temple terrace, a lilac arboretum, excellent magnolias, annuals, perennials, and water-lily pools. The conservatory (four display houses and two growing houses) features cycads, bromeliads, orchids, ferns, economic plants, a very good bonsai collection, and an equally good collection of cacti and succulents—especially the dwarf and miniature varieties. The gardens are excellent, no matter the season; but flowering is heaviest from mid-April through June. Garden: May through October; weekdays, 9:00 A.M.–6:00 P.M., Saturday, Sunday, and holidays, 10:00 A.M.–6:00 P.M.; winter: weekdays, 10:00 A.M.–4:00 P.M.. Saturday, Sunday, and holidays, 10:00 A.M.–4:30 P.M. Conservatory: weekdays, 10:00 A.M.–4:00 P.M.;

137

Saturday, Sunday, and holidays, 11:00 A.M.–4:00 P.M. Small fees are charged for the conservatory on Sundays; for the Japanese hill and pond garden on weekends; and daily for the Ryoanji Garden.

Central Park, from 59th Street to 110th Street, between Fifth Avenue and Central Park West. A huge $2\frac{1}{2}$-by-$\frac{1}{2}$-mile tract that is completely landscaped with trees, shrubs, meadows, and lawns, and containing several ponds and a lake. There is delightful conservatory garden on the site of the old greenhouse at 105th Street and Fifth Avenue, where seasonal displays are exhibited. Other informal plantings are distributed throughout the park areas. Particularly good are the magnolias and flowering crab apples in spring (as are the hawthorns along the river in Riverside Park). As part of the landscaping there are scattered groups of lilacs and heather, as well as a Shakespeare Garden and a Ramble. Daily, sunrise–sunset.

Channel Gardens, Rockefeller Center, Fifth Avenue at 49th Street. The center was the first large project to use landscaping at both street and rooftop levels. The Channel Gardens, really an allée between several buildings, have 6 formal beds and fountains and benches; the rooftops, among them, have nearly 2 acres of gardens. More than 20,000 plants are displayed in the Channel Gardens: lilies in the spring, tropical plants in the summer, chrysanthemums in the fall, and a special illuminated display during the Christmas season. Among the mini-park gardens on the rooftops are raised tree beds, sculptures, a reflecting pool, fountains, lawns, and clipped hedges. The Channel Gardens are open at all times; the roof gardens must be visited on special tours, for which a fee is charged.

The Cloisters, Fort Tryon Park, Northern Avenue and Cabrini Circle, 10040. Medieval gardens faithfully and beautifully reproduced. Iris is featured in the Cuxa Cloister, Christmas plants in the Saint-Guilhem Cloister, herbs in the Bonnefont Cloister (140 kinds), fragrant herbs in the courtyard—70 of them from the list that Charlemagne made up for his own château garden, and 80 more from old herbal lists. Tuesday through Saturday, year round, 10:00 A.M.–5:00 P.M. Sunday, winter, 1:00 P.M.–5:00 P.M.; summer, 1:00 P.M.–6:00 P.M. Holidays, 1:00 P.M.–5:00 P.M. A donation is required.

Ford Foundation Indoor Garden

Opposite: *The Cloisters*. Above: *Channel Gardens*

Courtyard Gardens

Courtyard Gardens, Frick Collection, 1 East 70th Street. One of several courtyard gardens in New York City, and of its kind the most outstanding. Built of limestone and several kinds of marble, it has a central fountain, and flowering plants and shrubs that are moved in as required (gardenias, cinerarias, and exotic foliage plants). Tuesday through Saturday, 10:00 A.M.–5:00 P.M. (summers to 6:00 P.M.) Sunday and holidays, from 1:00 P.M. Closed major holidays. Fee (includes entrance to the museum).

Dyckman House Park and Museum, 4881 Broadway. A garden of boxwood hedges, flowers, fruit trees, and a grape arbor. Reminiscent, as is the house, of early Dutch designs. Tuesday through Sunday, 11:00 A.M.–5:00 P.M.

Ford Foundation Indoor Garden, 320 East 43rd Street, 10017. Eleven stories high, the building encloses an indoor garden containing trees, flowers, shrubs, and vines that will bloom most of the year. The garden is surrounded on two sides by L-shaped office wings, and on the other two sides by ten-story-high glass walls. Southern magnolias and jacaranda, azaleas and camellias, helxine

and Korean grass are among the very numerous collection of plants. A cistern collects water for ration usage in summer. Monday through Friday, 9:00 A.M.–5:00 P.M.

Fort Tryon Park, 190th Street and Overlook Terrace. There are 8 miles of paths in this 67-acre park, and a garden of heather, a formal garden, and informal drifts of perennials and summer annuals against a background of hemlock, beech, chestnut, and oak. An excellent garden of a type not often found in cities. A pleasant walk in spring, especially along the paths that lead ultimately to the Cloister Gardens. Daily, sunrise–sunset.

Garden of Enid, Institute of Physical Medicine and Rehabilitation, New York University, First Avenue and 34th Street. A greenhouse, complete with a selection of tropical and subtropical plants, which is used by the patients of the hospital, both children and adults, as a form of therapy, either emotional or physical. Daily, 9:00 A.M.–5:00 P.M.

Horticultural Society of New York, 128 West 58th Street, 10019. An active organization that collects and distributes horticultural information by means of lectures, displays, an excellent library, trips, and garden club meetings; it takes an active interest in the city's horticultural needs. Daily, 9:00 A.M.–5.00 P.M.

New York Botanical Garden, Bronx Park at 200th Street, 10458. The garden maintains 239 acres of landscaped grounds with 15,000 kinds of plants. The collection is so vast that home gardeners in New York may have spent years enjoying this wealth of plant material in the midst of a great borough without having seen half of the plants. The formal gardens are either near the conservatory or the museum and include the lilac and magnolia collections and the Thompson Memorial Rock Garden, which extends over $3\frac{1}{2}$ acres and contains 1,200 varieties of plants. There are informal and formal flowers beds, a good peony collection, and an outstanding rose garden that was recently completed. A magnolia grove, dwarf conifers (200 varieties), a lilac collection; the native trees are excellent.

Day lilies, iris, and dahlias have rewarding settings. Especially good in the spring is the liriodendron-lined roadway up to the museum building. The last stand of hemlock forest in the city can be found here along the edges of the Bronx River. The conservatory houses about 2,000 kinds of plants under 2 acres of glass. A palm house, a rain forest, economic plants, a fern house, orchids, cycads, cacti and succulents, and seasonal displays are worth seeing. Two large water-lily pools are just in front of the conservatory, partly shielded by two glass wings. The museum provides excellent learning opportunities for both children and adults, splendid displays, one of the best horticultural libraries, and a research program that has rarely been excelled. There is always plenty to see during any month of the year, but May and June are good months for the outdoor flowers, October and November for the chrysanthemums and fall flowers. Park: daily 10:00 A.M.–one-half hour before sunset. Conservatory: daily 10:00 A.M.–4:00 P.M. Fee only for parking.

Queens Botanic Garden, 42-50 Main Street, Flushing, 11355. On the 26 landscaped acres are a rose garden, an ericaceous garden, a fragrance garden, dwarf conifers, and an excellent collection of rhododendrons. There is a tulip display in spring, roses in summer, and chrysanthemums from mid-September to mid-November. Green-

Below: *New York Botanical Garden.* Opposite: *Hammond Museum Oriental Stroll Garden*

New York Botanical Garden

Above: *Bayard Cutting Arboretum*

house. Daily, 9:00 A.M.–dusk.

Van Cortlandt Manor and Garden, Broadway and 246th Street. A formal Dutch garden reminiscent of the eighteenth century.

Wave Hill Center for Environmental Studies, 675 West 252nd Street, The Bronx, 10471. A 28-acre area in upper New York City, with wildflowers and a nature trail; it is landscaped with a rose garden, an herb garden, an aquatic garden, a palm court, and three greenhouses. From mid-April to mid-November: Thursday through Sunday, 9:00 A.M.–5:00 P.M. Fee.

NIAGARA FALLS: *Rose Garden, Hyde Park.*

NORTH SALEM: *Hammond Museum, Deveau Road, 10560.* The museum has built on 3½ acres an Oriental Stroll Garden, with charming Oriental plantings, and a reflection pool, a Zen garden, and a dry waterfall. From May 30 to October 30: Wednesday through Sunday, 11:00 A.M.–5:00 P.M. Fee.

OAKDALE (SUFFOLK Co.) *Bayard Cutting Arboretum, Montauk Highway, 11769.* An outstanding pinetum with massed plantings of broadleaf evergreens and wild-flower gardens on 690 acres. About 75 of the acres are

landscaped, including many rhododendrons that were planted in 1887, a rose garden, lilacs, holly, azaleas, mountain laurel, dogwood, and native shrubs. A cypress swamp is interesting to naturalist-minded gardeners. Among the specimen trees are weeping hemlocks, Cilician firs, spruces, and aspens, and many one-of-a-kind evergreens. Blooming starts in March and climaxes in mid-June. From April 15 to October 30: daily, 9:00 A.M.–6:00 P.M. Winter: Daily, 9:00 A.M.–dusk. Fee.

OLD WESTBURY: *Old Westbury Gardens, Old Westbury Road, 11568.* A beautiful home and estate of 100 acres started in 1905. Landscaped somewhat in the manner of old English manor houses with five gardens. Avenues of lindens and beech, a pinetum, a wildflower preserve and trail; and such specimens as Korean pines, Atlas cedars, and cucumber magnolias. The formal gardens have several subgardens: a boxwood garden, a cottage garden, a rose garden, and a walled Italian Garden (which has a lily pond), trees, and 2 acres of perennial and annual borders. More than ample plantings of azaleas and rhododendrons, and a wealth of lilacs and

New York Botanical Garden

primroses. A child's garden with a small thatched cottage is a joy, particularly for adults. From early May to late October: Wednesday through Sunday and holidays, 10:00 A.M.–5:00 P.M. Fee.

OSSINING: *Kitchawan Research Laboratory, 712 Kitchawan Road, 10652*. Operated by the Brooklyn Botanic Garden (NYC), a 235-acre preserve for laboratory studies and trails for nature study and conservation education. Write to the Director's office of the Brooklyn Botanic Garden for permission to visit the preserve.

The garden also manages the *Teatown Lake Reservation, Spring Valley Road, 10562*. A Langley teacher-training-program.

OYSTER BAY: *Planting Fields Arboretum, Planting Fields Road, 11771*. An abundance of plants (5,500 kinds) on 409 acres; about 150 of the acres are landscaped plantings. Magnificent specimen trees (silver linden, cedar, weeping hemlock, European beech) and a rhododendron walk of great splendor. The teaching gardens have shrubs arranged alphabetically—a sort of simplified synoptic garden. The collections include azaleas, dwarf conifers, hollies. The display greenhouses keep collections of begonias, orchids and other tropical plants, cacti and other succulents, and camellias. The seasonal flowers reach a peak between April and early June. Gardens: daily, 10:00 A.M.–4:00 P.M. Greenhouses: Monday through Friday, 10:00 A.M.–4:00 P.M.; Sunday, 1:00 A.M.–4:00 P.M. Fee.

POUGHKEEPSIE: *Vassar College, Raymond Avenue*. The campus has been landscaped with many trees, both native and from other areas, which are now mature and and very beautiful. There is also a Shakespeare Garden. Daily.

ROCHESTER: *Cobbs Hill Park*. Many lilacs and Chinese shrubs. Rochester was once the center of a plant quarantine station, and many of the plantings in the parks are irreplaceable. (See Durand-Eastman Park, below). Daily.

Durand-Eastman Park, Kings Highway. Between the two parks, Durand and Highland, there are 500 acres of planting and more than 4,000 species and varieties of plants. The plant features are flowering crab apples, cherries, magnolias, dogwood, fragrant snowbell, conifers, roses. The peak of flowering will be sometime between late April and early May. Daily, dawn–dusk.

Garden of Fragrance, Museum of Arts and Sciences, 687 East Avenue. Some 100 varieties of herbs arranged in 8 beds coincidental to their uses: culinary, aromatic, medicinal, etc. The roses in the garden illustrate pictorially their history from 1,000 B.C. to the first hybrid tea. There are special beds for the Chinese and Victorian roses. Daily, 9:00 A.M.–sunset.

Highland Park, Mount Hope Avenue and South Goodman Street. The park covers 125 acres and includes many mature rare shrubs and trees: European hornbeam, Asiatic maple, Turkish hazelnut, hawthorn, and holly. The named lilac varieties (500) are among the best in the country. Covering nearly 22 acres, with nearly 2,000 lilacs, varieties dating back to colonial times as well as most of the great double-flowering varieties are included. A special day each year is set aside in their honor. There are many exciting garden displays: azaleas, rhododendrons, roses, peonies, tulips, annuals, chrysanthemums. The Lamberton Conservatory has seasonal displays against a background of 40,000 plants kept regularly in the conservatory. Park: daily, dawn–11:00 P.M. Conservatory: daily, 9:00 A.M.–5:00 P.M. For information about Lilac Sunday (and the Monroe County Arboretum), write to Monroe County Parks Bureau, 375 Westfall Road, Rochester, N.Y. 14620.

Maplewood Rose Garden, Lake Avenue. Roses, hawthorns, flowering crab apples. Daily.

Poet's Garden, Werner Castle Grounds of the Garden Center, 5 Castle Park Avenue. An attractive garden center.

ROSLYN: *William Cullen Bryant Preserve.* Formerly the Frick Estate and the Clayton Pinetum. As yet, it is not open to the public. For information, write to the Nassau County Recreation and Parks Division, Eisenhower Park, East Meadow, N.Y. 11554.

SARATOGA SPRINGS: *Congress Park.* Italian garden, annuals and perennials.

Petrified Sea Gardens, Route 29. A large rock garden in an extraordinary park of petrified plants; a water-lily pool and seasonal floral displays. May through October: 9:00 A.M.–6:00 P.M. Fee.

SCHENECTADY: *Jackson Garden of Union College, Union Street, 12308.* Evergreen and wildflower gardens;

Opposite, above, and below: *Old Westbury Gardens*

a rose garden. Specific collections include anemones, ferns, primulas, tree peonies, tuberous begonias, and annuals. The garden (20 acres) was started 125 years ago, and many of the plants—such as mountain laurel, lily of the valley, and the old-fashioned flowers—have pleasant histories. April through November: 9:00 A.M.–sunset.

SOUTHAMPTON: *Parrish Art Museum, 25 Job's Lane*. A small arboretum of unusual trees and shrubs. May through October: Tuesday through Saturday, 10:00 A.M.–4:45 P.M. Winter: Thursday through Saturday, 10:00 A.M.–4:45 P.M. Sunday, all year, 2:00 P.M.–4:45 P.M.

SYOSSET: *Christie Pinetum*. Not as yet open to the public. Information can be secured from the Nassau County Recreation and Parks Division, Eisenhower Park, East Meadow, N.Y. 11554.

SYRACUSE: *Edmund Mills Rose Garden, Thoren Park*. About 10,000 roses (275 varieties) on 3 acres; in addition, tulips, an annual garden, a perennial garden, a garden of culinary and medicinal herbs. Particularly lovely when the gardens are illuminated at night. Daily, daylight hours.

Burlington Memorial Gardens. Alpine plants.

TARRYTOWN: *Lyndhurst, 635 South Broadway, 10591*. A Gothic mansion set down on 67 acres of attractive landscaping. The arboretum has trees planted during the previous century, primarily native trees and those from countries whose climate was comparable to the Tarrytown region. Gingko, star magnolia, weeping beech, larch, and linden. A rose garden, good wisterias, nature trails, and a greenhouse—the largest in the country when it was built—now to be restored. From April 1 to October 31: daily, 10:00 A.M.–5:00 P.M. Fee.

Sunnyside, Route 9D, just below Lyndhurst, deserves a visit if only for the landscaping, which is good, and because it is close by.

TUXEDO PARK: *Sterling Forest, Route 210, 10987*. Established as a commercial enterprise, the gardens are well maintained in the midst of a forest. Color is a feature, and it changes with the seasons. Tulips (nearly a million of them) and other spring bulbs; annuals and tuberous begonias, many in baskets hanging from trees; chrysanthemums for fall. Also a rose garden, a water garden, and a poetry garden. From May 1 to late October: Daily, 9:30 A.M.–6:00 P.M. Closed rest of the year (although part of the area becomes a ski ground in winter). Fee.

Sterling Forest Gardens

North Carolina

ASHEVILLE: *Biltmore House and Gardens, Route 25, 28803.* An extraordinary French Renaissance château (365 rooms) and 35 acres of formal gardens. Actually there are 11,000 acres of the estate left from the original grant of 125,000 on which George Washington Biltmore built his mansion. The approach road is through a stand of pine and hemlock, edged with rhododendrons and mountain laurel. Although the arboretum is not unusual, the gardens, based on Vaux-le-Vicomte, are very special. These include a magnificent 4-acre enclosed English garden with espaliered walls, one of the finest gardens of its type in the country; an Italian garden, with pools and water lilies; a rose garden (5,000 bushes); an azalea garden of native species (one of the best collections); plus English ivy, wisteria, and excellent boxwood. Bulbs and peonies provide bright interest in the spring; iris later. There is an orchid display in the greenhouse, whose exterior is circled with holly. Daily, 9:00 A.M.–6:00 P.M. Closed from December 15 to February 1. Fee.

University Botanical Gardens, University of North Carolina, W. T. Weaver Boulevard, 28806. The botanical gardens— the largest in the Southeast—are located on the university campus on a 10-acre site. The plant species grown here, limited to those native to North Carolina, now number about 2,000 of the 3,000 known species. The gardens are primarily a source for study, a center for horticultural information, and a focus for conservation efforts. Beautifully landscaped; two great lawns backed with many varieties of trees and shrubs, a bog garden, a fragrance garden, an herb garden, walks and shelters and wildflowers. A small greenhouse is nearby. Daily, dawn–dusk.

Graggy Gardens on Blue Ridge Parkway (about 17 miles north of Asheville, at milepost 364.6). Nearly 600 acres of Catawba rhododendrons at an elevation of 6,000 feet. Peaking around the middle of June, give or take a week. The sight of so many wild rhododendrons (and patches of flame azaleas) is almost too much to be believed. These natural gardens are as good as any formal or informal planting in the country.

Also, in the nearby *Pisgah National Forest*, the mountain laurel in mid-June is a pink delight.

BATH: *The Bonner House Meditation Garden.* In North Carolina's oldest town, an 18th-century home largely

Tryon Palace Restoration

surrounded with gardenias, wisteria, crape myrtle, and azaleas; there is a quiet retreat that gives its name to the entire garden. Oyster-shell paths. Tuesday through Saturday, 10:00 A.M.–5:00 P.M. Sunday, 2:00 P.M.–5:00 P.M. Fee.

BLOWING ROCK: *Martha Franck Fragrance Garden, North Carolina Rehabilitation Center for the Blind.* An acre of raised beds, easily accessible and designed especially to overcome the major handicap of the blind. It is filled with fragrant flowers, herbs, and bulbs. Students are encouraged to touch, feel, and taste—and to enjoy the the fragile perfumes. The distinction here is not so much in the plants in the garden as in the novelty of a garden tailored to the physical needs of the blind and the handicapped.

BOONE: *Daniel Boone Native Gardens, Horn in the West Drive, 28607.* An extensive collection of native plants, largely in an informally landscaped setting so that they may easily be located and studied. There is a large rockery and pool, a grassed allée lined with blueberry and pink and white dogwood, and 14 varieties of azaleas. A dry wall of dicentra, columbine, iris, pinks interspersed with ferns. A wishing well, a reflection pool surrounded with rhododendrons, kalmia, and conifers; and a bower of violets and ferns. A rustic bridge leads to a woodland path where shade-loving wildflowers may be found. July and August: Daily except Monday, 9:00 A.M.–7:00 P.M. May, June, September, and October: Daily except Monday, 9:00 A.M.–5:00 P.M. Fee.

CHAPEL HILL: *Coker Arboretum, University of North Carolina Campus, Laurel Hill Road, 27514.* A 5-acre arboretum of native and ornamental trees and shrubs. Once a swamp, now drained, it has a collection of 350 different kinds of temperate-zone woody plants. Daffodils and crocus are used for underplanting. Daily, 8:00 A.M.–5:00 P.M.

The North Carolina Botanical Garden, University of North Carolina, Laurel Hill Road, 27514. Started in 1952 with 70 acres, the botanical garden now includes 329 acres of virgin forest, mature pines, woodlands, fields, a stream, and trails for displaying the native plants of North Carolina in their natural settings. There are Oconee bells—the shortia that was lost for over a hundred years—Venus's fly-traps, purple rhododendrons, witch

Elizabethan Garden

148

Sarah P. Duke Gardens

The Gourd Museum

hazel, dog trilliums, jack-in-the-pulpits, trout lilies, yellow-fringed orchids and other endangered species, and rare plants. Daily, 8:00 A.M.–5:00 P.M.

CHARLOTTE: *Rhododendron Gardens, University of North Carolina, Route 49.*

CHERRYVILLE: *The Iron Gate Garden.* So named because of the intricate ironwork of its gate. The garden has 5 acres of flowering plants and an outstanding collection of day lilies.

CLEMMONS: *Tanglewood Park.* Among many other tourist attractions, an arboretum with fragrance gardens. Daily.

DURHAM: *Sarah P. Duke Gardens, Duke University, 27706.* The gardens are at the west entrance to the campus on 55 acres of land. Surrounding them are pines and magnolias, evergreen shrubs, and naturalized daffodils. There is a rose garden, an azalea court garden, a wisteria pergola, terraces, a rock garden, the Hanes iris garden, a grass and sky garden, and the Bloomquist garden. Peak flowering begins in mid-April and lasts through mid-May, with flowering crab apples, cherries, dogwoods, redbud, and spring bulbs. Annuals and perennials and begonias are featured in summer, and a large chrysanthemum show may be seen in the fall. Winter is accompanied by firet horns and their brilliant berries, nandina, winter jasmine, and holly. These are essentially gardens for continuous bloom. An Oriental tea house is planned for the near future. Daily, 8:00 A.M.–sunset.

FUQUAY SPRINGS (VARINA): *The Gourd Museum, Route 55, 27526.* The growing and display of gourds, from miniatures to giants. For those who like gourds, the 12-acre home and museum of gourds provides a wealth of fantastic shapes and unexpected uses—from cups to musical instruments. Daily, summer, 8:00 A.M.–10:00 P.M.; winter, 8:00 A.M.–6:00 P.M.

GREENSBORO: *Anniversary Garden.* A natural garden with a variety of plants, trees, and wildflowers—azaleas, rhododendrons, iris, peonies, and day lilies that show best from April to May and into June.

MANTEO: *The Elizabethan Garden, Roanoke Island, 27954.* Located near the site of the "Lost Colony," the 10½-acre garden includes a park of native shrubs, trees, and flowers enclosing a formal garden of clipped hedges

Above, and opposite page: *Tryon Palace Restoration*

Poets and Dreamers Gardens

North Carolina Botanic Garden

and perennials. In the formal area there is a sunken garden, a mount, and a terrace garden with appropriate statuary, with paths winding unexpectedly by wild-flowers—all reminiscent of Elizabethan pleasure gardens. Yet the garden is neither a restoration nor a replica of other, older gardens; it is one that might have been developed by the settlers of the Lost Colony if they had survived and thrived. There is round-the-year color: camellias are featured through fall and winter; April brings masses of azaleas and dogwood, flowering fruits, and spring bulbs; summer is noted for gardenias, fragrant herbs, crape myrtle, day lilies, hydrangeas, and hundreds of ferns and wildflowers tucked under shrubs and trees. Daily, 9:30 A.M.–4:30 P.M.; to 6:30 P.M. when there are performances of an historical play. Fee.

NEW BERN: *Tryon Palace Gardens, 1618 Pollock Street, 28560.* Built in 1767–70, the palace was burned by accident 28 years later and lay in ruins until restoration began in 1952. It is a magnificent example of careful research and painstaking restoration. The original gardens were influenced by the English gardens of the mid-18th century, and these principles have been

followed meticulously, using only plant materials imported or known locally prior to 1770. Native American plants such as magnolia, yaupon, myrtle, wild cherry, laurel, and wild sweet crab were particularly useful ornaments in the gardens. The clipped edging hedges of yaupon must be seen to be believed. Plantings of dense shrubbery and trees, of different heights, flank the lawns. Two private (or privy) gardens that can only be seen from the house and away from prying eyes are now known as the Green and the Kellenberger gardens. There are walls for espaliered fruits and a kitchen garden in which both flowers and vegetables are intermingled—small French strawberries, for example, vie with fragrant roses. The Maude Moore Latham Garden is unique, the most ornately geometrical of the gardens; flower beds of different shapes are bordered with clipped yaupon and filled with colorful flowers, and each bed is separated from the others by intricate brick paths. The Kellenberger Garden is a rectangle encircled with brick walls on which Confederate jasmine, cruel vines, and pyracantha form a background to the flower beds. The Green Garden has an extraordinary clipped hedge

of yaupon shaped rather like a double cross. Hawks Allée, leading to the house, is filled with low flowering plants, especially lilies and clipped holly and Cherokee roses. A work garden has hotbeds and a shade house strung with growing gourds. There is a topiary hedge near the patio that is delightful. Within the present limits of the estate, there are three subsidiary gardens near the palace gardens: the Stevenson House Garden—a green garden with white flowers; the Jones House Garden, with raised beds of camellias, azaleas, gardenias, and creeping phlox; and a third garden at the Stanley House, a sort of enclosed town house garden, with brick walls enclosing trees, shrubs, and tulips, hyacinths, damask roses, daffodils, peonies, candytuft, lavender, and many other plants dear to the hearts of old-fashioned gardeners. Tuesday through Saturday, 9:30 A.M.–4:00 P.M. Sunday, 1:00 P.M.–4:00 P.M. Closed Thanksgiving, December 24 to 26, and New Year's Day. Fee.

PEARSON'S FALLS: *A botanical sanctuary.*

PINEHURST: *Clarendon Gardens, Linden Road, 28374.* The largest collection of hollies in the United States (more than 200 varieties). Iris and azaleas along the woodland paths. Chrysanthemums in November, and camellias from fall to January. Daffodils, hyacinths, dogwood in the spring. Crape myrtle, phlox, day lilies in summer. Daily. Sunday: 1:00 P.M.–5:00 P.M.

RALEIGH: *All Faiths Chapel Garden, Dorothea Dix Hospital.* A planned and planted garden for year-round interest to hospital patients as well as visitors.

North Carolina State University Horticultural Science Test Gardens, 27607. Many roses are grown from both the All-America selections and from newly named varieties. The gardens also conduct plant trials for annuals and bedding plants. The university manages the *Grandpappy Holly Arboretum* at New Bern, an official arboretum of the Holly Society of America.

Raleigh Rose Garden, Pogue Street. A garden of 2,000 bushes that reach a flowering peak in May-June.

WRAL Gardens, Western Boulevard. A large landscaped area featuring many azaleas. Daily.

RED SPRINGS: *Flora MacDonald Azalea Gardens, Vardell Hall Junior College.* A very old campus garden of mature, native azaleas and their hybrids. Daily.

REIDSVILLE: *Chinqua-Penn Plantation, Wentworth Road.*

An English country house with formal gardens and rose gardens. From March 1 to December 15: Wednesday through Saturday, 10:00 A.M.–4:00 P.M. Sunday, 1:00 P.M.–4:00 P.M. Fee.

SALEMBURG: *Laurel Lake Gardens.* Azaleas, camellias, and hollies in informal gardens; a nursery. Daily.

SALISBURY: *Poets' and Dreamers' Garden, Livingston College.* Special plantings that honor noted poets. A Biblical garden consisting of herbs and flowers mentioned in the Bible. A Shakespeare garden accomplishes much the same thing in relation to Shakespearean writings. A fountain, illuminated at night. And an international garden with shrubs and flowers of other countries. Daily.

SOUTHERN PINES: *Carolina Orchids.* Some 70,000 plants (10,000 different kinds) in the greenhouses of a well-known grower. Tours each Monday through Friday, 2:00 P.M.–4:00 P.M.

WAYNESVILLE: *Freelander Dahlia Gardens.* One of the largest displays of staked dahlias; and also many roses and chestnut trees. Open only during the flowering season (late summer).

WILMINGTON: *Airlie Gardens, Wrightville Beach Highway.* On 155 acres, formal and informal gardens that may be viewed from an automobile. Landscaped against the pines, hardwoods, and live oaks are magnolias, azaleas, camellias—especially japonicas—and wisteria. A lake, its banks lined with azaleas, has a bridge hung with banksia roses. Daily. Fee.

Greenfield Gardens, Carolina Beach Highway (South 3rd Street), 28401. Around a 125-acre lake are thousands upon thousands of azaleas, camellias, dogwood, roses, water lilies, daffodils, holly, hawthorn, and flowering crab apples. The home of an azalea festival and a storybook zoo for children. Daily.

WINNABOW: *Orton Plantation Gardens, Route 133, 28401.* Many fine specimen trees, among them live oak, camphor tree, and pine. Quiet paths shaded by live oaks wind through 3 acres of informal gardens. There is a stroll garden, a sun garden, a water garden, a garden of only white flowers, Japanese and Indian azaleas, dogwood, camellias, roses, fragrant plants, and annuals and perennials. Flowering is excellent in April and picks up again in the fall. Only the gardens are open. Spring and summer: daily, 8:00 A.M.–5:00 P.M. Fee.

WINSTON-SALEM: *Reynolda Gardens of Wake Forest University, Reynolda Road, 27109.* The gardens, on 148 acres with 1,000 varieties of plants, are interesting for the 4-acre formal garden with its flowering cherries, magnolias, bald cypress, and boxwood, and for the collections of junipers and hollies. A pool and a tea house are at the far end of the greenhouse range which has a collection of ivies intriguing to hobbyists. Weeping Japanese cherries are planted along the walks. Visits to the gardens are best made in spring or in fall. Daily, dawn–dusk. Fee.

North Dakota

AMIDON: *Columnar Cedars.* Growing near a burning coal vein, these cedars, related to Rocky Mountain junipers, are the only ones known to grow in a columnar shape. There is no known reason for the phenomenon. The hills and plains, here and elsewhere in North Dakota—where once great forests flourished—have an astounding range of wildflowers. Some 2,000 kinds have been catalogued—cacti and yuccas, dogwood and American plums, prairie rose and phlox, cornflower, Mariposa lily, and innumerable others, many of them garden and rock garden favorites.

DUNSEITH: *International Peace Garden, Route 2, 58329.* Astride the Canadian-American border, and symbolizing the peace between the two nations, the 2,300 acre tract is beautifully landscaped with ornamental shrubs, trees,

tulips, lythrum and other summer perennials, thousands of bedding plants, gladioli, and asters. Around the central buildings there are 7 levels of terracing leading downward, alongside water plantings, to a clover-shaped sunken garden of 2,000 roses. The garden is best known for its international music programs. April through November: daily.

MINOT: *Theodore Roosevelt Park and Zoo, 1215 4th Avenue, 58701.* Among other local attractions, 10 acres of formal lawns and a sunken garden. May through September: daily, 6:00 A.M.–10:00 P.M. October through April: 9:00 A.M.–9:00 P.M.

WAHPETON: *Chahinkapa Park, 1st Street and 7th Avenue.* Pleasant gardens in addition to a zoo and an aviary. Daily.

International Peace Garden.

Ohio

AKRON: *Stan Hywet Gardens, 714 North Portage Path, 44303.* An authentically styled Tudor mansion on 65 acres, of which 35 acres are in gardens and lawns and orchards. A rose garden, an English walled garden. a rhododendron walk, a birch tree lane, terraces, pools, and statuary. A good selection of tulips (20,000) yearly; daffodils (50,000), forsythia, and wildflowers in the spring, followed by flowering crab apples, flowering fruit trees, and lilacs. Then rhododendrons and azaleas, iris (350 varieties), peonies (400 kinds), daylilies, gladioli, and finally dahlias and chrysanthemums (8,000 massed plants) to end the season. Tuesday through Saturday, 10:00 A.M.–4:15 P.M. Sunday, 1:00 P.M.–5:00 P.M. Fee.

BERKEY: *Secor Park Arboretum, RR 1, 93504.* Flowering trees and shrubs and six nature trails in a woodland area of 500 acres. Ornamentals: magnolias, an evergreen grove, and native trees. Greenhouse. Weekdays, 9:00 A.M.–5:00 P.M. Saturday, Sunday, and holidays, 11:00 A.M.–6:00 P.M.

CANTON: *Garden Center, Stadium Park.* A Japanese garden and masses of tulips in the spring, chrysanthemums for the fall, and in between those seasons, peonies. The Center itself has many floral displays. Daily, 9:00 A.M.–5:00 P.M. Closed holidays and during August. *Zoological and Botanical Gardens, 12th Street, N.E.* Daily, 10:00 A.M.–4:00 P.M.

CHILLICOTHE: *Adena Gardens.* The Colonial garden has 40 varieties of roses, all known before 1813, and many perennials of the same period. From April 1 to October 31: daily except Monday, 9:00 A.M.–4:30 P.M.

CINCINNATI: *Ault Park, Heeking Avenue.* A garden of 1,800 roses, old-fashioned and modern, and a recognized rose demonstration garden. A dahlia trial garden (1,000 kinds); extensive borders of peonies and annuals. Flowering crab apples and flowering cherries. The emphasis in this garden is on flowering.

The Garden Center of Greater Cincinnati, 2715 Reading Road. Provides an excellent center of horticultural activities, even in subzero weather. Model plantings: roses, grasses, and evergreens; and a garden for the blind. Monday through Friday, 9:30 A.M.–4:30 P.M.

The Hinkle Gardens, nearby, have flowering trees and shrubs, basic perennials, day lilies, iris, and peonies. Daily, 7:00 A.M.–11:00 P.M.

Ault Park

Top: *Mount Airy Arboretum.* Above: *Sooty Acres Botanic Garden*

Krohn Conservatory, 950 Eden Park Drive. Display areas and 6 seasonal shows (some unusual) in the 20,000 square-foot conservatory. The regular collection (over 700 varieties and species) includes: tropical shrubs, ferns, aroids, cacti, succulents, orchids, palms, and an arrangement of plants representative of a tropical jungle. The shows (each lasting two months): pre-spring, Easter, Mother's Day, summer, Mum, Christmas. Monday through Saturday, 10:00 A.M.–5:00 P.M. Sunday, 10:00 A.M.–6:00 P.M. (Special night hours for Easter and Christmas.)

Mount Airy Forest and Arboretum, 5083 Colerain Avenue, 45223. Also located in Ault Park, (see above), the tract includes 1,500 acres of man-made forest, the first municipal reforestation project in this country. The arboretum section, 120 acres, includes more than 1,700 species of trees, shrubs, and ground covers. Special attractions: the Green Garden, a display of many ground covers; the Braam Area, a collection of azaleas and rhododendrons; the Daisy Jones Garden, in which the perennials are gathered; the Garden of the States, in which there is a tree, shrub, flower—the official

plants—for each state. The collections are arranged within landscaped areas, and many of them are somewhat arranged in family groups. Arboretum: daily, 7:00 A.M.–dusk. Forest: daily, 7:00 A.M.–11:00 P.M.

Sooty Acres Botanic Garden, Reading Road and William Howard Taft Avenue. Now more correctly known as the Cornelius J. Hauck Botanic Garden. Once a private garden, it has many interesting and rare plant specimens—for example, the Lea oak and the Manchurian sawtooth oak. Of considerable interest is the dwarf evergreen garden with over 50 varieties of pine, spruce, fir, and other conifers. Monday through Friday, 10:00 A.M.–4:00 P.M. Closed holidays.

Spring Grove Cemetery, 4521 Spring Grove Avenue, 45232. This cemetery, as well as those in Massachusetts, Ohio, and in several Southern states, was included in a campaign during the last century to make such places beautiful. As a result, there are many unrivaled specimen trees in these cemeteries. Here one can see a rose garden, a collection of American hollies, and many cultivars of of English ivy; and bulbs in spring and annuals in summer. An extraordinarily lovely 400 acres of land-

Above and opposite: *Franklyn Park Conservatory*

Western Reserve Herb Society Garden

scaping. Daily, 8:00 A.M.–5:00 P.M.

Winton Woods, 10245 Winton Road, 45231. A wildflower reserve; guided tours only (Spring). Also included at the same address are additional guided tours through Sharon Woods and the Miami Whitewater Forest.

CLEVELAND: *Rockefeller Park, East Boulevard and Liberty Street*. Nineteen nations are represented in the Cultural Gardens (40 acres), each with a garden distinctively styled with plants and sculptures, representing the backgrounds of Cleveland's diverse citizenry. Included are an Italian hillside garden, a Hebrew garden with rock plants from Palestine, a Hungarian garden, and gardens symbolic of Greece, Poland, Germany, and other countries. In addition, there is a Brotherhood Garden and a Shakespeare Garden. A large greenhouse is used for the propagation of park plants and for special displays.

Rockefeller Park Greenhouse, 750 East 88th Street. Special sections are devoted to tropical plants, economic plants, palms, ferns, cacti, and orchids. Lavish shows are also held of plants characteristically associated with various seasons. (Monday through Saturday, 8:00 A.M.–

4:00 P.M. Sunday, 8:00 A.M.–5:00 P.M.)

A Japanese Garden to the north of the greenhouse entrance is an exotic arrangement of walks, benches, a waterfall, a pool, shrubs, trees, and an authentic Japanese well. Rhododendrons and azaleas are profusely planted along the borders.

Talking Garden for the Blind is on the north side of the greenhouse. It places emphasis on fragrant flowers, scented foliage, and textures. Visitors are encouraged to feel, sniff, even crush those leaves whose fragrance must thus be released. There are also talking boxes with tape-recorded information for both sightless and sighted persons alike.

Western Reserve Herb Society Garden, Garden Center of Greater Cleveland, 11030 East Boulevard, 44106. Herbs arranged by their uses—dye plants, fragrant herbs, culinary herbs, medicinal plants—in a knot garden and surrounding beds. A rose garden and a rose trial and cutting garden, pools for aquatics. Hyacinths and an exceptional tulip garden in early spring; wallflowers in May. In June, alliums, blue-flowered chives, catnip, scented geraniums, and historical roses. The design of

the garden was adapted from early monastery gardens and castle-keep gardens of the Middle Ages. Monday through Friday, 9:00 A.M.–5:00 P.M. Sunday, 2:00 P.M.–5:00 P.M.

COLUMBUS: *Floriculture Garden of Ohio State University, Route 62.* The Demoyne Tulip Garden, and pot-grown chrysanthemums in the test gardens.

Franklin Park Conservatory, 16000 East Broad Street. Trees, plants, and flowers foreign to the Ohio climate are grown in a tropical atmosphere. Special displays at Easter, in autumn, and at Christmas. No one knows how or why the conservatory reached Columbus from the 1893 World's Fair in Chicago (the records were burned in the Columbus fire); and few can recall the time in 1926 when the conservatory also housed the zoo animals, including monkeys and an elephant, while new quarters were being prepared for them. Monday through Friday, 9:00 A.M.–4:00 P.M. Saturday and Sunday, 9:00 A.M.–5:00 P.M.

Park of Roses, Whetstone Park, High Street and Hollenback Drive. On 13½ acres there are 36,000 rose bushes of 425 different varieties—a rose fantasia. This is one of the country's largest collections, and also includes an excellent group of old-fashioned favorites and a rose testing garden. Adjacent to the garden is the headquarters of the American Rose Society, where visitors are always welcome during business hours. Completing the park's horticultural holdings are 5½ acres featuring perennial gardens and flowering crab apples. The floral peak occurs in June. From May 30 to October 15: 10:00 A.M.–dusk. (Sometimes the gardens have been lighted in the evening.) Fee.

DAYTON: *Dayton Council Garden Center, 1820 Brown Street.* There are 26 gardens in this Center. Daily.

James M. Cox, Jr. Arboretum, 6733 Springboro Pike, 45449. A recent (1967) addition to the country's arboretums, but effective planting and display of trees, shrubs, and vines overcomes many of the handicaps of youthfulness. The arboretum (164 acres) has a very good collection of flowering crab apples, a lathhouse display area, and a greenhouse. The shrub collection is being arranged in synoptic groups. Daily, dawn–dusk.

GATES MILLS: *Orchid Conservatory, Neill Greenhouses, Inc., 2045 SOM Center Road.* Hundreds of orchids and such tropicals as a ginger tree, vanilla, Persian plum—rarely seen in the Ohio area.

KENT: *Wolcott Lilac Gardens, 450 West Main Street.* A collection of tulips, peonies, and more than 100 different varieties of lilacs. Fee.

LAKEWOOD: *Oldest Stone House, Lakewood Park, 1200 Andrews Avenue, 44107.* The favorite flowers of a century ago: primroses, heartsease, bachelor's button, and others, that added color to the old-fashioned gardens. An herb garden that is laid out in an orderly manner, but in which flowers and herbs (and vegetables in those days) are mixed for fragrance and color and use. Wednesday and Sunday, 2:00 P.M.–5:00 P.M.

LORAIN: *Memorial Rose Garden, Lakeview Park, West Erie Avenue.* Some 4,000 hybrid roses (75 varieties) in 48 separate beds and laid out in a cycloid. A fountain lighted at night and a large concrete floral basket.

LUCAS: *Malabar Farm, Pleasant Valley Road.* The farm and home of author Louis Bromfield, which he developed from four worn-out farms into one of the most productive farms in the country, thereby helping to develop better farming and agricultural practices. The lilacs around the home are now more than twenty years old, and visitors are welcomed, without charge, to see them. Monday through Saturday, 9:00 A.M.–5:00 P.M. Sunday, 1:00 P.M.–5:00 P.M. A fee is charged for the farm tour.

MANSFIELD: *Kingswood Center, 900 Park Avenue West, 44903.* An unusually attractive garden (47 acres), with an all-season interest and seasonal displays as well. The extensive collections of trees, shrubs, and plants are those most suitable for central Ohio. An American Iris Society Test Garden (1,000 cultivars), annuals and perennials in the formal gardens, roses (largely in a test garden), special dahlias (150 varieties), lilies (50 cultivars), day lilies (400 kinds), and 400 kinds of peonies; gladioli in abundance, and daffodils, tulips (a major display), wildflowers, and chrysanthemums (also a major display). A good collection of ornamental trees and evergreens. The greenhouses are devoted to a considerable number of columneas and cacti. Gardens: Daily, 8:00 A.M.–sunset. Kingwood Hall and the Library: Monday through Friday, 8:00 A.M.–5:00 P.M.; Sunday, 1:30 P.M.–4:30 P.M.

MENTOR: *Holden Arboretum, 9500 Sperry Road, 44060.*

Above and opposite: *Kingwood Center*

Part field and part woodland tract of 2,600 acres, with lakes, the arboretum has 6,000 different kinds of plants collected from all over the world. It serves as a nature center, a research and teaching center, and a study area for ornamentals. Noteworthy are the exotic nut trees, 200 kinds of ornamental fruit trees, conifers, hollies, acres of lilacs and rhododendrons, a hillside of azaleas, and maples. It is most colorful in May, when more than 200 kinds of flowering trees are in bloom, and in October, when foliage is colored. April through October: 10:00 A.M.–7:00 P.M. November through March: 10:00 A.M.–4:00 P.M. Fee.

The Wayside Gardens, 8605 Mentor Avenue. Something is always blooming here from early July to late in the fall. And the fields, especially when the phlox bloom, can be quite spectacular. Perennials, shrubs, roses, and special gardens of plants not as yet introduced to Ohio gardeners. Monday through Friday, during business hours. Saturday, until noon.

NEWARK: *The Dawes Arboretum, Route 5, 43055.* Privately endowed and dedicated to promote the planting of forest and ornamental trees, to increase knowledge, and to improve methods of cultivation, the arboretum encourages students from second-graders to golden-age gardeners. The cultivated areas have good collections of holly, hawthorn, viburnums, rhododendrons, and azaleas. There is a small tropical greenhouse. The balance of the 850-acre estate has a Japanese garden (complete with a lake and a meditation house) that, although designed in the Japanese classic tradition, has made excellent use of the hardier similar American plant materials—a most successful blending of Oriental tradition and American plants. The children's gardens—with a demonstration of maple-syrup collecting and making—have been most successful. School children from the elementary schools spend a considerable number of class hours learning their lessons in the arboretum, as well as learning lessons from the arboretum. Of special interest to visitors are the flowering crab apples and the magnolias, flowering in May. June is also colorful, and fall and winter are very exciting. Daily, sunrise–sunset.

SANDUSKY: *Washington Park.* Six intricate floral mounds are planted twice each season; and lighted by

Above, and below: *Dawes Arboretum*

Oldest Stone House Garden

Holden Arboretum

night.

STRONGVILLE: *Gardenview Horticultural Park, 16711 Pearl Road (Route 42), 44136.* The gardens are extensive and designed to provide gardening visitors with many ideas that may easily be adapted to their own home gardens. On the 16-acre tract there are many cultivars of flowering crab apples, spring gardens, annual and perennial gardens, water gardens, unusual maples and other trees underplanted with spring bulbs. The tuberous begonias are a delight to find in summer. Mid-spring is a good time to enjoy the many flowers. In 1949 the park was a barren parcel of blue and yellow clay; it has since been developed and maintained throughout the succeeding years by a single individual (and still is). This has been a prodigious accomplishment, particularly in soil reclamation and improvement; especially since the park is neither tax-supported nor endowed. The sole source of funds to date has been the admission and membership fees. Plans are now being developed to build a civic building to house the increasing number of volumes in the horticultural library and to provide space for horticultural lectures and meetings. Saturday

and Sunday, dawn–dusk. Other times by appointment (tel. 216-238-6653). Fee.

TOLEDO: *George P. Crosby Park Gardens, 2518 Morgan Road, 43615.* A collection of shrubs and trees, either specific to Ohio, or suitable for planting in the area.

R. A. Stranahan Arboretum, University of Toledo, 33 Birkhead Place, 43606. Native woodlands covering 47 acres.

Toledo Zoological Gardens and Greenhouses, Route 24. Year-round displays in the greenhouses. Collections of cacti, chrysanthemums, scented geraniums, and many varieties of tropical foliage plants. The outdoor gardens have a rose garden (400 different kinds), a lily pool, and the Edna Knight Memorial Garden.

VAN WERT: *Wassenberg Gardens, Route 30.* Growers of fine peonies, iris, and day lilies; also, a considerable number of Oriental poppies. Daily, 8:00 A.M.–5:00 P.M.

WARREN: *Rose Gardens, Perkins Park.* Nearby are formal gardens in W. D. Packard Park.

WOOSTER: *Secrest Arboretum, Route 250, 44691.* An Ohio Agricultural Research and Development Center, and an Agricultural Experiment Station affiliate. The arboretum's primary function is research on commercial

crops. But much of the 75 acres is filled with ornamental plants (1,800 kinds) that are important to home gardeners. Large and noteworthy collections of yews (100 cultivars), firs, spruce, and junipers (several silver twisted firs, dawn redwoods, and bristlecone pines); flowering crab apples (135 cultivars), flowering plums and peaches. The collection of ironclad and rosebay rhododendrons is more than good. Hollies (93 cultivars) in the test garden are well displayed and are to be expanded to 5 acres. On 2.7 acres there is a Garden of Roses of Legend and Romance, more than 500 kinds, including many that have been grown for centuries. Also worth noting is a distinguished allée of azaleas and a shade-tree evaluation plot (125 kinds) that may be useful in gardens or along roads. The second week in May is a good time to see the flowering crab apples, the

third week for rhododendrons. Daily, dawn–dusk.
YOUNGSTOWN: *Fellows Riverside Gardens, Mill Creek Park, 816 Glenwood Avenue, 44502.* Fifteen acres of the nearly 2,400 acres of the park are devoted to tulips and lilies, annuals, chrysanthemums, and old-fashioned and modern roses. Seasonal floral displays, with a wide variety of plant material. Daily, dawn–dusk.
The *Garden Center, 123 McKinley Avenue, 44509* (near Mill Creek Park).

ZOAR: *Zoar Village State Memorial, Route 212.* An experiment in communal living that lasted for 80 years. The formal community garden of the Separatists has been excellently restored. It is based on a description of the New Jerusalem in the Book of Revelations. Daily, 9:00 A.M.–dusk. Fee.

Oklahoma

MUSKOGEE: *Honor Heights Park*. Beautiful flower gardens, especially the banks of azaleas. Daily, dawn–dusk.

OKLAHOMA CITY: *Will Rogers Horticultural Park and Arboretum, 3500 Northwest 36th Street, 73112*. Over 100 kinds of plants in the gardens and more than 900 kinds in the arboretum area, which takes up 20 acres of the total 30. An azalea trail of all the available known varieties, junipers (250), holly (100), redbud (17 of the known cultivars), crape myrtle (21), and China hibiscus (115 varieties) The formal rose garden has 5,000 plants distributed among 340 varieties, including many old-fashioned roses. Many old-time favorites are in the Garden of Memory: peonies (68 varieties), cannas (40), and an extensive iris group (350 varieties).

The greenhouse collections include many cacti and other succulents, exotic foliage plants, and orchids. Daily, 8:00 A.M.–dusk.

TULSA: *Philbrook Art Center, 2727 South Rockford Road.* Behind the museum, spreading over 23 acres of land-scaped gardens, is an Italian Renaissance garden with clipped hedges, fountains, and a terraced waterway formally planted with shaped evergreens. Some topiary, ground covers, and woody shrubs. Below the terraces is an informal area of plants and a pool which leads to the small botanical gardens. Tuesday, 10:00 A.M.–5:00 P.M.; 7:30 P.M.–9:30 P.M. Wednesday through Saturday, 10:00 A.M.–5:00 P.M. Sunday, 1:00 P.M.–5:00 P.M. Closed legal holidays. Fee.

Will Rogers Horticultural Park and Arboretum

Oregon

BROOKINGS: *Azalea State Park*. The home of the Oregon azalea festival.

CANBY: *Ellis Farms*. One of the largest pansy growers in the country, with an extraordinary variety. Check with the office first, during the flowering season, before visiting the fields.

COOS BAY: *Shore Acres State Park*. The name of the estate originated with the previous owners, the Asa M. Simpson family, and was retained by the state of Oregon when it bought the property (637 acres) in 1942. There is a large formal garden, maintained by the state, which ends in a sunken garden that utilizes Japanese motifs. In addition to the local and regional plants on the estate, there are many exotic specimens brought to Coos Bay by the Simpson sailing fleet.

CRATER LAKE: *Castle Crest Wildflower Garden, 97604*. A marvelous display of wildflowers throughout the summer season, which, incidentally, is very short; few wildflowers appear before July 1. During early August literally thousands of Lewis monkey flowers bloom in the area, followed quickly by other species—elephant-head, Anderson's lupine, skyrocket gilia, and many many more. The garden has the status of a wildflower botanical preserve and is about ¼ mile from the park headquarters. Daily, during the season.

DODGE PARK: *Jan de Graaff's Oregon Bulb Farms, Dodge Park Boulevard*. Acres and acres of lily fields, a a sort of man-made wonder. June through September: Daily, but only to qualified specialists who have previously made a written request to visit the farms.

FLORENCE: *Darlingtonia Wayside State Preserve*. On the Oregon coast, just above Florence, the preserve is both unique and strangely beautiful. Thousands of hooded darlingtonias, massed along the meadow, and thrusting their red or orange spotted translucent hoods above the ground. They are an unforgettable sight in spring and summer.

MEDFORD: *Jackson and Perkins Rose Nurseries*. The growing and breeding fields of the world-famous rose nurseries. Many of the fields may be seen from the nearby roadways. Visits to the nurseries growing grounds should be confirmed in advance by letter.

PORTLAND: *Hoyt Arboretum, 4,000 S.W. Fairview Boulevard, 97221*. One of the nation's largest collections

Opposite: *Japanese Garden*. Above: *Azalea State Park*

International Rose Test Garden

of conifers, many species and varieties. The terrain is a rugged hillside above the city, which is naturally suited to the growing needs of the conifers. In addition to the more usual trees, there are the uncommon California nutmeg tree, the Western yew, the Santa Lucia fir, and the Siskiyou and Sitka spruces. On the arboretum's 214 acres there are other excellent collections. Douglas firs, hemlocks, cedars, dogwoods, madrones, as well as other native shrubs and flowers and ferns. Although the area was cleaned out, much of the natural growths was spared in order to give the arboretum a natural appearance. Daily, 8:00 A.M.–4:30 P.M.

International Rose Test Garden, Washington Park, S.W. Kensington Avenue. A spectacular that just grew when, after World War I, the European gardens were closed and the United Stated growers decided to install their own test gardens in the Portland area. The garden now has more than 10,000 roses, 520 varieties, in an area landscaped with azaleas, camellias, rhododendrons, and tulips. The rose beds are so arranged that viewing is easy, and recognition of the cultivars is made simple. The roses are most bountiful in June, but the Oregon season

is a long one because of the moist and temperate climate. Daily, sunrise–sunset.

Japanese Garden, Washington Park, S.W. Kensington Avenue (directly above the International Rose Test Garden). Mail should be addressed to the Japanese Garden Society at P.O. Box 3847, Portland, Ore. 97208. This is a unique garden, one of a kind and also one of the finest in the country. Within its $5\frac{1}{2}$ acres there are five separate gardens arranged in an over-all group. The gardens are an idealized conception of nature, using stones, water, and greenery in carefully reduced proportions and placement so as to create a serene beauty: the Flat Garden, the Sand and Stone Garden, the Moss Garden, the Tea Garden, and the Strolling Pond Garden. The entire garden area is surrounded by woodlands, and one fence of azaleas introduces a touch of spring color into the gentle greens, as does a spectacular Japanese maple in the fall. Each of the gardens tells a story. The rock-studded ponds and irregular terrain of the Strolling Pond Garden symbolize the world in miniature, and the crane and tortoise denote long life and good health for the visitors. On the edge of the Flat Garden is a

Above and below: *Japanese Garden*

polished stone inscribed with haiku verse in Japanese characters: "Here I saw the same soft spring as in Japan." During the high summer days there is a shuttle bus that transports visitors from the parking lot to the gardens without charge. From Easter through October: Weekdays, 10:00 A.M.–4:00 P.M. Saturday and Sunday, 12:00 noon–6:00 P.M. (However, the schedule of hours is somewhat variable.) Fee.

Rhododendron Society Gardens, S.E. 28th Avenue (1 block north of Woodstock Avenue). Mailing address: P.O. Box 14773, Portland, Ore. 97214. One of the country's finest collections of rhododendrons and azaleas in a beautiful woodland and lake setting. The society's garden is located in part on a 4-acre island in Crystal Spring Lake and on the nearby shore (3 acres). More than 2,000 plants have been planted, representing nearly 600 species and cultivars, including all of the familiar rhododendron and azalea hybrids and the less well-known species which vary from ground-hugging mats to tree-like specimens with huge leaves. Many of the smaller species and hybrids are planted in a rock garden; and a cool house protects the tender rhododendrons that are on display. Within the larger garden, a particularly spectacular group is the massed planting of Rhododendron Cynthia, now over 20 feet tall. As a background and cover, there are Douglas firs, flowering cherries, oaks, maples, magnolias, a dove tree, franklinia, and dogwood. April through September: daily, 8:00 A.M.–8:00 P.M. October through March: daily, 8:00 A.M.–4:30 P.M.

Sunken Rose Garden, Peninsula Park. More than 15,000 roses in formal beds, separated by grass and gravel walks.

SALEM: *Bush's Pasture Garden, High Street and Mission Street.* Roses, peonies, azaleas, flowering cherries, flowering crab apples, hawthorns, and many of the original fruit trees once planted in the pasture's orchard before it became a park. Daily.

Schreiner's Iris Gardens. Breeders and growers of very beautiful iris plants.

Pennsylvania

ALLENTOWN: *West Park.* An 8-acre arboretum and culture center with hundreds of native and exotic trees and shrubs.

Trexler Memorial Park Greenhouses, 18105. Greenhouses with rare tropical and subtropical plants. A chrysanthemum show in mid-November.

AMBLER: *Temple University Gardens, Ambler Campus, Meeting House Road, 19002.* The formal gardens, adjacent to the woodlands, are now 45 years old and have the look of well-cared-for maturity. Within the 10-acre area, the four herbaceous borders (80 feet each) provide bloom from April to November, and are good examples of the art of perennial gardening, now almost a lost kind of gardening in many areas. Two other borders, filled with annuals, supply much of the summer color. A planted dry wall, an allée of Japanese cherries, an herb garden, and 45-year old boxwood hedges. The Louise Stine Fisher Memorial Garden has 110 varieties of dwarf conifers and other unusual dwarf plants, including such species as rhododendrons, boxwood, heather, Hinoki cypress, and juniper. The collection of trees and shrubs extends through the center of the university campus, with 700 species and varieties of natives and ornamentals: maple, honey locust, juniper, and representative groups of hollies (English, American, Japanese), forsythias, and roses as accents. Daily, all year.

AMBRIDGE: *Old Economy Village and Gardens, Route 65.* A church that has no pastor, a steeple clock with no minute hand—relics of an adventure in communal living which failed, but which left a legacy of peace and dedicated vigor, practical gardens of unequaled excellence, and flower gardens with reflecting pools, paths, and labyrinths. The formal gardens have a graceful pavilion and a grotto; the flowers are largely those of the early 19th century. There is an excellent kitchen garden in which flowers, herbs, and vegetables are grown. A greenhouse has some of the structural aspects of the original glass house. Monday through Saturday, 8:30 A.M.–5:00 P.M. Sunday, 1:00 P.M.–5:00 P.M.

BERWICK: *Elan Memorial Park, 203 East Front Street, 18603.* A 55-acre arboretum associated with the cemetery; together they possess 2,000 kinds of plants. The collection of flowering trees and lilacs is excellent; many, many kinds of annuals are used in 50 beds for summer

Longwood Gardens

displays, around which evergreens are used informally. The greenhouse shelters cacti, hoyas, and camellias, Both the arboretum and the greenhouse are located near Lime Ridge on Route 11-S. Daily, daylight hours.

BETHLEHEM: *Rose Garden and Sayre Park Arboretum.*

BRISTOL: *Pennsbury Manor.* William Penn's home has a garden somewhat reminiscent of his times: herbs, old hollies, and perennial and annual gardens.

BUTLER: *Jenning's Blazing Star Nature Reserve, Route 8.* The reserve, 280 acres, was established to provide for a 3-acre relict area of natural prairie in which the blazing star was making a sort of last stand against men. Some 20 acres of forest have been cleared to provide a more favorable setting for the blazing star's further development. The balance of the acreage has been left to show most of the native plants of an eastern deciduous forest. The reserve is managed by a unique organization, the Western Pennsylvania Conservancy, which is doing a great deal in other areas also to save Pennsylvania's natural forests. Daily.

DOYLESTOWN: *Burpee's Experimental Garden, Fordhook Farms, New Britain Road.* The test gardens were originally established in 1888, and have been continued as a productive and interesting way of testing new vegetable and flower products. Many bulbs and annuals by the thousands make a brilliant display during the spring and summer months. May through October: daily, 8:00 A.M.–4:30 P.M.

ELIZABETHTOWN: *Masonic Homes Gardens.* Beautiful formal gardens that have received the Pennsylvania Distinguished Garden Award. Fountain and reflecting pool with aquatic plants and water lilies, 12 beds of roses and 2 large rose arbors, plus 16 other flower beds for annuals and perennials. The arboretum, with many rare and exotic trees, borders the gardens on two sides; the collection includes conifers, cypress, dogwood, and native trees. Daily, but first visit the administrative office.

ERIE: *Asbury Woods Outdoor Laboratory, 38th and Asbury Road, 16506.* A wonderland of nature.

GREENSBURG: *Greensburg Garden Center, 951 Old Salem Road, 15601.* A young, well-designed center whose arboretum is planned to display (and demonstrate) proven ornamentals of known hardiness for area gardeners. There is now a small collection of flowering

Haverford College

Hershey Rose Garden and Arboretum

Mill Grove

Temple University Gardens

trees, evergreen and deciduous shrubs, and ground covers. In a protected "mini-climate" the center is growing dove trees, nandina, trifoliate orange, and similar less hardy plants as an experiment.

HARRISBURG: *Italian Lake.* A variety of flowering plants around a small and beautiful lake; spring bulbs, flowering trees, and annuals. Daily.

Municipal Rose Garden. Now more than 7,500 rose bushes in a wide variety of hybrids. Daily.

Another rose garden is nearby at the *Executive Mansion.* Monday through Friday, 9:00 A.M.–11:30 A.M.

Ridley Creek State Park. Located near the headquarters of the park are three famous gardens designed by the Olmsted brothers (1924) who planned so many of the great gardens. There is a formal perennial garden, a formal rose garden, and a topiary garden. More than 30 varieties of plants, shrubs, and trees have been used to create the backgrounds of the gardens: boxwood, yew, holly, lilacs, and azaleas; as well as sycamores, hawthorns, flowering cherries, and others. Spring and early summer are good visiting dates.

HAVERFORD: *Haverford College, College Avenue, 19041.*

A campus arboretum of large, mature trees and an outstanding collection of evergreens. The Wolman Walk is planted with more than 240 species and varieties of trees and shrubs (including massed rhododendrons). The core of the campus has both native and foreign trees, some over 150 years old. The college was originally landscaped in 1834 in the English Reptonian tradition, which has been adhered to ever since. Daily.

HERSHEY: *Hershey Rose Garden and Arboretum, 17033.* An outstanding rose garden of 42,000 plants and 1,200 varieties, peaking from mid-April to May. Old-fashioned roses are displayed by themselves; a nearby bed of green-petaled roses is quite astonishing. Spring begins in the garden with a tulip spread: 30,000 bulbs, and 1,500 varieties. Then come azaleas and rhododendrons, which are followed by thousands of annuals, then chrysanthemums (200 cultivars). Day lilies, lilies, iris, and other perennials are used to provide even more continuity. In the arboretum, and elsewhere within the landscaped groups, are hollies (100 kinds), the Hohman collection of dwarf evergreens, and unusual deciduous trees as well as conifers. There are also many

flowering cherries, flowering shrubs, magnolias, and empress trees. The garden and arboretum cover 23 acres. From mid-April to December 1: daily, 8:00 A.M.–7:00 P.M.
HOOKSTOWN: *Wildflower Reserve, Route 30, Raccoon Creek State Park (The Western Pennsylvania Conservancy).* A 300-acre reserve which offers 500 species of wildflowers and ferns and trees. It has been frequently described, along with several other small reserves, as the last stand of wildflowers. The reserve has two formerly cultivated fields in which the European daisy has naturalized itself. The wooded area contains many of the natives that have been introduced to cultivation, and many more examples of native trees and plants indigenous to the Pennsylvania area. From April 1 to fall: daily except Monday, 10:00 A.M.–sunset.
KENNETT SQUARE: *Longwood Gardens, 19348.* The gardens combine the best of the New World's rolling hills and native trees with the best of the Old World's influence on formal gardens, fountains, and the vast conservatory. The gardens are magnificent any time of the year, winter included, when snow is on the ground, and the greenhouses are filled with flowering plants and

special displays. Longwood probably has the widest scope of activities of all American gardens. It offers a varied group of educational activities, from lectures to intensive training, for college undergraduates, post-graduates, and students from other countries. There is an open-air theater for concerts, ballets, operas, and plays. These activities, together with the extraordinary plant collections (more than 12,000 kinds of plants), the landscaping and outdoor gardens and pools and fountains, the greenhouse and conservatory displays, and the arboretum, make Longwood's 350 cultivated acres one of the greatest gardens in America. The outdoor gardens combine woodland paths with colorful formal gardens and special attractions: a rock garden, an herb garden, a topiary garden, a heather garden, several rose gardens, even a vegetable garden and wildflowers. Heather and other ericaceous plants, as well as dwarf conifers and other conifer slow growers are used as accent plants. The Italian Water Garden was influenced by the design of the Villa Gamberaia near Florence, but native hemlock was substituted for the original cypresses. The fountain system, covering about 5 acres with

Swiss Pines

pools and canals, is outlined with Japanese holly and clipped Norway maples. The fountains are illuminated with colored lights every Tuesday, Thursday, and Sunday evenings for a half hour (mid-May to mid-October). The arboretum dates back to the original owners (ca. 1800) and includes such special trees as the tulip tree, the Kentucky coffee, and the cucumber magnolia. Also noteworthy are the pinetum and an avenue of empress trees that flower magnificently in May. The conservatory and display greenhouses (16) provide year-round color and interest. In the main conservatory, the seasons are recognized with six displays of special plantings: spring, Easter, summer, fall, Christmas, and winter. Summer: hybrid lilies and tuberous begonias, fancy-leaved caladiums, pink cannas, standards of lantana and fuchsia and pelargonium among the tall tree ferns. Autumn: vast cascades and uprights of chrysanthemums (a fantastic sight). Winter: the camellia collection, which is outstanding, and acacias. Permanent displays are featured in the Tropical Terrace Garden, the Rose House, the Fern Passage, the Desert House, the Economic House, and the Orchid House

(one of the most popular). Other indoor displays include cycads, bromeliads, palms, and an indoor collection of mild-climate roses, azaleas, and rhododendrons; there is also an orangerie. There is really no time when the gardens do not have some sort of splendid floral show, so the choice of dates for a visit depends entirely of the whim or the hobby of the visitor. The chysanthemum show for example, is almost not to be believed; anyone will be sure to enjoy it. Gardens: daily, year round, 8:00 A.M.–dusk. Conservatories: daily, 11:00 A.M.–5:00 P.M. (some scheduled displays run later). Organ concerts, originating in the ballroom next to the conservatory, are given each Sunday between 3:00 P.M. and 5:00 P.M.

KYLERTOWN: *Rolling Tree Farm and Arboretum.* A 20-year-old reclamation project; 70 species and varieties of trees planted on reclaimed land, which was once strip mined. Essentially this is the work of one man on 180 acres of infertile soil, and a demonstration of what can be done elsewhere. pines, firs, spruce, deciduous flowering trees. June through October: daily.

LANCASTER: *Holtwood Arboretum, Route 372.* A nature

Masonic Homes Gardens

study area and, at this time, a relatively small arboretum.

LIMA: *John J. Tyler Arboretum, 515 Painter Road, 19060.* Formerly the Painter Arboretum, the 700-acre estate still has trees surviving from that earlier period (1830), notably a cedar of Lebanon, ginkgos, and sequoias. There are now some 4,000 kinds of plants and trees in the arboretum. Thousands of bulbs, many culinary herbs, and a garden of fragrance for the blind. A large planting of rhododendrons, azaleas, dogwoods, and dwarf conifers; wonderful old yews and tree peonies. Visitors usually arrive in April and May to see the flowering trees and shrubs. Daily, sunrise–sunset.

LUDLOW: *Olmstead Gardens.* A wide variety of flowers and 12,000 tulips.

MALVERN: *Swiss Pines, Charleston Road, RRD 1, 19355.* Five hundred acres of which 11 are developed (more are planned) into a sort of group of individual gardens near the Colonial tea house. A rose garden, a very good herb garden (110 kinds), a heather garden (150 kinds), and heaths (200). The Japanese Garden, for which Swiss Pines is best known, has a stream and a pavilion (Shingon), a "long-pine" tea house with its own enclosed

garden, evergreen plantings, Oriental shrubs, and many stone sculptures. The tea house is authentic, since it was crafted in Japan and assembled at the gardens. In addition, there is a bamboo grove and a collection of rare dwarf conifers. From mid-March to mid-December: Monday through Friday, 10:00 A.M.–4:00 P.M. Saturday, 9:00 A.M.–12:00 noon. Possibly a fee.

MOUNT ALTON: *Mount Alton Arboretum, Pennsylvannia State University, 17237.* A 36-acre arboretum with more than 300 species of trees and shrubs; many natives, and many from Asia and Europe. Daily.

NEWTOWN SQUARE: *Charles E. Ellis School for Girls, 19073.* A campus arboretum of 300 acres, planted with hundreds of unusual shrubs and trees; most of them are hardy to the area and are either native or non-native varieties that offer exceptional landscape values. The conifers are particularly well represented. Daily.

NORTH EAST: *The Farm of Paschke, RRD 1, 16428.* One of the extraordinary chrysanthemum farms in the country (there are several) with 10 acres of field-grown bushes and a fine lathhouse display area where flowering plants are massed. Flowering begins in late August and peaks

18th-century Garden

in October. Daily during the growing and flowering season.

OHIOPYLE: *Bear Run Nature Reserve.* Another of the Western Pennsylvania Conservancy's operations. A varied natural area in which wildflowers abound and are easily seen and recognized along 9 miles of trails. The reserve has often been described as the most scenic and one of the most botanically important areas in the country. Among the trees are many varieties of oaks, excellent specimens of black cherry, hickory, sour gum, hop hornbeam, and other garden familiars. The shrubs consist of extensive stands of rhododendrons, pink azaleas, dogwood, spice beech, etc. And it is rich in herbaceous materials: daisies, lilies, cardinal flowers, and a hundred more. A truly extraordinary natural garden. Daily, 10:00 A.M.–6:00 P.M.

Ferncliff Park. Its 100 acres are a nucleus for further expansion in the area. A project of the Western Pennsylvania Conservancy group, the park contains many rare specimens of plants. Also many of the commonly grown ornamental trees that are found there as natives are studied for further useful information about both conservation and home uses. Red, scarlet, white, and black oak, tulip trees, and the cucumber tree are some that will be encountered. Daily.

PHILADELPHIA: *Awbury Arboretum, Aquarium Drive, 19130.* Native plant materials and nonnatives of similar hardiness (110 species and varieties). Daily, sunrise–sunset.

Barnes Foundation Arboretum, 300 Latche's Lane, Merion Station 19066. An excellently displayed dwarf conifer garden; collections of cotoneasters, magnolias, peonies, viburnums, and ferns (80 species) on 12 acres (3,000 species and varieties of plants). Daily, 9:00 A.M.–5:00 P.M. *by appointment only.* Requests may be made to P.O. Box 128 at the above address.

Fairmount Park. The park is the largest landscaped city park in the world (7,832 acres); and could be considered the largest city arboretum (3,000,000 trees). Among the outstanding gardens in the park are: *The Horticultural Hall Gardens* which feature many of the nation's rarest trees, and which were planted in 1876; *The Japanese House and Garden* complete with pond, fish, bridge and extensive planting; *Glendinning Rock Garden,* in which azaleas, flowering cherries, and flowering crab apples make a pleasant background for rock plants; *Mount Pleasant Mansion* whose colonial garden is much the same today as it was 200 years ago; *Cedar Grove Herb Garden*, a re-created farm garden; and the magnificent cherry blossom display along the east bank of the Schuylkill River. Daily, sunrise to sunset.

John Bartram's Garden, 54th Street and Elmwood Avenue, 19143. Although the garden is now part of a park, it was the site of America's first botanic garden of any value. None of the planting dates from 1700, but a yellowwood and a gingko may have been planted by Bartram's son William. A visit here, though the area is charming, is more for a sense of history. Daily, 8:00 A.M.–4:00 P.M.

Independence National Historical Park (gardens), 311-13 Walnut Street, 19106. The park takes in a rather large section of the city, preserving many old homes and several churches, bank buildings, and other units (20 of them in all) clustered around and near Independence Hall, in the heart of the old city. Plants, shrubs, and trees growing by these buildings and homes or in their gardens provide an astonishingly accurate list of plants that were known to Colonial Philadelphia. Indeed, the only substitutions that have been made were to replace some old and stringy Colonial garden plants with their more compact and lovelier descendants. A walk through the area should really start at park headquarters at 311 Walnut Street, where questions can be answered and information about the park and the gardens is provided. Then, but not necessarily in this order, visit the:

Deshler-Morris House, 5442 Germantown Avenue. The garden is a typical large city garden of the period, with excellent large trees and specimens of tree forms of boxwood.

St. Joseph's Church Yard, 4th and Walnut Streets. Plantings of northern red oak with an undercover of serviceberry and euonymus, golden-rain trees, Japanese snowball, and English holly, with English ivy as a ground cover.

18th-century Garden, 325 Walnut Street. The headquarters of the Pennsylvania Horticultural Society. A visit to this headquarters, one of the four most influential horticultural societies in the country, is definitely indicated. Although the gardens are part of the national park system, the society developed and maintains them.

Magnolia Tribute Garden

The garden was designed to reflect the spirit of Colonial Philadelphia, and consists of three separate sections: a formal garden with walks and parterres filled with flowers, a small orchard, and an area reserved for vegetables and herbs and cutting flowers. The style is unmistakably English, because the 18th-century Philadelphian who was successful emulated the British upper class of the preceding century. Native plants in this garden: rhododendron, clethra, bayberry, hawthorn, winterberry, and holly. And among the exotics: ginkgo, chrysanthemums, and roses (from China); fruits (European); geraniums (South Africa); and such annuals as ageratum, zinnia, cosmos, salvia (Central America, probably by way of Portugal).

Bishop White Garden, 3rd and Walnut Streets. Another typically 18th-century garden with a mixed planting that expressed a Philadelphian's Colonial taste.

Pemberton House Yard, Chestnut and Orianna Streets. In this garden the early Philadelphian began to incorporate fruit trees into the garden plan.

DAR Rose Garden, between Walnut and Spruce Streets. The garden is dedicated to roses, particularly the old varieties that provide continuous bloom from mid-May to December.

DAR Bulb Garden (near the rose garden) consists of varieties that are native as well as those brought over by the early Colonials, or imported by John Bartram.

Magnolia Tribute Garden, Locust Street, between 4th and 5th Streets. A melange of 13 saucer magnolias, azaleas, English oak, American holly, cotoneaster, rhododendron, and English ivy.

Visits to these gardens in Independence National Park may be made from dawn to dusk, daily; or at times that the current occupants of the houses may determine.

Mary Garden, Our Mother of Consolation School, Chestnut Hill. An interesting garden if only because of the wide variety of flowers with religious names.

Zoological Society Rose Garden, 34th Street and Girard Avenue.

Morris Arboretum, 9414 Meadowbrook Avenue, Chestnut Hill, 19143. Flowering trees, shrubs, and azaleas planted on a hillside (175 acres) in a Philadelphia suburb. A collection of native Pennsylvania trees and nonnatives of similar hardiness. Conifers, hollies, and witch hazel;

Japanese Garden

gardens of heath, heather, roses, medicinal plants; a fern house and a laboratory (in all, about 3,500 different kinds of plants). Weekdays, 9:00 A.M.–4:00 P.M. Saturday and Sunday, 9:00 A.M.–5:00 P.M. Fee.

POTTSTOWN: *J. and R. Orchids, Chestnut Hill Road, R.D. #2, 19464.* Specialists in phalaenopsis and paphiopedilums. Daily during business hours.

PITTSBURGH: *Aviary-Conservatory, West Park, Sherman Avenue and West Ohio Street.* A tropical forest, under glass, in which exotic birds are allowed to fly freely. Daily, 9:00 A.M.–4:30 P.M. Fee.

Equitable Plaza. Two acres of open promenades with spray pools and fountains, 90 varieties of shade trees, hundreds of shrubs, and thousands of flowers. Excellent urban planning.

Mellon Square Park. An oasis of trees, fountains, and waterfalls built on top of a 6-level underground parking garage. On the nearly 1½ acres are two large areas and one small one for floral displays: spring bulbs, annuals, and chrysanthemums.

Phipps Conservatory, Schenley Park, 15213. The conservatory spreads over 2½ acres of glass and is sectioned into 12 display houses. The special shows—spring, fall, and Christmas—are beautifully styled and presented and have become bywords for magnificent floral displays in many countries. The exhibition rooms are lavish with cascading plants, formal and informal plantings, and horticultural specimens arranged in garden settings. Nearly a half-mile of paths wander through steaming jungles, Oriental splendor (Japanese garden), modern and old-fashioned gardens, natural gardens, tropical water gardens, and the symmetry of a French parterre. There is an outstanding collection of orchids largely from Indochina. Outdoors there are lily ponds and a series of terraced herbaceous gardens and grouped shrubs. Daily, 9:00 A.M.–5:00 P.M. During show periods, 7:00 P.M.–9:00 P.M., at which time a fee is charged.

READING: *Reading Public Museum Botanical Garden, 500 Museum Road, 19602.* The landscaping around the museum is as much a part of the botanic gardens as are the surrounding 25 acres. Spring flowering trees, especially lilacs, of which there are 200 varieties. Summer annuals and fall chrysanthemums carry much of the garden color. Formal gardens and a peony

Phipps Aviary Conservatory

Opposite, and above: *Phipps Conservatory*

garden; a special section for cacti and subtropical economic plants. Daily, sunrise–sunset.

SCRANTON: *Nay Aug Floral Gardens and Greenhouse, Arthur Avenue and Mulberry Avenue.* Excellent gardens that surround the Everhart Museum and its pools; multicolored flowers, usually fragrant. Greenhouse. Gardens: daily. Greenhouse: daily except Monday, 9:00 A.M.–2:00 P.M.

STATE COLLEGE: *Pennsylvania State University Experimental Gardens.* Also known as University Park. The campus test gardens are restricted to studies of All-America rose trials, All-America annuals selections, and chrysanthemum selections. June through October: daily, 8:00 A.M.–sunset.

SWARTHMORE: *Arthur Hoyt Scott Horticultural Foundation, Swarthmore College Campus, Chester Road, 19081.* The arboretum is spread over the 300-acre campus, encompassing 5,000 species and varieties of plants. A remarkable collection, well integrated with the campus landscaping; it should be seen, preferably, during April and May. Much of the collection consists of flowering trees and plants that bloom in the spring. Flowering crab

apples, lilacs, magnolias, rhododendrons, tree peonies, and the Dean Bond rose garden. Daily, sunrise–sunset.

VALLEY FORGE: *Valley Forge State Park.* In addition to its significance in American history, Valley Forge has some of the best stands of dogwood in the country, and is considered by those who have seen the flowers in early May as unequaled anywhere. There are more than 50,000 pink and white dogwood in the park; and a particularly beautiful group, Dogwood Grove, is located along both sides of Inner Line Drive, near the New Jersey monument. Rhododendrons and mountain laurel are present also in profusion along the wooded areas. Daily, dawn–dusk.

Mill Grove, Audubon, 19407. An attractive estate of 130 acres along the Perkiomen Creek, where Audubon spent his first years in America. Six miles of trails and special plantings of trees and shrubs attractive to both birds and gardeners. More than 400 species and varieties of flowering shrubs and plants. Daily except Monday, 10:00 A.M.–5:00 P.M.

WALLINGFORD: *Taylor Memorial Arboretum, 10 Ridley Drive, Garden City, 19086.* There are very good trial

Valley Forge State Park

Star Roses

gardens in which plants and shrubs are tested for their suitability to the area home gardens. An herb garden; displays of azaleas, camellias, and hollies; and an excellent public education program. The arboretum covers 32 acres, with 1,500 varieties of plants. Daily, sunrise–sunset.

WASHINGTON CROSSING: *Bowman's Hill State Wild Flower Preserve, Washington Crossing State Park, 18977.* A notable development of a natural area in which all the native plants of Pennsylvania are represented. In this sense, the preserve is a botanical garden as well as an arboretum. Paths and trails through the 100 acres lead to more than 1,000 species of plants: wild azaleas, bluebells, attractive herbs (many of which are used in pharmaceutical preparations), and ferns and trees representative of the area. Daily, sunrise–sunset.

WEST CHESTER: *David Townsend House.* Spacious gardens originally planted by David Townsend (1806). Tuesday, Thursday, and Saturday, 1:00 P.M.–4:00 P.M.

WEST GROVE: *Star Roses, 19390.* Each year from July through September millions of rose blooms are on display at the Conrad-Pyle Company's 600-acre growing fields (just south of West Grove). It is possible to drive around many of the fields; for more personal viewing of the "Star" roses make arrangements with the management. The lovely and formal Robert Pyle Memorial Rose Garden, with its collection of 3,500 select roses, is near the

Garden Center, which is open daily from late June to early October. The garden center itself, though commercially oriented, has nice displays and a lathhouse in which a wide selection of other ornamental plants are available. Daily, 9:00 A.M.–5:00 P.M.

Adjacent to the rose fields is the Red Rose Inn, whose original grant included the payment of one red rose each year as rent, a gracious gesture that the Conrad-Pyle Company has maintained in a yearly ceremony.

WESTTOWN: *Westtown School Arboretum.* Fifty acres of native trees and a conifer collection.

WHITEHALL: *Bart's Bonsai Nursery, 522 Fifth Street, Fullerton, 18052.* One of the most complete collections of aged (and beginning) Bonsai. Daily, during business hours.

WILKES-BARRE: *The River Commons Flowering Cherry Display.* Along both sides of the Susquehanna River, as it flows by the city, thousands of Kanzan cherries have been planted. In early May the massed pilgrimage to see the flowers has resulted in a three-day festival.

WOMELSDORF: *Conrad Weiser Park.* Five acres of display gardens; and, nearby, the home of Pennsylvania's ambassador to the Indians, for whom the park was named.

WYNCOTE: *Curtis Arboretum and Park, Greenwood Avenue and Church Road.* Marked trees and shrubs, two ponds, and a Memorial Grove. Daily, 9:00 A.M.–9:00 P.M.

Rhode Island

BARRINGTON: *Llys-Ys-Rhosyn, 93 Rumstick Road*. One of the largest private rose gardens in the East; nearly 7,000 roses in many varieties on $11\frac{1}{2}$ acres. Karl P. Jones, who opened his gardens to the public, is a rosarian of excellent background. May through November: daily, during the daylight hours.

CENTRAL FALLS: *Jenks Park, 580 Broad Street*. Like many parks, it features roses; cockscomb and other annuals during the summer. Daily, year-round.

CRANSTON: *Dialogue Garden, Oaklawn Avenue and Spring Lane Road*. The garden is a physical symbol of the Dialogue Group, an organization of several religious faiths. Its circular form denotes unity. Significant plants from the Bible, suitable to the New England climate, were selected to help express the views of the group. Russian olive, cotoneaster (burning bush), rock spray, scarlet firethorn, rosebay rhododendron. A redwood arbor for meditation is being covered with wisteria. Daily. *Winsor Azalea Garden, 44 Marden Street*. On the shores of Fenner's Pond, the gardens of azaleas and rhododendrons have been open to the public for nearly 30 years as a courtesy of the Ralph T. Winsors. For about three weeks in early May (usually beginning on the tenth), the garden is open daily from 10:00 A.M. to 10:00 P.M.

EAST GREENWICH: *Varnum Gardens, General James Mitchel Varnum House*. The garden is kept colorful with spring bulbs, annuals, and staple perennials—a pleasant acre of flowers within Colonial traditions. June: Sunday 3:00 P.M.–5:00 P.M. July through September: Wednesday and Sunday, 3:00 P.M.–5:00 P.M. Fee.

GREENE: *Greene Herb Gardens, Narrow Lane Road*. Various types of herbs—rosemary, lavender, santolina, thyme, and others—are sold at this garden the year round. But for the curious, the outdoor gardens, spring to fall, contain such historic or unusual herb beds as: English, Bible, Half Moon, Dye, Tea, Kitchen, Christmas, and City-of-Worms. Gardens: from May 1 to November 15, daily except Sunday, 1:00 P.M.–5:00 P.M. Greenhouses: all year.

KINGSTON: *Gardens and Greenhouses of the University of Rhode Island*. The university also maintains an Agricultural Experiment Station; but the gardens are administered by the Department of Horticulture. Special shows in the greenhouses include a Palm Sunday Flower

The Elms

Show, and a fall Flower and Garden Show (usually a student display). Within the planting grounds: spring bulbs (tulips and daffodils), summer roses and annuals, fall chrysanthemums. Ornamental perennials and shrubs for a background. Gardens: daily, all year, daylight hours. Greenhouses: Monday through Friday, 8:00 A.M.–5:30 P.M.

MIDDLETOWN: *Whitehall House*. Only flowers suitable to the period (18th century) are grown, with emphasis on those that bloom in July and August to coincide with the time that the house is open to the public. July and August: daily, 10:00 A.M.– 5:00 P.M. Fee.

NEWBURYPORT: *Knapp-Healy House, 47 High Street*. An early nineteenth-century home with a beautiful old garden in the rear; some of the original boxwood and a gazebo still survive.

NEWPORT: *The Breakers, Ochre Point Avenue*. A fabulous mansion styled as a 17th-century Italian villa with appropriate planting. The sunken gardens with their famous parterres were removed during World War II because of a lack of help. But many other points of horticultural interest remain. There are particularly fine specimens of Japanese maple, copper beech, and pin oaks in rows. The formal area is enclosed, and a sense of seclusion is enhanced by borders of rhododendron, mountain laurel, dogwood, and other flowering shrubs. May through November: daily, 10:00 A.M.– 5:00 P.M. Fee.

Château-sur-Mer, Bellevue Avenue. A lavish Victorian villa whose grounds are landscaped in much the same romantic, turn-of-the-century traditions. From mid-April to Memorial Day: Saturday and Sunday, 10:00 A.M.– 5:00 P.M. From Memorial Day to mid-November: daily, 10:00 A.M.–5:00 P.M. Fee.

The Elms, Bellevue Avenue. A copy of an early 18th-century French château, with formal sunken gardens, designed by a French architect. There are bronze and marble statues, playing fountains, great lawns, terraces, and a tea house. A magnificent collection of shrubs and trees from all over the world. Borders of clipped euonymus, and trimmed ornamental trees. English ivy ground covers, and paths edged with Pfitzer's juniper and arborvitae. Tulip displays in the spring, begonias for summer, and chrysanthemums in the fall are special

Wilcox Park

University of Rhode Island

The Breakers

Stephen Hopkins House

features of the sunken gardens. Daily, 10:00 A.M.–5:00 P.M. Fee.

Wanton-Lyman-Hazard House, Broadway and Stone Street. The gardens are only incidental to the house, the oldest dwelling in Newport. But there are displays of old boxwood, herbs, and other appropriate plantings of perennials and bulbs.

PAWTUCKET: *Marconi Gardens, Slater Memorial Park.* The sunken garden is surrounded by well-designed bridges and flower beds of annuals. The waterfall, surrounded by mountain laurel, dogwood, and rhododendron, is extremely picturesque. From mid-May to mid-October: daily, during the daylight hours.

Old Slater Museum Fiber and Dye Garden. A garden of herbs, dye plants, and fiber plants used before the age of chemistry. Examples of flax, cotton, China jute, kenaf, abaca, sisal, cabuya, and bowstring hemp. Dye plants are madder, indigo, woad, genista, marigold, pokeberry, lily of the valley, and others. Also, teasel—a thistlelike plant—used for raising the nap of woolens. Spring through fall: Tuesday through Saturday, 10:00 A.M.–5:00 P.M. Sunday, 2:00 P.M.–5:00 P.M.

PROVIDENCE: *A Biblical Garden, Temple Beth El, 70 Orchard Avenue.* Plants of Biblical authenticity and of special interest and significance in Old Testament stories in a 60-by-2 foot border. The garden has received two national awards for excellence. A weeping mulberry, an espaliered pyracantha in the shape of a Menorah, myrtle for ground cover, saffron crocus, dwarf juniper, and sage for Mosaic wisdom. Wormwood is represented, as is rue, spindel-tree, and Baltic ivy. Spring through fall: daily, dawn–dusk.

Garden for the Blind, 1958 Broad Street. A two-level garden with signs and plant labels in braille. Peppermint, lavender, marigolds, carnations, geraniums, and a selection of herbs. Plants are identifiable by scent, touch, and taste. The garden adjoins the Rhode Island Association for the Blind. Monday through Friday, 9:00 A.M.–5:00 P.M.

Japanese Garden, Pembroke College, Cushing Street. The garden, although accessible, is hidden from public view, having been so designed as to be viewed from the dining room of the college. Rocks, pines, dogwoods and grounds are so arranged as to be pleasing to the eye

Swann Point Cemetery

on a minute scale.

John Brown House, 52 Power Street, 02906. A Colonial-type garden surrounding a brick courtyard. Espaliered fruit trees and low-growing plants and shrubbery.

Roger Williams Park, Elmwood Avenue. Formal gardens and open woodlands, small lakes. Special displays of tulips and azaleas, begonias, and chrysanthemums in their corresponding seasons. Rose garden and greenhouses.

Close to the Elmwood entrance is the *Betsy Williams Cottage,* a gambrel-roofed Colonial home densely covered with aged wisteria.

Shakespeare's Head, 21 Meeting Street. A serene garden that owes much of its appeal to its Colonial design. The garden is old-fashioned in its flowers and walled, which provides a sense of privacy. The major plantings are of herbs, boxwood, dogwood, and quince trees. The building houses the Rhode Island Federation of Garden Clubs, and it is a nice gesture to ask their permission before entering the garden.

Stephen Hopkins House and Garden. A restoration of the 18th-century garden. A parterre garden that is entered by descending five stone steps at either end. The geometric pattern and the 8-foot wall give the garden an air of austere formality not usually associated with Colonial gardens. Wednesday and Saturday, 1:00 P.M.–4:00 P.M.

Swann Point Cemetery, 585 Blackstone Boulevard. Like those in several other cemeteries of the period, the gardens were planned for beauty. So well has this been accomplished at Swann Point that it has become a botanical preserve for the nearby schools. On its 200 acres there are more than 300 kinds of trees and shrubs, many of which are not from the area but which have acclimated themselves. Greenhouses are operated at Swann Point, with special shows put on in the garden area near the chapel. A tulip display during the third week of May, and a chrysanthemum exhibit in mid-October. Daily, sunrise–sunset.

WESTERLY: *Wilcox Park, Grove Avenue.* The 32 acres adjoin the Memorial and Public Library in the center of the city. The park has fine water-lily gardens with a long season of bloom, from July to October, and fine English oaks, hemlocks, and a collection of trees native to Rhode Island.

WICKFORD: *Smith's Castle (near Cocumscussoc).* An 18th-century, design-winning garden. It is not a restoration, but a re-creation of what might have been there originally. All plant materials are from 18th-century listings. Old roses: cabbage, moss, and damask; perennials such as early peonies, spicy pinks, and herbs of many varieties; annuals: pot marigolds, globe amaranth, and the fragrant "cherry pie." Monday through Wednesday, Friday and Saturday, 10:00 A.M.–5:00 P.M. Sunday, 1:00 P.M.–5:00 P.M. Fee.

WYOMING: *Meadowbrook Herb Garden, Route 138.* Over 200 herbs are grown in the greenhouses, the outdoor formal gardens, and the fields. A variety of culinary, medicinal, and ornamental herbs, which are harvested and processed into richly fragrant herb teas that are sold in the herb shop attached to the greenhouses. Daily, 1:00 P.M.–6:00 P.M.; at other hours by appointment only.

On following page
Clock-wise from top right:
Olu Pua Gardens, Kalaheo, Hawaii
Montreal Botanic Gardens, Montreal, Canada
Butchart Gardens, Victoria, Canada
Legislative Building Gardens, Regina, Canada
St. Thomas Gardens, Charlotte Amalie,
U.S. Virgin Islands

South Carolina

CHARLESTON: *Boone Hall Plantation, Christ Church Parish, Route 17-N.* A ¾-mile avenue of moss-draped oaks and a mansion flanked by formal gardens of azaleas and camellias, with garden walks made from plantation bricks. Monday through Saturday, 9:00 A.M.–5:00 P.M. Sunday, 1:00 P.M.–5:00 P.M. Closed Thanksgiving and Christmas. Fee.

Charles Town Landing. A 200-acre landscaped park that has several additional attractions (an animal forest, a theater, etc.). It is the site of the first English colony in South Carolina; and the present site of an 80-acre garden, essentially English in design, which contains some of the most impressive oaks in the Low Country of the Carolinas. Hundreds of other trees and shrubs have been added, so that the result is, for all practical gardening purposes, an arboretum of considerable loveliness nearly in the center of the town. Daily.

Hampton Park. A sunken garden, rose-bordered walks, camellias, and azaleas. Daily.

Magnolia Gardens and Nurseries, Route 4, 29407. Notable for the superb azaleas and the world's largest collection of camellias, with lagoons and a bridge draped with wisteria—a sort of fairyland dropped into a setting of unrivaled beauty. The gardens were once listed in an early Baedeker as one of the three most attractive sights in the New World, the others being Niagara Falls and the Grand Canyon! Of course, this was at the turn of the century. The gardens are part of an 80-acre estate (25 acres of gardens and 16 acres of lawn); the remainder is farmed as a wholesale nursery. Many live oaks, magnolias, and bald cypresses for backgrounds. Many camellias (1,000 varieties, mostly japonica), some of which date back to 1843, the azaleas five years later; initially planted by a clergyman to regain his health, he developed the basic plan of the gardens as they exist today. Some of the camellias are now so large that they are considered as trees instead of shrubs. Since many of camellia flowers go with the coming of warm weather, it is advisable to see them during late February or early March at the latest. The fame of the garden is largely due to its massed azaleas, blooming in mid-March. Sometimes the fallen azalea petals so cover the paths that a visitor seems to be engulfed in color. Spring is also welcomed with daffodils, jonquils, spiraea,

Magnolia Gardens

Bomar Water Gardens

Magnolia Gardens

Middleton Place Gardens

flowering quince, and forsythia. Of flowering trees there is a profusion: Oriental magnolias, flowering crab apples, dogwood, redbud, and many others. Grouped with the trees are pockets of climbing jasmine and Cherokee and banksia roses. From February 15 to May 1: daily, 8:00 A.M.–5:00 P.M. Fee.

Middleton Place, Route 4, 29407. An old plantation home with gardens of azaleas and camellias, thought to be the oldest landscaped gardens in the country. The gardens were begun in 1741 and finished in 1751, when elegance and natural plantings were the marks of a great garden. The plant explorer André Michaux brought the first camellias in the New World to Middleton; three of the four original plants still survive. Nearby these historic camellias is one that is thought to be the largest in the world. Sixty-five acres of the 6,000-acre estate (the plantation is a working farm) are in terraces and parterres, open gardens, and massed displays of camellias (a camellia allée is justly famous) and azaleas (35,000 on a single hillside). Within the formal area there is a Moon Garden, an Octagonal Garden, a Secret Garden, and a Sundial Garden; butterfly lakes; a giant crape

myrtle, a bamboo grove, and a garden of rare camellias that is a delight to connoisseurs. There are also many fine Southern magnolias and an oak thought to be nearly 1,000 years old. Some trails lead through natural woods to a bald-cypress lake; others carry the visitor into the "farm"—an area filled with 19th-century artifacts and farming tools. Daily, 8:00 A.M.–5:00 P.M. Fee.

CHERAW: *Bomar Water Gardens.* The gardens were developed around a series of spring-fed lakes and ponds, and a waterfall. The spring that feeds the gardens' lily ponds maintains an exact temperature of 70° F. The land areas are amply planted with azaleas and well-grouped native trees. Daily. Fee.

CLEMSON: *Clemson University Ornamental Area, Route 123 (or Route 93), 29631.* Many species of ornamentals are grown, both for display and for educational uses. There are annual variety trial gardens in summer; a pioneer garden, and a wildflower garden. The research area is landscaped with azaleas and camellias, other shrubs, and lawn grasses. The greenhouse has a collection of orchids (700 varieties and species). In the Ornamental

Middleton Place Gardens

Area, trails lead through the shrub-trial planting to a tea house, a wildflower garden, and a bog garden; a special trail for the blind has been established here also. The Pioneer Complex is historical and authentic; an early log cabin has been built, much as the first white Americans built their homes, complete with out-buildings and split rail fence. The garden is a year-round pleasure; informal plantings of herbs, flowers, native vines and fruits, and vegetables—all typical of the kitchen gardens of the pioneers. The Variety Trial Garden: a 2½-acre plot with 48 separate beds, a show place for plants, and a testing ground for the newest varieties of annuals. Petunias seem to dominate the trials, but others are well represented; ageratum, celosia, dahlia, geranium, marigold, salvia, pansies, snapdragons, sweet peas, and zinnias. In the perennial area the gardens are planted with peonies, iris, day lilies, chrysanthemums, and 280 varieties of daffodils being checked for hardiness, stems, and floral characteristics. With such an agglomeration of plants there is no true peak floral period; there are flowers 8 to 9 months out of the year, beginning with April. Daily, sunrise–sunset.

COLUMBIA: *Memorial Gardens.* Azaleas, camellias, superb boxwoods, and a walled garden.

University of South Carolina Gardens, Sumter Street. There are actually two small gardens on the campus. The Sumter Street garden has beautiful azaleas, camellias, and roses and clipped hedges of dwarf holly. The other garden (entered through a small doorway in a brick wall between Marion and Bull streets) has a fountain and formal beds of floribunda roses that are bordered with sasanquas and azaleas. Daily, all year.

Don't overlook the garden of the *Columbia Museum of Art, 1519 Senate Street*, with its collection of 50 species of South Carolina plants. Or the *Boylston Gardens*, with their formal boxwood, white azaleas, and flowering bulbs.

GEORGETOWN: *Belle Isle Gardens.* Of the 5,000 acres many have been devoted to landscaped grounds planted with azaleas, camellias, bamboo, wisteria, dogwood, magnolia, and many other Southern trees and shrubs; flowering plants are grown in parterres. November through August: daily, 8:00 A.M.–6:00 P.M. Closed Christmas. Fee.

GREENWOOD: *Park Seed Company Gardens, Route 254.*

When flowers are at a minimum in summer, the 10-acre test gardens of the Park Seed Company are filled with blooms. Their All-America selections are announced during the last week of July—which has become a sort of a festival in the area. Daily, Monday through Friday, 8:00 A.M.–4:30 P.M. Closed holidays.

HARTSVILLE: *Kalmia Gardens, Route 151*. So named for the mountain laurel, *Kalmia latifolia*, the dominant flowering shrub in the gardens. Essentially a 24-acre arboretum with 700 varieties and species of trees and shrubs native to both the Up-Country and the Low-Country areas. Daily.

MURRELLS INLET: *Brookgreen Gardens, Route 17, 29576*. The garden was originally conceived as a background for sculptures, and its later development has clearly been influenced by this purpose. There are 340 large marble, bronze, and aluminum statues by 178 artists. The acreage (10,000 acres) is largely a wildlife and wildflower sanctuary, of which 300 acres have been provided for the gardens and the sanctuaries. Of the 700 kinds of plants that have been introduced or were natives, most are hollies and live oaks. But there is also a dogwood garden, a palmetto garden (of great charm), and a rose garden. Well represented are magnolias, crape myrtle, oleander, camellias and azaleas, jasmines. A live-oak walk bordered with clipped ivy has an almost unbelievable grandeur. The total effect is of an outdoor museum that is both beautiful and satisfying. Daily, 9:00 A.M.–4:45 P.M. Closed Christmas. Fee.

OAKLEY: *Cypress Gardens, 29466*. Magnificent cypress, masses of Indian azaleas (40 kinds) and Kurume azaleas from Japan, and 300 cultivars of camellias provide a floral peak around mid-March to mid-April, although the camellias begin flowering earlier. Drifts of daffodils, narcissus, pockets of *Daphne odorata*, and sweet olive combine to add a gentle fragrance, in which the perfume of the yellow jasmine is dominant. The real exhibit is the imposing cypress trees growing in their natural habitat and azaleas on the banks of the swamps, both reflected in the inky black waters. The flower-transformed swamp and the majestic trees seem to create the impressive grandeur of a great cathedral in which the devotional candles are the flaming azaleas. From February 15 to May 1: daily, 8:00 A.M.–dusk. Fee.

Cypress Gardens

Brookgreen Gardens

Brookgreen Gardens

Glencairn Gardens

ORANGEBURG: *Edisto Memorial Gardens, Route 301-S, 29115.* Created less than 40 years ago from a dismal swamp along the edge of the Edisto River, the 90-acre gardens now have magnificent roses (6,000 bushes and 110 varieties, plus a rose test plot), which come into full bloom around the middle of April. This is also about the correct time to see the azalea-lined trails, the dogwood, crape myrtle, wisteria, and other early-blooming ornamentals such as the flowering crab apples. Daily.

ROCK HILL: *Glencairn Gardens, Charlotte Avenue and Crest Street.* The northernmost of the formal gardens in South Carolina, with terraced lawns, landscaped flower beds, a fountain, and a reflecting pool surrounded by tall trees. It is restful in any season, and ablaze in the spring when its famous azaleas and dogwood bloom.

Late April is a good visiting period, but the planting does have year-round interest. Daily, sunrise–sunset.

SUMMERVILLE: *Summerville Municipal Gardens, Junction of Routes 17 and 78.* The informally planted azalea gardens are as sumptuously rich as those gardens built on a grander scale. One of the main varieties is the pinkish "Pride of Summerville." Daily.

SUMTER: *Swan Lake Gardens, West Liberty Street.* Noted for its 6 million Japanese iris and innumerable Dutch iris, which bloom in the spring. Also notable for the lake's families of swans—white mute English swans and the black Australians. Other plants: Egyptian lotus, sweet anise, bay blossom tree, yellow jasmine, gardenia, wisteria, and pleasantly grouped maples for fall foliage colors. Daily, 8:00 A.M.–5:00 P.M.

South Dakota

BROOKINGS: *McCrory Gardens, South Dakota State University, Route 14-E, 57006.* The gardens are part of the campus grounds, and are used for demonstrations of home improvement, for testing plants, trees, and shrubs, and for research and instruction. But both students and the public are always invited to visit the gardens even if only for the purpose of enjoyment or relaxation. The plantings are nearly all of hardy ornamentals: trees, shrubs, regional annuals and perennials, vines and turfs that are suitable for landscape use in the Great Plains. The Pharmaceutical Gardens contain an interesting group of herbs and plants used in the manufacture of drugs and patent medicines. Tobacco plants are grown as pollution indicators, and have indicated at least a modicum of polluted air in South Dakota. Daily, 8:00 A.M.–8:00 P.M.

GARY: *Fragrance Garden for the Blind.*

MITCHELL: *Hitchcock Park, 901 East Hansen Street.* The park's formal gardens are planted with annuals dahlias, delphiniums, lilies, roses, and tulips, surrounded by groups of local and imported trees. Daily.

RAPID CITY: *Sioux Park, Story Book Island, Canyon Lake Road.* A very well-landscaped area that includes much of the children's zoo, also on the island.

SIOUX FALLS: *McKennon Park, 21st Street and 2nd Avenue.* The oldest formal gardens in the city, covering $18\frac{3}{4}$ acres and with nearly 11,000 plants.
Sherman Park, Kiwanis Avenue. Great Plains Zoo and Cactus Gardens. The only surprising thing about a cactus garden so far north is that many gardeners are not aware of the fact that many varieties of the cactus family are native to those areas. Part of the gardens and the waterfall nearby are made of native quartzite stone.

VERMILLION: *Stetwold Mum Grower Gardens 108 East Main Street.* A commercial nursery with a fine selection of hardy chrysanthemums—and iris—which do well in the great Plains climate zone. Several acres of field-planted chrysanthemums.

WEBSTER: *Petunia capital of the world.*

Pharmaceutical Gardens

Tennessee

CHATTANOOGA: *Reflection Riding, Route 148.* A wild-flower preserve of 300 acres, several lakes, and natural woods at the foot of Lookout Mountain. It is designed to be viewed entirely from an automobile along the 3-mile scenic drive where at least 45 varieties of trees and 60 kinds of wildflowers are identified by easily readable signs—a sort of modified arboretum that precludes walking. There are many native trees and shrubs, including stands of azaleas, dogwood, and shad-blow, and such trees as wild cherry, sassafras, black walnut, and others. A very peaceful and lovely natural area rescued from the oblivion of industrialization; lovely in spring or fall, especially as the maples and hickories and tulip trees turn scarlet and gold. Daily, summer, 7:30 A.M.–dusk; winter, 8:00 A.M.–6:00 P.M. Fee.

COLUMBIA: *James Knox Polk Home, 303 West 7th Street.* The garden is patterned after the large estates of the 19th century; formal areas are backed with natural drifts of shrubs and trees. The four gardens consist of a Court Garden with an iron fountain; a formal garden with Southern flower favorites and bordered in boxwood and brick paths somewhat along the lines of similar gardens at Williamsburg; a natural garden, with statuary and beds of tulips; and a cutting garden, where peonies and lily of the valley are established as well as other flowering plants. Daily, 9:00 A.M.–5:00 P.M. Fee.

GATLINBURG: *Great Smoky Mountains National Park, 37738.* An area extraordinarily rich in flowering plants, shrubs, and trees that have meant much to gardening and to gardeners. The lovely flame azalea and mountain laurel (May-June), rose-purple rhododendrons (mid-June), white rhododendrons (June-July), dogwood and redbud (mid to late April); and wildflowers of many species (a total of 1,500 kinds of flowering plants). Guide maps and information may be secured from the park headquarters in Gatlinburg. Daily.

KNOXVILLE: *Blount Mansion, 200 West Hill Avenue.* An 18th-century garden. Fee.
Ivan Rachoff Gardens, Tennessee Federation of Garden Clubs, 1943 Tennessee Avenue, N.W. Rock garden, azaleas, many varieties of bulbs, dogwoods. Daily.

MEMPHIS: *Memphis Botanic Garden, Audubon Park, 750 Cherry Road, 38117.* Originally the W. C. Paul Arboretum (87 acres). A very pleasant Japanese Garden,

Reflection Riding

the Michie Magnolia Garden, with 80 varieties; the Ketchum Iris Garden; roses (3,500 kinds). Special collections include azaleas, flowering crab apples, and hollies. There are special plantings of daffodils, day lilies, and dahlias. Also a tropical conservatory with staple items, and a cool house for the camellia collection. Spring and fall are the best viewing seasons. Monday through Saturday, 9:00 A.M.–5:00 P.M. Sunday, 2:00 P.M.–5:00 P.M.

Southwestern Arboretum, Southwestern College of Memphis, 38117. Some 100 acres of native woody species of shrubs and trees.

NASHVILLE: *Belle Meade Mansion.* A 24-acre remnant of a once great plantation, retaining its spacious lawns intact, its century-old rock garden, and 125 varieties of trees.

Childrens Museum, 724 2nd Avenue, South. A native wildflower garden done in wax by artist Paul Marchand. Much more appropriate for adults, although delightful for children, too.

Hermitage, Route 70-N. Home and gardens of Andrew Jackson, considered to be one of the outstanding examples of early American landscaping in the area. The garden (a 1-acre square bisected by brick walks) was designed by Rachel Jackson and contains, in addition to magnolias and hickories, more than 50 varieties of plants that were available to gardeners in the previous century, predominantly iris, lilies, peonies, pinks, roses, hyacinths, and jonquils, and shrub favorites such as crape myrtle, chionanthus, cotinus (smoke trees). Daily, 9:00 A.M.–5:00 P.M. Closed Christmas. Fee.

Tennessee Botanical Gardens and Fine Arts Center, Inc., Cheek Road, 37203. This is one of the more delightful garden-art associations since it is not so much a mélange as it is mutually supportive; each occupies its own space, but their proximity provides an easy access of one to the other. Daffodils, day lilies, iris, azaleas, peonies, and chrysanthemums. The Julia Bainbridge

Greenhouse of camellias; and another greenhouse for an orchid collection. An arboretum arrangement of flowering crab apples and hollies, forest trees, and handsome boxwoods. Fountains, streams, pools, and ponds. The Tretschler evergreen planting; the Howe Garden of Wildflowers. Brochures of the garden and the museum describe their relationship most accurately as "a joining of gardens and arts for greater enjoyment and understanding of both." Tuesday through Saturday, 10:00 A.M.–5:00 P.M. Sunday, 1:00 P.M.–5:00 P.M. Fee.

OAK RIDGE: *University of Tennessee Arboretum, 794 Bethel Valley Road, 37830.* Some 600 kinds of plants on 25 cultivated acres. Dwarf conifers and a shrub garden; a planting of heaths and hollies and dogwood (37 varieties). Spring is most colorful. Monday through Friday, 8:00 A.M.–4:00 P.M.

ROAN MOUNTAIN: *Rhododendron display.* The finest display of Catawba rhododendrons in the country is found near the top of Roan Mountain. The climate, moist and temperate, and the soil conditions are ideally suited to the plants, and they bloom more profusely here than elsewhere. Some of the early travelers and botanists have described "rhododendron thickets so tangled that it is difficult to pass through them, if at all." There is a good road to the top of Roan Mountain from nearby Elizabethton or Johnson City. Check with the Chamber of Commerce in the area for the best flowering dates, which may change from time to time.

SIGNAL MOUNTAIN: *Rivermont Orchids, James Boulevard.* One of the classic orchid nurseries, with well-grown stock and a good variety of plants. Thursday only.

SMYRNA: *Sam Davis Memorial Home, Route 41.* A formal garden—essentially a green garden—whose walks are bordered with shaped cypress and flanked with pleasant groups of trees. Daily. Fee.

Texas

ABILENE: *Iris Trail*. Special iris gardens are designated as show gardens each April, and usually have among them more than 900 varieties of iris, including all of the winners of the Dykes Award of the American Iris Society. Although Abilene has been noted for its iris, it is most unusual to find so many varieties in relatively so small an area. One of the gardens, the *McMurray Iris Garden on Sayles Boulevard and South 16th Street*, is an American Iris Society Symposium show place. It has only iris plants selected yearly by the Iris Symposium as the most beautiful; each year 100 new Symposium selections are added. For information, contact the Chamber of Commerce, 341 Hickory Street.

AMARILLO: *Amarillo Garden Center*. A recently completed and an attractive headquarters. Visitors are welcomed during business hours.

Rose Garden, Memorial Park, South Washington Street. A 20-acre park adjacent to Amarillo College, with a lovely garden pavilion and many roses. Daily, during daylight hours.

AUSTIN: *Fiesta Gardens, Town Lake Park*. Lavish displays of exotic plants; and famous for the Bluebonnet Trails.

Laguna Gloria Art Gallery Garden. An Italianate building surrounded by beautifully styled gardens. Tuesday through Saturday, 10:00 A.M.–12:00 noon; 2:00 P.M.–5:00 P.M.

State Complex, midtown area. Forty-six acres of immaculate landscaped grounds; stately shade trees, flower gardens. Daily.

Zilker Gardens, Zilker Park. A large park (391 acres) of which a considerable portion has been set aside for formal gardens and the *Austin Area Garden Center*. The Center is a most remarkable building of native stone, hewn timbers, and inside paneling of wood. The Hamilton Azalea Garden: 20,000 square feet of rugged hillside landscaped with beds of azaleas. The Rose Garden: its borders are informal and constructed of native stone, and hold 65 varieties of roses. The Oriental Garden: a delicate balance between water and plant materials, with a series of cascades and lotus ponds, a tea house, and a "bridge-to-walk-over-the-moon." Still to come: a fragrance garden, a water garden, parterres, a cactus garden, an orchid house, and a botanical greenhouse. But there is plenty to admire and a good

194

Memorial Rose Garden

Opposite: *Fort Worth Botanic Gardens*. Above: *Ima Hogg Home*

Fort Worth Botanic Gardens

deal to learn. Daily.

BROWNSVILLE: *Gladys Porter Zoo, Ringgold and 6th Street.* Following the new concepts of naturalness, the zoo has placed its animals in natural backgrounds and has thereby developed an interesting collection of subtropicals, palms, and native Texas plants. Daily, Fee. *Tropical Nursery, 1925 Central Boulevard.* One of only several nurseries to breed crotons, it has developed an interesting collection of these exotic foliage plants. The growing grounds also contain many other tropical foliage plants.

CLEVELAND: *Hilltop Herb Farm, 77327.* Located in Sam Houston National Forest area, the herb farm is a delightful place to visit. An Herb Garden, a Mary Garden, an English Garden, a Wheel of Thyme Garden—among others; and surrounded by oaks, magnolias, redbud, and dogwood as well as vines, tuberous begonias, and ferns. Daily, year round; though spring and early summer are best.

COLLEGE STATION: *Texas A & M University Arboretum and Trial Grounds.* More than 800 species and varieties are on display in the arboretum and greenhouse

(largely for shows). The university is responsible for testing and evaluating trees, shrubs, and plants that may be profitably introduced into the area. Daily. *Garden of Biblical Plants, First Methodist Church.* The garden is located between the church and the parsonage.

CONROE: *Walton Gardens, off Route 75.* A seasonal floral showcase where thousands of flowering plants appropriate to each season are displayed. Daily, except Saturday. Fee.

DALLAS: *Cloister Garden, 3300 Mocking Bird Lane.* *Dallas Garden Center, Forest and 1st Street, State Fair Grounds, 75226.* A relatively new 7½-acre center with well-established gardens. The Collier Garden of Perennials; the Garden of Day Lilies; Scruggs Herb and Scent Garden; iris, rose, and water gardens; Herbert Marcus Garden; Shakespeare Garden; and a Little Mexico Garden of Color. There is also a garden room of tropical plants and an indoor garden display. Weekdays, 10:00 A.M.–5:00 P.M. Saturday and Sunday, 2:00 P.M.–5:00 P.M. Closed Christmas. *Lambert Gardens, 3800 Northwest Highway.* Interesting plant materials.

Above: *Palmetto State Park.* Below: *Cactus Garden, Judge Roy Bean Visitor Center*

Owens Fine Arts Center, Southern Methodist University Campus. A court garden and a sculpture garden of contemporary Italian sculptures. Monday through Saturday, 12:00 noon–5:00 P.M. Sunday, 1:00 P.M.–5:00 P.M.
EDINBURG: *Fitzpatrick's Cactus Gardens, Highway 281.* Twenty acres of cactus plants from all over the world; an imposing sight to delight cactus hobbyists. Daily.
FORT WORTH: *Botanic Garden, Forest Park, 3220 Botanic Garden Drive, 76107.* A display greenhouse with ferns, house plants, and orchids, and a 90-acre park area in which more than 2,500 kinds of plants are grown. (By some estimates the total plant count runs to 150,000, including 150 varieties of trees, 14,000 rose bushes, and 500 varieties of flowering trees—enough to keep even the most knowledgeable visitor busy.) A rose garden hedged with dwarf yaupon, iris and herb gardens, a fragrance garden, and a cactus garden. A 1-acre Japanese Garden is presently being developed. There are good collections of holly and crape myrtle. Mid-May and June are pleasant months to visit the arboretum and, particularly, to become aquainted with the garden center. Arboretum: daily, sunrise–sunset.

Greenhouses: Monday through Friday, 7:30 A.M.–4:00 P.M. Garden Center: daily, 8:00 A.M.–4:00 P.M.
HENDERSON: *The Wood Box House and Garden.* A typical east Texas woodland (37 acres) planted with English boxwood, dogwood, redbud, and (most likely) a million narcissi.
HOUSTON: *Garden Center, Herman Park.* Gardens of fragrance, herbs and perennials, roses.
Aline McAshan Botanical Hall and Arboretum, Voss Road and Memorial Drive, 77055. Primarily a children's center for the study of conservation and field botany, and an adult workshop in plant-animal relationships. There is an adjoining greenhouse. The arboretum (200 acres, with 235 varieties of woody plants) is largely a mixed forest of native deciduous trees with nature trails and appropriate instructions. Near the hall is an herb garden and a collection of hollies. Arboretum: daily, 8:00 A.M.–6:00 P.M. Botanical Hall: Monday through Saturday, 8:30 A.M.–5:30 P.M; Sunday, 1:00 P.M.–5:30 P.M.
Ima Hogg Home, 2940 Lazy Lane. Formal gardens with spacious lawns, clipped hedges, and many ornamental and native trees and shrubs. A circular garden is bisected

Chrysanthemum Gardens

to make arc-shaped beds filled with perennials, some annuals, and dwarf herbaceous plants. Tours are arranged by advanced reservation with the Museum of Fine Arts, 1001 Bissonnet.

River Oaks. A residential area of Houston that is particularly colorful during the azalea season (March). Visitors may ride or walk through the well-marked area when the gardens are officially open for the Azalea Trail. For information, contact Houston's Visitor Council (tel 713-224-5201).

Sam Houston Historical Park, 515 Allen Parkway. A 21-acre park set aside as a monument to the early history of Texas, including landscaped grounds and gardens and restored historic buildings. Monday through Friday, 10:00 A.M.–4:00 P.M. Sunday, 1:30 P.M.–4:30 P.M. Fee.

JACKSONVILLE: *Hamlin's Gardens, Route 17S.* Thousands of azaleas, dogwood, and redbud which—during the blooming season only (March)—may be seen by arrangement with Mr. Harold Hamlin.

JEFFERSON: *Excelsior House.* A hotel that has been in continuous operation since the 1880s. It has a pleasant court garden with brick paths, a fountain, and a pool; the garden has a wisteria arbor, dogwood, and elegant small shrubs. Daily.

LANGTRY: *Cactus Gardens, Judge Roy Bean Visitor Center.* Many of the Southwestern native trees and shrubs—and a very good cactus garden—are on display at this attractive botanic garden. Wide pathways, raised and terraced beds, and interpretive plaques make the garden easily seen and keep visitors well informed. Daily, sunrise–sunset.

LAREDO: *Cactus Gardens, 3201 San Bernardo Avenue.* One of the most extensive collections of cacti.

LUBBOCK: *Chrysanthemum Gardens, Texas Technological College Campus.* Each October the Campus is alive with colorful drifts of chrysanthemums (over 40,000 plants). The planting is actually part of a city-wide program to make Lubbock the city of chrysanthemums. Special brochures and planting advice are provided for all home gardeners, and technical assistance is available. The result: a city-wide panorama of color in the fall.

LULING: *Palmetto State Park, Route 183.* A rare botanical garden of 173 acres along the banks of the San Marcos River. Quaking bogs, wild orchids, water lilies, graceful

ferns, many palmettos, and some rare plants not found elsewhere. The park is a field laboratory for several universities. Daily. Fee.

MISSION: *The All-Poinsettia Show.* Now 25 years old, the December display of poinsettias is the only one of its kind in the country. From the poinsettia fields to the city's displays, poinsettias of red, yellow, cream, and pink may be seen.

Sharon Estate. Acres and acres of orange and grapefruit groves surrounding the mansion and the beautifully terraced formal gardens and spacious lawns. Many native trees and colorful shrubs and brilliant flowers.

McALLEN: *Valley Botanical Garden, Route 83, 78501.* A garden for the healthy to regard with awe, since most of the work is accomplished by garden trainees who are either physically handicapped or mentally retarded. Indeed, the purpose of the garden is provide work and educational assistance for such young people. Within the 20-acre estate there are herb and rose gardens, a sunken garden, and a collection of native shrubs and trees of the southwestern area of Texas. Rarely seen in Texas: sweet olives, sugarberries, and ebony trees

can be viewed in the garden and their white blossoms admired in the spring. Bluebonnets in large fields, bougainvillea everywhere. The Hughs Cactus Garden has a remarkable collection of cacti native to the Southwest, and the citrus arboretum has specimens of every type of citrus tree grown commercially. Daily, 8:00 A.M.– 5:00 P.M.

MONAHANS: *Monahans Sandhills State Park, Route 80.* Some 4,000 acres of wind-sculptured sand dunes and one of the largest oak forests in the nation—which is not at first apparent. The oldest trees are barely 3 feet tall but their roots may descend as far as 90 feet in search of water to sustain their miniature surface growth. Daily. Fee.

PALESTINE: *Davey Dogwood Park.* About 400 acres of picturesque landscape (and paved roads) and more dogwood than is usually seen in one area. Late March. Daily.

PANTHER JUNCTION: *Big Bend National Park.* For gardeners or others who wish to see the most flowers in one place, Big Bend in March-April provides an exhilarating opportunity. More than 1,000 kinds of

The Alamo Gardens

plants, such as acacias, cacti, lupines, giant daggers, yuccas, and many rare plants. Because of the difference in elevation and topography, wildflowers bloom almost continuously from spring to fall; but the high season is early in spring, and it can provide floral drifts and fields of flowers that may be seen for miles. Daily, sunrise–sunset.

PECOS: *Desert Botanical Garden, Pecos Municipal Park.* Plants, shrubs, and trees native to the area; cactus, other succulents, and arid climate plants are in the majority. Daily, sunrise–sunset.

SAN ANTONIO: *Brackenridge Park, North St. Mary's Street, 78212.* Walk or ride the mini-train to the Chinese Sunken Gardens, a monument to Oriental design transferred to the Occident. Created from a quarry, the park now has pools and a pavilion, terraced gardens stone walkways, and spiraling steps. Water lilies, dwarf shrubs, and tropical plants. The garden is expertly designed and skillfully maintained. Daily.

Mission Gardens. The Spanish influence, with trees and shrubs and the sparse use of garden materials, may be seen at *Mission Concepción (807 Mission Road)* and *Mission San José (701 East Pyron).* Daily, 10:00 A.M.–6:00 P.M. Fee.

Paseo del Río (The River Walk). Along the banks of the San Antonio River, as it passes through the city, there are flowers and shrubs and trees beautifully arranged, arched Venetian bridges, and paved walkways leading from grove to grove, from outdoor café to outdoor café. A rock garden, a cactus garden, groups of tropical foliage plants. The promenade has been called "beauty by the mile." Daily, until the shops close, and later.

Spanish Governor's Palace, 105 Military Plaza. A courtyard garden typical of the Spanish Extremadura, with a fountain and lilies, pebbled walks, and subtropical plants. Monday through Saturday, 9:00 A.M.–5:00 P.M. Sunday, 10:00 A.M.–5:00 P.M. Fee.

Zoological Gardens, 3903 North St. Mary's Street, 78212. Animals in landscaped areas that have many excellent plants typical of the area or similar to those in the countries from which the animals came originally. April through October: daily, 9:30 A.M.–6:30 P.M. November through March: daily, 9:30 A.M.–5:00 P.M. Fee.

The Alamo Gardens, Alamo Plaza, East Houston and South Alamo Streets. Small but luxurious gardens. Monday through Saturday, 9:00 A.M.–5:30 P.M. Sunday,

Tyler Rose Farm

10:00 A.M.–5:30 P.M. Fee.

TYLER: *Rose Park, West Front and Boone Streets*. A terraced park, transformed from red clay gullies and filled with native pines, oaks, and shrubs, enhanced by graveled paths and streams, fountains and reflection pools. It surrounds a 22-acre rose garden (36,000 bushes, 500 varieties). The rose beds are symmetrical, edged with concrete borders; some beds are terraced. Each bed contains from 20 to 60 rose bushes (and is devoted to a single variety). Some of the unexpected delights of the garden are a bed of "green-petaled" roses, some very tall tree roses, and mini-roses in a raised bed, so tiny that each flower is barely the size of a dime. Within the garden area there is also the Vance Burks Memorial Camellia Garden and the Jacob Johnson Conservatory, with lavish tropical exotics: anthuriums, bromeliads, cycads, tree ferns, and many others. The Garden Center, which overlooks the park, is a good place from which to plan a visit. Daily, sunrise–sunset.

WEATHERFORD: *Chandor Gardens, West Simons Street*. The Chandor home sometimes called "White Shadows," was the home of Douglas Chandor the portraitist. The gardens are a lesson in creativity and persistence. The original soil was caliche, a peculiarly intractable former sea bed, which was replaced with tons of soil. Live oaks were imported and native trees—and others hardy and suitable—were planted. Hedges of roses were introduced; then groups of lilacs and crape myrtle, and columns of magnolias. Formal and informal gardens were constructed, streams and rock walls added, and garden ornaments (some homemade, including a Ming-type dragon whose porcelain body scales were cooked in a kitchen oven) were set in place. A soft, beautiful and curiously protective, romantic garden for such a difficult climate. Daily. Fee.

WEST COLUMBIA: *Varner-Hogg Plantation, Route 35*. A Greek Revival home with formal and informal gardens. Much of the planting was accomplished with subtropicals. Tuesday, Thursday through Sunday, 10:00 A.M.–12:00 noon; 1:00 P.M.–5:00 P.M. Fee.

WESLACO: *Link Nursery and Floral Company, Route 83*. An unusual planting of subtropical shrubs and trees—especially the flowering species. An intricate system of paths leads through the nursery grounds and provides easy access to the plant materials. Daily.

Utah

FARMINGTON: *Field Station of the Utah State University*; and an agricultural experiment station for evaluating ornamentals and other crops for use in Utah. Daily, all year.

FILLMORE: *Rose Gardens, Territorial State House State Historic Monument, Center Street*. One of the loveliest rose gardens in Utah is next to the statehouse. The statehouse, built of red sandstone quarried in the mountains east of Fillmore, was to be the west wing of the Capitol, but Salt Lake became the capital city. The statehouse is surrounded by large trees, lawns, and flowers, and has a handsome rose garden. Daily, except during the winter months.

OGDEN: *Municipal Grounds*. The second city of Utah is famous for its municipal gardens and, especially, for the Christmas display on the grounds. The gardens are formal in design, with steppingstone walks, dwarf shrubs, and many potted plants for interest and color.

SALT LAKE CITY: *Garden Center, Sugar House Park, 1600 East 21st Street South*. Excellent flower beds and lawns, and a nice group of trees. The Garden Center is very active, with shows during most of the year.

Governor's Mansion, 1270 Fairfax Road. Gardens and trees. *House of Bonsai, 1625 East 6400 South*. In addition to the bonsai, there is a pleasant garden-yard.

International Peace Garden, Jordan Park, 1060 South 8th West. Initiated in 1939 to honor the Americans of foreign origin living in Salt Lake City, the gardens now have 19 nations represented. Each national garden was created and planted by local representatives of that culture, and at their own expense. The British garden is formal, with clipped hedges and rectangular rose beds, and has the British crown displayed in flowers. Canadians used wood logs and pine trees. The Chinese garden has a pagoda, graceful bridges, and special plantings of small shrubs. Lebanon planted cedars of Lebanon. The Germans used massive gates, linden trees, and stonework. Holland planted masses of tulips. And so on for the other gardens, altogether a remarkable collection of national talents displayed along the banks of the Jordan River. Daily, sunrise–sunset.

Iris Gardens, Lindsay Gardens, 9th Avenue and M Street. A small and well-balanced collection.

Liberty Park, 10th South and 6th East. Some very beautiful

Temple Gardens

raised flower beds at Park Headquarters.

Memory Grove Park, at the foot of Capitol Hill (City Creek Canyon). The estate of Brigham Young, with a meditation chapel in a setting of native shrubs and trees.

Rose Gardens, Holy Cross Hospital, 10th East and 2nd South. The municipal rose garden, with more than 10,000 bushes and a correspondingly large number of varieties, and particularly the most recent All-American selections, Some very fine old specimens of historic roses. Daily, sunrise–sunset.

State Arboretum of Utah, University of Utah, 84112. A remarkable collection of woody plants assembled on the campus as part of the university's landscape. Many of them were, and are, part of the continuing evaluation of trees suitable for Utah. Some 440 varieties of trees are represented (a total of more than 5,500). There are several prominent planting areas and groves: The *U* Circle, Cottom's Gulch, the Sill House, North Campus Road Park, South Heating Plant Park (where the exciting and attractive new hybrid oaks are established), Chapel Glen, and a new area— Red Butte—now being developed. Other than natives, there are many trees of special interest to both botanists and gardeners: aspen, umbrella catalpa (a grafted top to give it a rounded look), empress trees, hinoki cypress, Chinese date, and many others. In Chapel Glen there is an herb garden, and a rose garden near Spencer Hall. It takes visitors about two hours to make the self-guided tour, for which an admirable pamphlet is issued. Daily, sunrise–sunset.

Temple Gardens, Temple Square, Church of the Latter-Day Saints. Among all gardens, secular or religious, the Temple Gardens rank very close to the top—not for size, but for the quality of the planting and its arrangement. This garden, as well as others among Mormon churches, has received many garden and national citations, the most recent being for a church-office-building garden planted on top of an underground garage, close by the Temple Gardens. As with all Mormon gardens, a special office of the church is responsible for the landscaping. Most often the gardens will be formal, cool and shaded, with grass and trees, and it is so planned that there is a pleasant sequence of bloom from spring through summer, making full use of annuals

Above: *Rose Garden, Territorial State House.* Below: *International Peace Garden*

Opposite: *Temple Gardens.* Above: *Ogden Municipal Grounds*

and perennials. Daily. Special tours are available.

SPRINGDALE: *Zion National Park, 48767.* One of the best "natural" gardens in the West, featuring the Hanging Gardens—plants growing up and down the canyon walls. The park is a flower show from spring well into summer. Cacti, yuccas, Zion moonflowers, white evening primroses, and "pygmy forests of conifers" are to be found here. In May and June, the flowering plants in the hanging gardens are outstanding. In summer, the plants at the higher elevations come into bloom (the park is on the northeast edge of the Mohave Desert) and sometimes last into the winter. On the whole, however, spring is the best time for flower watchers.

Daily during the season.

TORREY: *Capitol Reef National Park, 84775.* Most national parks are by way of being botanical gardens or arboretums, some more than others, as with Capitol Reef. Its naturally rocky terrain and high elevations have developed plant life similar to that of the high Sonoran Desert of the Southwest. As a result there are many lupines, globe mallows, cliff roses, serviceberries, clematis, Fremont berries, and many others, both common and rare, particularly along the Hickman Bridge Trail. Some shrubs and trees have achieved the stature of specimens: single-leaf ash, snowberry, dwarf yucca, buffalo bush, Mormon tea, and serviceberry.

Vermont

BENNINGTON: *Memorial Gardens*. Interesting plant material.

BRATTLEBORO: *Naulahka*. Home of Rudyard Kipling, with a perennial garden in the English tradition.

CHARLOTTE: *F. H. Hosford Nursery, Inc*. Flowering shrubs and plants characteristic of the region.

EAST BURKE: *Burklyn*. The former estate and home of Elmer Darling (a Vermont lumberman). A natural landmark whose landscaping is evocative of the Vermont hills.

MARSHFIELD: *Groton State Forest, Route 2*. Beautiful stands of rhododendrons are a delight during the early summer. Daily. Fee.

NORTH BENNINGTON: *McCullough Mansion and Gardens*. A white clapboard Victorian house among tall trees and landscaped grounds. July through October: Tuesday through Friday, Sunday, and holidays, 10:00 A.M.–5:00 P.M. Fee.

OLD BENNINGTON: *Bennington Museum*. A courtyard garden with sculptures by contemporary artists.

PEACHAM: *Garden in the Woods*. Another area under the control of the New England Wildflower Society (Framingham, Mass.). It is a bog and woodland filled with choice native orchids.

READING: *Stone Chimney Gardens*. Numerous herbs, primroses, delphiniums, and other perennials. The herbs flower from June to November, before and after the perennials, filling in the seasonal floral gap. May through November: daily.

RUPERT: *Merck Forest Foundation*. A 2,600-acre reserve (enjoyed by both hikers and skiers) that is being used for an investigation into the relationship between forest and farm, discovering which plants and shrubs provide the best wildlife sustenance and cover and are beneficial to the natural ecology of the area.

ST. JOHNSBURY: *Fairbanks Museum of Natural Science, 83 Main Street*. A Victorian Gothic red sandstone building on grounds landscaped with appropriate shrubs and trees. Monday through Saturday, 9:30 A.M.–4:30 P.M. Sunday, 1:00 P.M.–5:00 P.M. Closed holidays.

SHELBURNE: *Shelburne Museum Garden, Route 7*. A collection of homes, buildings, and memorabilia of New England that has been assembled on well-landscaped grounds. Old-fashioned roses, a fine herb garden, apple trees, and lilacs. Hollyhocks and a rose garden shaped like rose petals (Prentis House). A natural rock garden. From May 15 to October 15: daily, 9:00 A.M.–5:00 P.M.

SPRINGFIELD: *Hartness House Inn and Gardens*. Formerly a governor's mansion, now an inn and restaurant in a landscaped setting.

WAITSFIELD: *Bundy Art Gallery*. Meadows and forests in which sculptures are placed on grassy knolls, in pine coves, along paths in the woods, and by a spring-fed lagoon. July and August: Monday, Wednesday, Saturday, 10:00 A.M.–5:00 P.M. Sunday, 1:00 P.M.–5:00 P.M.

WILLIAMSTOWN: *Robinson Gardens*. Terraces and rock walls set with rock plants, peonies, phlox. April through October.

Burklyn

Virginia

ASHLAND: *Scotchtown, Route 685.* Home of Patrick Henry; a frame house and grounds of the early Colonial period (mid-18th century). Monday through Saturday, 10:00 A.M.–5:00 P.M. Sunday, 2:00 P.M.–5:00 P.M. Fee.

BLACKSBURG: *Virginia Polytechnic Institute Arboretum, 24061.* A 60-acre collection of ornamental and native shade trees and a special section of dwarf plants.

BLUE RIDGE PARKWAY: *Craggy Gardens, Milestone 24064.* The gardens, reached by a trail, are rhododendrons at their best and loveliest in nature. Check with the visitor center at the milestone for dates. Together with Roan Mountain in Tennessee, Craggy Gardens is one of the wonders of rhododendrons in the East.

BOWLING GREEN: *Hampton Manor.* An unusual garden designed by Salvador Dali.

BOYCE: *Orland E. White Research Arboretum, Blandy Experimental Farm, University of Virginia, 22620.* A collection of conifers, evergreens, woody trees, and shrubs representing 50 botanical families, logically arranged and well landscaped, and 5,000 kinds of plants on 123 acres. Barberry, magnolia, rose, saxifrage, aster, honeysuckle—arranged by families—as well as other groupings. The flowering trees come into bloom by late April; there are iris and day-lily collections for summer; and fall foliage appears by mid-October. The arboretum conducts a research program in genetics, and one with irradiation. Greenhouses. The arboretum is not open to the public, but visitors who are interested in the plant collections are welcome, provided prior arrangements are made. It is wise to make reservations well in advance by writing to P.O. Box 85 at the above address.

BURROWSVILLE: *Brandon, Route 613.* Another house of great charm, part of which was designed by Thomas Jefferson. The gardens (beyond a 300-foot lawn) are primarily boxwood and tulip trees, and a group of exotic trees brought from the West Indies 300 years ago. An ancient, gnarled mulberry tree remains as a reminder of the attempt to establish a silk industry in America. Two great cucumber trees and a well-sodded walkway frame the view of the James River. A Virginia Garden Club horticulturist describes these green gardens as the "most glorious ever created." Beyond the gardens is an 1,800-acre working farm, where visitors are also invited. Daily, 9:00 A.M.–5:30 P.M. Fee.

Bryan Park Azalea Garden

Above: *Orland E. White Research Arboretum.* Top: *Oatlands*

CHARLES CITY: *Shirley Plantation, Route 5, 23030.* An 800-acre James River agricultural estate that has remained in the possession of the same family for nine generations. Grains and Hereford-Angus cattle. The grounds are pleasantly landscaped. Daily. Closed Christmas. Fee.

Westover. A Georgian building of almost exquisite simplicity (its doors, chimneys, and iron scroll gate are world-famous, and its Indian escape tunnel has provided interesting speculations). The old boxwood gardens are excellent, and the row of 100-year-old tulip poplars very lovely in spring. Gardens: daily, 9:00 A.M.–6:00 P.M. Fee.

CHARLOTTESVILLE: *Ash Lawn.* The home of James Monroe, designed by Thomas Jefferson. Century-old boxwood gardens; borders and plantings that are well preserved and possess great charm as only such established boxwood gardens can. A 300-year-old oak tree and a 150-year-old pine dominate the gardens. Daily, 7:00 A.M.–7:00 P.M. Fee.

Monticello, Route 53. Thomas Jefferson's home and gardens faithfully restored according to his original plan, both in design and in plants used. The lawn, a large

asymmetrical oval, is surrounded by tree plantings in front of which are flower gardens and a walkway. The buildings, so characteristic of plantation homes, were joined by Jefferson to make an all-weather promenade, as well as to conceal the utilitarian structures. March through October: daily, 8:00 A.M.–5:00 P.M. November through February: daily, 9:00 A.M.–4:30 P.M. Fee.

FREDERICKSBURG: *Kenmore, 1201 Washington Avenue, 22401.* The restored home and gardens of Betty Washington Lewis, George Washington's sister. The flower gardens feature 18th-century types of flowers. From March 1 to November 15: daily, 9:00 A.M.–5:00 P.M., other months to 4:30 P.M. Fee.

The Mary Ball Washington House, 1200 Charles Street. The home of George Washington's mother. An old English garden with boxwood and flowers; tulips, pansies, phlox, roses. Daily, 9:00 A.M.–5:00 P.M. Fee.

GLOUCESTER: *Daffodil Farms.* Daffodils are a major commercial product on the acreage around this town, often called "Little Holland." The farms produce a crop of bulbs that is shipped world-wide. Several growers have exhibition gardens in which more than 1,500

Oatlands

varieties of daffodils are grown. The Chamber of Commerce (P.O Box 296) has information and guide maps.

LANCASTER COUNTY: *Christ Church.* An excellent example of a restored church building and disciplined landscaping that is historically correct.

LEESBURG: *Morven Park, Old Waterford Road, Route 2, 22075.* The old iron gateway and the boxwood gardens are probably the finest of their kind in the country. A magnolia-shaded reflecting pool; a parterre sundial garden with specimen yews and miniature boxwood; tulips in the spring. The terraces and paths are paved with handmade bricks. A grassed nature trail, edged in many places with shoulder-high boxwood, leads, in spring, to areas filled with wildflowers. Daily, April through October: Monday through Saturday, 10:00 A.M.–5:00 P.M. Sunday, 1:00 P.M.–5:00 P.M. Fee.

Oatlands, Route 2, 22075. The mansion and the formal gardens are from the Federal period—a classical American style that has rarely been equaled in elegance. The enormous boxwoods are impressive, and the gardens, later expanded, are evocative of the best of the Colonial period. The original bowling green has been transformed into a boxwood allée, with a reflecting pool at one end and a gazebo at the other. The parterres, edged with boxwood, are also a later development, but consistent with history, as is the balustrade that now encloses the front terrace. From April to mid-May is a good time to see the gardens, when they are bright with tulips, daffodils, lilies, and perennials, but they are equally noble as green gardens at any time of the year. From April 1 to October 31: Monday through Saturday, 10:00 A.M.–5:00 P.M. Sunday, 1:00 P.M.–5:00 P.M. Fee.

LORTON: *Gunston Hall, Route 1 (or Route 95), 22079.* Built late in the 18th century. Both the house and the gardens are of unusual design. The elaborate gardens of clipped boxwood parterres and the arrangement of the shrubs and trees are typical of the formality of English gardens. The allée of 12-foot boxwood is magnificent, and the view of the Potomac from the door of the mansion, framed by the allée, is unforgettable. Daily, 9:30 A.M.–5:00 P.M. Fee.

MONTROSS: *Stratford Hall, Route 214.* A working plantation and the historic structure that was once the

home of generations of Lees and the birthplace of Robert E. Lee. The gardens on each side of the house, east and west, have ancient boxwood, flowering shrubs; an herb garden, and a kitchen garden. Daily, 9:00 A.M.–5:00 P.M. Closed Christmas. Fee.

MOUNT VERNON: *The Mount Vernon Gardens, Mount Vernon Memorial Highway, 22121*. The restored gardens now remain substantially as George Washington designed them, although they deteriorated badly after his death. The estate was ultimately purchased by the Mount Vernon's Ladies Association of the Union, and so carefully and successfully have the gardens and the outbuildings been restored that they are today the best remaining example of the social and economic life of the 18th century. Of all the original planting, only six trees survive; but the replacements serve as well or better than the originals may have done. The courtyard of the house opens on the bowling green, which itself is surrounded by a serpentine of native and exotic trees. Behind the trees, actually hidden by them, are the flower gardens and kitchen gardens—looking much as they must have appeared to George Washington,

who designed them and had them planted. The entire handling of the gardens is a bold use of space. The estate is a sort of New World version of an old English country house. From March 1 to September 30: daily, 9:00 A.M.–5:00 P.M. From October 1 to February 28: daily, 9:00 A.M.–4:00 P.M. Fee.

Woodlawn Plantation, Route 235, 22121. A home given by George Washington to Nellie Custis and Lawrence Lewis—his wife's granddaughter (whom he had adopted) and his nephew, whom she had married. There is a collection of roses from the last century's favorites, and two parterre gardens that reach a peak of bloom by late May. Two nature trails wind through the woodlands. Daily, 9:30 A.M.–4:30 P.M. Closed Christmas and New Year's Day. Fee.

NORFOLK: *Adam Thoroughgood House, 1636 Parrish Road*. The oldest brick house in America, with a reconstructed 17th-century garden of great beauty. The present gardener-guide dresses in a costume of the period and is so authentic in his speech and actions that many visitors are left slightly bewildered, particularly so because the house is one of the few in America which

seems to have an authentic ghost. April through June, September through November: Monday through Saturday, 10:00 A.M.–5:00 P.M. Sunday, 11:00 A.M.–5:00 P.M. July and August: daily, 10:00 A.M.–10:00 P.M. December through March: daily, 12:00 noon–5:00 P.M. Closed Christmas and New Year's Day. Fee.

Lafayette City Park, 35th Street and Granby Street. Greenhouses and a conservatory. Monday through Friday, 7:00 A.M.–4:30 P.M. Saturday, 8:30 A.M.–5:00 P.M. Sunday, 10:00 A.M.–5:00 P.M.

Norfolk Botanical Gardens, Airport Road, 23518. Sometimes romantically, though incorrectly, called the "Gardens-by-the-Sea", or the "Home of the International Azalea Festival," which takes place in April. The botanical gardens—which meet the rigid specifications of such installations—have a collection of about 700 different kinds of plants on 160 landscaped acres, and miles of foot trails and paths. Azaleas (250,000 plants), camellias (700 varieties), crape myrtles, rhododendrons, roses in profusion. An authentic Japanese garden, a holly garden, and a collection of plants often mistaken for holly. Heather gardens and heath garden plantings. A gazebo provides an over-all view of the Colonial gardens, expertly pruned in the manner of such gardens. Orchids are displayed in a fiberglass greenhouse. In addition, there are hundreds of companion plants and plantings: hemlocks, white pines, junipers, and an underplanting of daffodils by the thousands. The gardens have also undertaken to introduce new plants to the area, demonstrating ways of using them in home gardens, and provide a considerable program of training for professional gardeners. By virtue of the planting, there is no single best time to see the gardens. Some plants will always be in bloom, although April through June is considered the most colorful. From April 1 to Labor Day: daily, 10:00 A.M.–5:00 P.M. Sunday, 11:00 A.M.–6:00 P.M. For winter schedules, which vary, phone the Chamber of Commerce (703-622-2312).

RICHMOND: *Agecroft Hall, 4305 Sulgrave Road, 23221.* A 500-year old Elizabethan half-timbered Tudor manor house that was transported to Richmond in 1926. The gardens are in keeping with the mansion. There are 23 acres of woodlands, lawns, and ornamental boxwood gardens. Tuesday through Friday, 10:00 A.M.–5:00 P.M.

Norfolk Botanic Gardens

Top: *Maymount Park*. Above: *Chippokes*. Right: *Bryan Park Azalea Garden*

Sunday, 2:00 P.M.–5:00 P.M. Closed legal holidays. Fee.
Bryan Park Azalea Garden, Bryan Park, Hermitage Road and Bellevue Avenue. A swampland that was developed into a park in the early 1950s. Many of the azaleas are from that time as well, given to the park department by Richmond home gardeners. There are now over 45,000 plants, about 50 species and varieties, on the 20 acres of recovered land. Features of the park include a small lake, a spray fountain, a stream, and a huge floral cross (50 by 30 feet) made up of red and white flowering azaleas. Dogwood serves as a background for all the planting. A distinction of the park is that it is possible to drive through it, slowly, making it possible for many handicapped people to see the azaleas during the peak bloom from mid-April to mid-May. Daily, sunrise–sunset.
Gladsgay Gardens, 6311 Three Chopt Road, 23226. Five acres of small gardens, each designed around a specific theme; and a large collection of azalea hybrids and rhododendrons. Visiting is *by appointment only*; and each visit should be confirmed by writing to Dr. Wheeldon at the above address.

Historic Garden Week; Headquarters, *The Garden Club of Virginia, Room 3, Jefferson Hotel (P.O. Box 1397), 23211.* This incredibly successful gardening project has become a permanent, state-wide event, with the proceeds going to the preservation, restoration, or reconstruction of historic homes and gardens. Visiting the lovely private gardens of Virginia is an experience that should be repeated several times, since it is impossible to see more than a few of them in one week. Special maps and guidebooks are prepared each year in advance, and they may be secured by writing to the Garden Club of Virginia at the above address. Daily, the last week of April. Fee.
Maymont Park, Hampton Street and Pennsylvania Avenue. An Italianate garden—with a pergola, fountains, and statuary—that has all the classic beauty and charm of old Italy. Below the water cascades of the Italian Garden is the Japanese Garden, serenely cool, with a pagoda, lily ponds, and appropriate shrubbery. Daily, 10:00 A.M.–5:00 P.M.
Nordley Mansion, Windsor Farms.
St. John's Mews, Carrington Square on Church Hill. A pleasantly restored historic area, well landscaped. Daily.

Virginia House, 4301 Sulgrave Road. A Tudor house moved in 1925 to Virginia. The extensive gardens overlook the James River. Herb gardens, a loggia, a bowling green, a rose garden edged with dwarf boxwood, an azalea garden, sunken garden, a water garden planted with Japanese iris and lotus, and, toward the river, a meadow with seasonal wildflowers. Daily. Fee.

Wilton, Grove Street. A Georgian mansion of the mid-18th-century moved to its present location and appropriately landscaped. Monday through Saturday, 10:00 A.M.–5:00 P.M. Sunday, 2:00 P.M.–5:00 P.M. Fee.

STAUNTON: *Woodrow Wilson Birthplace, 24 North Coalter Street*. A Victorian garden of exquisite beauty. Brick walkways and bowknot flower beds bordered in clipped boxwood. Tulips and iris in season, with background shrubbery and small trees. It is by no means a large garden, but the perfection of its design makes it a period piece from the late 19th century. June through August: Monday through Saturday, 8:30 A.M.–6:00 P.M. Sunday, 9:00 A.M.–5:00 P.M. September through May: daily, 9:00 A.M.–5:00 P.M. Closed Sunday during December, January, and February.

SURRY: *Chippokes Plantation State Park*. The gardens are considerable (6 acres) and are believed to have the largest collection of crape myrtle in the country, and the ancient cedars are certainly among the largest in the country. Magnolias and boxwood and the crape myrtle are used as backgrounds for spring bulbs, azaleas, and hollies. The old mulberry trees are leftovers from the experiment to produce silk. The kitchen gardens are a pleasant sight and one that should induce the construction of more like them across the country. Prior to becoming a state park, the plantation was a working farm for 300 years, and it has continued to function as such. From Memorial Day to Labor Day: daily except Monday, 10:00 A.M.–6:00 P.M. Fee.

Rolfe-Warren House, Smith's Fort Plantation, Route 10. A reproduction of a 17th-century yard with enclosed gardens.

WAYNESBORO: *Swannanoa Gardens, Route 250*. A rather fabulous marble Italianate Renaissance palace-museum with terraced sculpture gardens and marble steps. A rose-covered marble pergola enclosed with native trees and ornamental shrubs. Formerly the

headquarters of the Walter Russel Foundation. Daily, summer, 8:00 A.M.–dusk; winter, 9:00 A.M.–5:00 P.M. Fee.

WILLIAMSBURG: *Carter's Grove Plantation, Route 60.* A young woman from France who visited the plantation in 1778 wrote: "We stopped at a famous place called Carter's Grove . . . one of the most elegant habitations in Virginia." And so it remains today, a superb lesson in what may be accomplished with green gardens and vistas. Daily.

Colonial Williamsburg. The most notable and famous restoration of Colonial homes and gardens in the country, and the most extensive. Begun in 1926, it has since cost $89 million, thus making it also the most expensive. It is without question among the most beautiful restorations and reconstructions in the country, totaling 500 buildings and houses, and 100 lovely gardens, on 170 acres. The restorations have been made according to historic plans, and the gardens utilize plant materials prevalent 200 years ago. These are the homes and gardens that Englishmen in the Virginia colony built to remind themselves of their homeland and that, to them, represented order and security. The gardens of the governor's palace cover 10 acres and include seven gardens characteristic of the Colonial period: elaborate and geometrical parterres, a formal boxwood garden, a bowling green with stately catalpas, a ballroom garden, a fruit garden, a holly maze (patterned after the maze at Hampton Court Palace), and terraced gardens sloping toward the canal and the fish pond. There are many green gardens at Williamsburg, a custom brought from England, and earlier from Holland. Such gardens required a minimum of maintenance and looked well all year. Yaupon, an American holly, replaces its English counterpart, and live oak, Southern magnolia, and boxwood (both tree and dwarf varieties) are the mainstays of this cool and elegant type of landscaping, along with evergreen ground covers such as periwinkle. There is topiary, more statuesque than ornate, which adds a variety of pleasant shapes. Pleached arbors of beech and hornbeam make welcome summer retreats. Vegetable and herb gardens acquire pleasing shapes, ornamental as well as practical, and usually are planted with cutting flowers as well. Spring is Williamsburg's most colorful season, with thousands and thousands of bulbs: tulips and crocus, narcissus and other bulbous flowers; the flowering shrubs and trees are usually spring ornaments— dogwood, redbud, catalpa, horse chestnuts, and, later, magnolias and crape myrtle. The summers, moistly humid and warm, are best served by the cool greenery, and fall by the autumn-colored foliage. Walking tours of the gardens begin in March and end on the last day of November; they are conducted Monday through Friday, at 10:30 A.M. and at 2:30 P.M. There is a fee. There is also an annual Williamsburg Garden Symposium, a five-day exploration of horticulture, with garden experts lecturing on garden design and other garden subjects. For information about this April program, write to the Registrar, Box C, Williamsburg, Va. 23185.

Washington

ABERDEEN: *Grays Harbor Arboretum, Grays Harbor College, 98520.* Rhododendrons and conifers on 79 acres. Daily, 9:00 A.M.–9:00 P.M.

BLAINE: *Peace Arch State Park.* The flower gardens are on both sides of the border between the United States and Canada, and symbolize the peace between the two nations with the longest unfortified border in the world. Daily in summer.

BURLINGTON: *Chuckanut Gardens, Route 1-5.* Plants, shrubs, and trees native to the Pacific Northwest; flowering bulbs and perennials. From mid-April to September 30: daily, 8:00 A.M.–dusk. The gardens are illuminated from 9:00 P.M. to 11:00 P.M., June through September.

CARSON: *Wind River Arboretum, U.S. Forest Service, 98610.* On 11 acres; conifers (123 species), 22 species of broadleaf trees, and 76 species of pinus, larix, picea, abies, tsuga, cedrus, and sequoia. Daily.

KENT: *South King County Arboretum, 98031.* A collection of magnolias, maples, and native plants and trees of the Northwest. Daily.

HOOD CANAL: *Rhododendrons* may be seen growing wild along the banks of the canal (an inlet of Puget Sound seen from Route 101). And more rhododendrons grow on Whidbey Island. Daily.

LONGMIRE: *Hudsonian Meadow Flowers, Mount Rainier National Park, 98397.* Mid-June ushers in the flower season on the meadows as the earth is cleared of snow and patches of avalanche fawn lilies appear, then western pasqueflower and elkslip marigold. The growing season is brief, and the plants bloom and fruit in a matter of weeks. As the islands of land enlarge, between the snow patches, masses of early plants take over. So there are actually two seasons of bloom: late June to early July and late July to early August. Both seasons of bloom tint the meadows lavishly with color, beginning with the humble butterbur and ending with the blue gentian. Information and schedules are available at the visitor center. During the flowering season: daily, sunrise–sunset.

MOUNT VERNON: *Commercial Tulip Growers.* Many acres of tulips in the area make vivid splashes of color in spring.

OLYMPIA: *State Capitol Grounds and Gardens.* A sunken

Opposite, and top: *University of Washington Arboretum*. Above: *Peace Arch State Park*. Right: *University of Washington Arboretum*

garden and rows of flowering cherries. In the garden beds, the flowers are changed seasonally. A state greenhouse with attractive collections. Grounds: daily; sunrise–sunset. Greenhouse: daily, 8:00 A.M.–5:00 P.M., closed holidays.

PORT ANGELES: *Hurricane Ridge Flowers, Olympic National Park, 98362.* As with many of the Washington mountain parks, Olympic National Park has almost an overabundance of wildflowers from early June through early August. The fields of Hurricane Ridge, when the avalanche lily blooms, must be seen to be believed, and it is a breath-taking sight because the largesse of nature is so lavish. About 64 flowering plant families are represented in the park and, within them, 428 species. For example, there are 39 kinds of roses, 21 kinds of lilies, 38 kinds of heath, 31 kinds of trees, and so on. Over much of the park are dense thickets of cascade azaleas in the mountain hemlock zone. Information about the flowers and their blooming seasons may be secured at the visitor center. From spring to fall: daily, sunrise–sunset.

PUYALLUP: *Daffodil and tulip-growing fields.* (Also at Summer). During April and May the fields are at their best, with color almost from horizon to horizon. A portion of Route 162 swings around the fields, and it is possible to get some sort of an idea what 30 million daffodils and tulips look like en masse.

SEATTLE: *Conservatory, Volunteer Park, 15th Avenue East and East Prospect Street.* The conservatory has both a temperature house and a tropical house for exotics. Near the conservatory are the formal gardens, with backgrounds of Pacific and Eastern dogwood, oaks, maples, hemlocks, and firs. Conservatory; daily, 9:00 A.M.–5:00 P.M. Grounds: daily, sunrise–sunset.

Denny Park, 100 Dexter Avenue North. A little more than 4½ acres of flower gardens, largely seasonal. Daily.

Drug Plant Gardens, University of Washington, College of Pharmacy, 17th Avenue North, 98105. A very well planted and very extensive garden, one of the largest of its kind. About 1,500 species, arranged in formal gardens on 3 acres of land, each species having some degree of medical application or interest. Also, greenhouses and associated laboratories. In the search for new and better medicines, plants are important, and greater use is

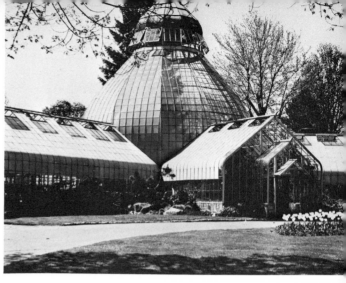

Mount Rainier National Park

Above: *Ohme Gardens.* Top: *Seymour Conservatory*

being made of them, so the drug plant gardens ensure material for research and for investigative purposes. The gardens are arranged somewhat by their uses: a "cascara circle" of similar plants; all-annual laxative plants; culinary and condiment herbs; nerve and muscle sedatives; medical stimulants; insecticides, etc. Daily, 8:00 A.M.–5:00 P.M.

Hiram M. Chittendon Locks Gardens, Lake Washington Ship Canal, 1519 Alaskan Way South, 98134. The locks are bordered by a 7-acre botanical garden, with flowers, shrubs, and trees from many lands—China, Tibet, Burma, India, and Europe. Many ground covers are featured. The gardens are part of a beautification program that is also developing other gardens and plantings along the banks of the ship canal from Shilshole Bay to Union Bay. Daily, 7:00 A.M.–9:00 P.M. During the warmer months.

Parsons Gardens, West Highland Drive and 7th Avenue North. A small planting (three-tenths of an acre).

University of Washington Arboretum, East Madison and Lake Washington Boulevard, 98105. Founded originally as a plant growth and testing center, the arboretum has developed an educational orientation toward introducing new ornamentals to the Seattle area and supplying supportive gardening information. The arboretum (200 acres) has an extremely large collection of rare woody plants and many fine specimen shrubs and trees (5,000 species and varieties of plants). Among them a collection of southern beech and Nootka cypress, and an intriguing group of the so-called "ice-cream tree"— an elm hybrid graft that grows in the shape of an ice-cream cone. A large number of azaleas (a walk through the azalea way is a sublime experience in mid-May), camellias, flowering cherries, flowering crab apples, California lilacs, magnolias, rhododendrons (700 kinds), conifers, hollies, maples, and pines. The Main Trail is lined with azaleas, flowering cherries, and eastern and western dogwood. The Waterfront Trail is a half-mile trail featuring semiaquatic plantings. A woodland garden, a rhododendron glen, and a world-famous Japanese garden, with a tea house, stone lanterns, a pond, and form-trained shrubs and trees typical of Japan. The Winter Garden flowers between October and March with witch hazels, viburnums, and heathers.

Hurricane Ridge Flowers

Summer is for mock orange, deutzias, cistus, silk trees, hydrangeas, stewartia, and clematis under lath. A display greenhouse. Arboretum: daily, sunrise–sunset, all year. Japanese Garden: from April 1 to mid-November, daily, 10:00 A.M.–dusk; winter, Saturday and Sunday only, 10:00 A.M.–dusk (fee). Greenhouse: Monday through Friday, 8:30 A.M.–4:00 P.M.

Woodlawn Park Zoological Garden and the International Rose Test Garden, Freemont Avenue and North 50th Street. Roses grow quite well in Washington, and the garden in Seattle is a good place to see them and learn their responses to the climate. Daily, 8:00 A.M.–sunset.

SPOKANE: *Finch Arboretum, 3404 Woodland Boulevard, 99204.* Conifers, flowering crab apples and other flowering ornamentals, the Corey Glen Rhododendron Gardens. March through September: daily, sunrise–sunset.

Manito Park, Grand Boulevard and 18th Avenue. The Duncan Gardens, formal gardens with seasonal flowers, are located within the park. These include a sunken garden, a large planting of roses, and many lilacs. (Within the city of Spokane, incidentally, there are many plantings of lilacs—a sort of specialty of both the city parks and city home gardeners—and a lilac festival takes place in mid-May.) The city greenhouse is also within the park. Daily, sunrise–sunset.

TACOMA: *Point Defiance Park Rose Gardens, North Pearl Street.* A 638-acre park of which about 500 acres are woodlands, the remainder either landscaped or supporting several public facilities. In addition to the roses, there are perennial borders, annuals, and arbors. Daily, 8:00 A.M.–dusk.

Seymour Conservatory, Wright Park, South I and G Streets, 98400. A classically shaped building from the early 1900s in which there is a constantly changing floral display. Within the three wings of the conservatory are native and exotic ferns, a collection of tropical foliage plants, and flowering trees and shrubs. Incidental to the collections are 2,000 orchid plants. Daily, 8:00 A.M.–4:20 P.M.

Wright Park also might be called a fledgling arboretum, since it has 111 varieties of trees among the total of 1,000 trees, flowering crab apples and flowering cherries, and some exceedingly large and tall camellias, as well as such trees as pawlonia, gingko, and katsura. Daily.

WENATCHEE: *Ohme Gardens, Route 2.* A beautiful and most unusual garden located on a 7-acre rocky outcrop overlooking the Columbia River. Stone paths and green lawns, mini-lakes, and spectacular alpine plants flowering in spring. There are summer plantings of flowers and flowering shrubs indigenous to the Northwest. From spring to fall: daily, 8:00 A.M.–dusk. Fee.

West Virginia

AURORA: *Cathedral State Park, Route 50.* A rare grove of old trees and one of the last stands of hardwoods. There is a mammoth hemlock, a gigantic black cherry, and a monstrous red oak, in addition to magnolias, sugar maples, and other natives that have taken their places in American gardens. The park has a generous undergrowth of ferns, violets, trilliums, trailing arbutus, and lady's-slippers—and acres of imposing stands of rhododendrons blooming from mid-June to mid-July. The nature trails are well organized to reveal much of the beauty of the 126-acre park. Daily.

BECKLEY: *Grandview State Park, Route 19, 25801.* The park consists of 878 acres of woodlands that have, among other tourist attractions, an extraordinarily fine stand of rhododendrons. Daily.

BERKELEY SPRINGS: *Cacapon State Park, 25411.* Extensive woodlands that are widely known for their spring displays of dogwood, redbud, ample mountain laurel, fragrant honeysuckle, wild azaleas, and other wildflowers. It is more than a happenstance that the parks of West Virginia are so located that wild or natural gardens are nearly everywhere one looks. The climate of the state is moist and favorable to such flowering plants and shrubs. And there always comes a time when the garden tourist needs the relief of wilderness foundlings and settings to balance the richness of formal gardens. Daily.

CHARLESTON: *Municipal Rose Garden, Davis Park.* More than 500 roses, in about 50 varieties. A well-displayed small garden.

Sunrise Garden Center, 746 Myrtle Road. The center is the hub of gardening activities in the Kanawha Valley, especially so with its programs and gardens. The lovely seasonal displays at the President Kennedy Memorial Garden, the abundance of shrubs and trees, and the miscellaneous flowering plants on the 16-acre estate enhance the center's reputation. The Iris Garden (April-May) has many species; the roses (300) are well-selected hybrids (mid-May to fall); and the Belmont Memorial Garden utilizes a floral mix for continuous bloom—tulips, azaleas, rhododendrons, crape myrtle, and hollies. The Hershe Garden demonstrates the usefulness of ground covers, small shrubs, and small ornamental sculptures. The nature trail provides yearly

Cathedral State Park

Top: *Cranberry Glades Botanical Area.* Above: *Holly River State Park*

Huntington Galleries

interest. Tuesday through Saturday, 10:00 A.M.–5:00 P.M. Sunday, 2:00 P.M.–5:00 P.M.

CLIFFTOP: *Babcock State Park, 25822.* Walking trails to rhododendrons that are overwhelming in numbers and magnificent blooms (June-July). And other wildflowers, particularly the bright orange jack-o'-lanterns that glow in the dark and their equally phosphorescent spores, whose fountainlike ejection has given rise to more horror stories than can be remembered. Daily.

DAVIS: *Blackwater Falls State Park, 26260.* A preponderance of hardwoods and very large areas of rhododendrons and other wildflowers. It is in this park that the West Virginia wildflower pilgrimage is held each year during the third week in May.

HACKER VALLEY: *Holly River State Park, 26222.* American holly is found here in unusual quantities— enough, in fact, to warm the hearts of holly enthusiasts. Also, some 2,000 other plant species, not the least of which are the pink lady's-slippers and other wild orchids, flaming pink azaleas, wild geraniums, acres of mayapples and jack-in-the-pulpits. It is best to visit in mid-spring. Daily.

HARPERS FERRY: *The Harper House and Gardens.*

HUNTINGTON: *Huntington Galleries, 8th Street Road.* An arboretum and the Virginia Cavendish Memorial Gardens, including a plant and a wildlife sanctuary. Five acres. Tuesday, Wednesday, Friday, and Saturday, 11:00 A.M.–5:00 P.M. Thursday, 11:00 A.M.–9:00 P.M. Sunday, 1:00 P.M.–5:00 P.M.

Municipal Rose Garden, Ritter Park.

JACKSON'S MILLS: *Stonewall Jackson Memorial Garden.*

MILL POINT: *Cranberry Glades Botanical Area, Monongahela National Forest, Forest Route 102.* Snakemouth orchids and pitcher plants, buck beans and sundews, grass pink orchids and bog rosemary—and hundreds of other unusual plants flowering during April and May or later, during the June-August period. A special board walkway makes many otherwise difficult areas easily accessible. Daily.

MONTGOMERY: *Tech Mountain Trails Arboretum, West Virginia Institute of Technology, 25136.* A preserve of natural woodlands.

MORGANTOWN: *West Virginia University Arboretum,*

Wheeling Garden Center

Evansdale Campus, Monongahela Boulevard, 26506. Primarily a 75-acre arboretum for native shrubs, but there is also a special collection of viburnums and a woodland with 500 kinds of plants. A planting of heaths, another of herbs, and one of ferns. Large stands of oaks and maples, and a particularly nice wildflower trail. Spring wildflower walks in April. Daily.

SHEPHERDSTOWN: *James Rumsey Monument.* The lilac garden which, with the Ionic column, honors Rumsey for his invention of jet-propulsion boats in 1787 is well worth a visit in early spring.

WESTON: *Jackson's Mill Museum and Garden, Route 19, 26452.* The exhibition illustrates pioneer life a hundred years ago; and nearby, in the 4-H camp, there is a formal garden. Daily, 8:00 A.M.–9:00 P.M.

WHEELING: *Frank Memorial Garden, Wheeling Park. West Virginia University Garden.*

Wheeling Garden Center, Oglebay Park, 26003. Formerly known as Waddington Farms, Oglebay Park became a city property in 1928, and has been developed into a model urban park of 800 acres, with many activities and attractions, not the least of which is the garden center. The center actively promotes interest in horticulture and provides advice on all garden activities. A greenhouse is maintained for exotics and for a special display of chrysanthemums in early November. There are trial gardens for iris, peonies, annuals, and roses. The arboretum, primarily of forest trees and rare shrubs, features pleasant nature walks both in spring and fall.

WHITE SULPHUR SPRINGS: *Greenbrier Hotel, 24986.* West Virginia's oldest and most fashionable hotel in a lovely spa setting, where for those interested there are some unique, native plants to be seen. Two miles west of the hotel is a marked area where many rare plants have been found (and rediscovered), among them box huckleberry, which botanists believe may have lived there unchanged for the last 6,000 years. It was discovered by the French botanist Michaux in 1790—and lost, then rediscovered in 1800-05—and lost again, although local residents had always known of the plant and relished its berries in jams and pies. But they knew it as juniper berries, not as the lost box huckleberry of botanists. Finally relocated in 1921, it has been marked for preservation. In this area of West Virginia the box huckleberry exists as a sort of ground cover for rhododendrons, blooming in April and May. A whole area of box huckleberry is unique in that it is not made up of many single plants, but of one plant with many underground runners—many plants, as it were, with a single common root system. Hence it is unable to propagate itself by cross-pollination. Other rarities are the mountain pimpernel and the swordleaf phlox—not garden plants, perhaps, but very interesting to a gardener. The spa has tulips in the spring, rhododendrons in May, and chrysanthemums in the fall; and the boxwood is excellent the year round. Daily.

Wisconsin

EAU CLAIRE: *Putnam Park Arboretum, Wisconsin State University, 54701.*

HALES CORNERS: *Alfred L. Boerner Botanical Gardens, Whitnall Park, 5879 South 92nd Street, 53130.* On nearly 500 acres the botanical gardens have more than 12,000 kinds of plants—which makes them a major installation. Also the nature of the floral planting, the arrangements, and the results in sheer beauty equally makes the gardens second to none in the country. The formal gardens are planned to demonstrate the uses as well as the beauties of the plant materials, or to subordinate those same materials to ornamental structures such as pools or sculptures. A pinetum, a long mall of shrubs, pools with hardy water lilies and ringed with an almost fabulous collection of flowering crab apples (there are 1,105 trees in the total collection, 237 species and varieties). One of the country's largest herb gardens, and most likely the loveliest in both planting and design (1,500 kinds of herbs), a bog garden, and an artificial prairie. The lilac garden (1,173 plants and 401 species and varieties) is bordered with 50,000 tulips (175 varieties), and when the blooming periods of the two areas coincide (early May), the resulting color is almost overwhelming. A rock garden, formal and semiformal rose gardens (about 5,000 plants and 375 varieties), and both herbaceous and tree-peony gardens. The walled annual garden is a mixed glory, as are the perennial gardens and borders. Day lilies, iris (456 kinds), dahlias, tuberous begonias, chrysanthemums; dwarf fruit trees, and a street-tree arboretum. As part of the instructional program the gardens maintain mulch, grass, and hedge demonstration plots. The test gardens and the trial gardens (annuals, perennials, dahlias, roses) are officially recognized and well planned for ease of observation. All in all, an extraordinary botanical garden of great beauty that cannot and should not be characterized solely by plant names and quantities of plant varieties. Any month from early April to mid-winter is a good month to visit the gardens, although most visitors try to catch the flowering crab apples, lilacs, and tulips. Daily, 8:00 A.M.–dusk.

KENOSHA: *Lincoln Memorial Botanical Garden.*

LA CROSSE: *Riverside Park, Front Street.* Gardens on the river front.

University of Wisconsin Arboretum

Olbrich Botanical Gardens

Above: *Horticultural Conservatory.* Top: *Kinn River Canyon Arboretum*

LAKE GENEVA: *Chrysanthemum Test Gardens, 53417.*
MADISON: *Olbrich Botanical Gardens, 3330 Atwood Avenue, 53701.* An 11½-acre garden as part of a 100-acre park. Flowering crab apples and other flowering shrubs (May), roses (June), a dahlia trial garden and a dahlia exhibition garden (July until frost). There are annual and perennial displays near a fountain that is illuminated in the evenings. A small display greenhouse with tropical plants. Daily, 7:00 A.M.–sunset.

University of Wisconsin Arboretum, 1207 Seminole Highway, 53706. Collections of evergreens, woody shrubs and trees, woodlands, wildflowers, and prairie studies. Although the arboretum's connection with the university makes it primarily a teaching and research installation, its tree and shrub display gardens are well planned and laid out in more than 30 different plant communities, remarkably close together and relatively undisturbed by man. The prairie area (once a meadow), the woodlands, and the marshes, ponds, and lakes have been left untouched. In other areas, there are flowering crab apples and viburnums (both native and Eurasian) in abundance. Visits to the arboretum may be timed

for the flowering periods: wildflowers and flowering crab apples—early May; lilacs—mid-May; prairie flowers—summer. There are nearly 2,000 kinds of plants on the 1,200 acres; and a greenhouse. Also part of the arboretum are the *Longnecker Horticultural Gardens* (40 acres), where a magnificent lilac collection (250 kinds) is displayed in a landscaped setting. The other ornamentals are so arranged as to indicate their best areas of usefulness and beauty in home-garden plantings. Native trees are used to demonstrate their ornamental values as well as their hardiness. Daily, 8:00 A.M.–10:00 P.M.

MILWAUKEE: *Horticultural Conservatory in Mitchel Park, 524 South Layton Boulevard, 53215.* The handsome geodesic domes of the conservatory are usually the first objective of visitors; the three domes do have a sort of space-age look. But other than that, they are uniquely suited to their purpose of protecting and growing warm climate plants. The Show House has seasonal flower shows (six of them) in a temperate climate, and considerable background planting. The Tropical House contains a rain forest (or jungle). The Arid House has

Above and below: *Horticultural Conservatory*

Above: *University of Wisconsin Arboretum.* Opposite: *Alfred L. Boerner Botanical Gardens*

cacti and other succulents, and a desert complete with palms. The 60 acres surrounding the domes are landscaped with a formal sunken garden of parterres, a mall of roses (2,000), and another mall of perennial plants. Daily except Monday, 9:00 A.M.–9:00 P.M. Fee after 11:00 A.M.

Skittnal Park. Extensive flower gardens, including roses, tuberous begonias, chrysanthemums.

NEENAH-MENASHA: *Smith Park, Keyes Street, 54956.* Formal gardens and outdoor picnic facilities.

OSHKOSH: *Paine Art Center and Arboretum, 1410 Algoma Boulevard, 54901.* A Tudor manor house (art museum) on 25 acres of formal 18th-century English flower gardens; ornamental trees and shrubs, and special plantings of junipers, evergreens, and dwarf lilacs. Daily except Monday, 9:00 A.M.–5:00 P.M. (grounds only).

POYNETTE: *McKenzie Environmental Center, County Q Road, 53955.* A forest arboretum, with a model nursery, and nature trails. The emphasis of the center is on keeping the trees that the country has and replacing those that have been lost by negligent practices. November through March: Monday through Friday, 9:00 A.M.–5:00 P.M. April through October: daily, 9:00 A.M.–5:00 P.M.

PRAIRIE DU CHIEN: *Villa Louis, 521 North Villa Louis Road.* A mansion restored to its 19th-century splendor,

set in immense grounds. May through October: daily, 9:00 A.M.–5:00 P.M. Fee.

RIVER FALLS: *Kinn River Arboretum, RFD 3, 65022.* The objective of the arboretum is to test broadleaf evergreens and deciduous plants under the severe winter-summer conditions of the area. Most emphasis is placed on cacti, yucca, rhododendrons, azaleas, magnolias, boxwood, and hollies. At present the arboretum is not open to the general public; but tours may be arranged by writing to the director.

SOMERS: *Hyslop Foundation, Hawthorn Hollow, 53140.* A private arboretum, at present concerned with identifying, collecting, and planting perennials, shrubs, and trees. There are, however, nature trails in use. Daily, sunrise–sunset.

SPRING GREEN: *House on the Rock, Route 23, 53588.* A house built on a hill, with waterfalls, pools, trees "throughout the house." And a wildlife pond area. April through November: daily, 9:00 A.M.–5:00 P.M. Fee.

WISCONSIN DELLS: *Biblical Gardens, Route 12, 53965.* Thirteen scenes from the life of Jesus, with authentically costumed figures, against a background of cultivated flowers, wildflowers, and pines. From mid-June to Labor Day: daily, 9:00 A.M.–8:00 P.M. Fee.

Story Book Gardens, Route 12, 53965. Storybook characters for children; and flower gardens for adults. From June 26 to Labor Day: daily, 9:30 A.M.–7:00 P.M. Fee.

Wyoming

CHEYENNE: *Cheyenne Horticultural Field Station, Plant Science Research Division, 82001.* Horticultural crops are difficult to grow in the High Plains region of Wyoming, so there are no arboretums or botanic gardens in the state. Most horticultural plants are shipped into the state for private use; and garden attractions, if any, may sometimes be found around public buildings, or, most usually, at the homes of gardeners associated with or near a garden center. Nonetheless, many of the difficulties gardeners face in Wyoming may be as important and as interesting to learn about as the successes of the more horticulturally oriented states to the south. However, there are examples of good gardening to be found within such towns as Lovell, noted in the region for its roses; or among the garden club members of Casper, Buffalo, and Chugwater—whose combined efforts have developed ways and means of using hardier plants, such as iris, peonies, delphiniums, lilacs, and lupines, to good advantage. Be that as it may, visitors to the Cheyenne Horticultural Field Station are always welcomed during the working day and their questions are competently answered. Daily, 8:00 A.M.–5:00 P.M.

JACKSON HOLE: *Grand Teton National Park.* The Indian Paint Brush Canyon Trail is famous for its wildflower displays in June and July.

YELLOWSTONE: *Yellowstone National Park, 82190.* A check list of the flowering plants at Yellowstone, published by the Yellowstone Library and Museum Association, indicates an astounding wealth of flowering plants, from anemones and blazing stars to scarlet gilia and wild columbine. As a matter of fact, nearly all of the stages of plant history and development—from algae to climax vegetation—may be seen within the park, and not infrequently all seven stages (aquatic, sagebrush/grass, alpine/subalpine, Douglas fir, lodgepole pine, aspen, spruce/fir) may be found within yards of each other. Since all of these stages include some 2,000 species, this alone makes the park a botanical paradise and a natural botanic garden without a peer. However, many visitors forego the masses of trees and the rock-encrusted lichens for the alpine meadow flowers, of which there are many in the park. Usually they are found at the 10,000-foot level—a bit high, but easily reached on Mount Washburn, where the subalpine meadows are a summer riot of color due, in large part, to the fact that alpines are dwarfs and therefore seem to carpet the meadows in drifts and large patches during June and July. Later in the season, toward the end of September, the aspens become conspicuously colored. It is a policy of the National Park Service never to introduce exotics, but it does happen by accident, and they sometimes graduate to flowering status, since the plant population of the forests and meadows is not static. So the natural beauty of the wildflowers remains protected for all visitors to enjoy during the very short summers. A pleasure that may be equalled but never surpassed by man-made gardens. Daily, sunrise–sunset (during the season).

Puerto Rico

SAN GERMÁN: *Arboretum and Casa Maria Gardens of the Inter-American University*. A 20-acre arboretum with pleasant gardens and tropical flowers. The arboretum is made up largely of woody shrubs and trees that are natives of the island. A greenhouse for displays. Daily.

MAYAGÜEZ: *Federal Experiment Station Plant Collection*. Operated by the U.S. Department of Agriculture, the station maintains a collection of 2,000 kinds of plants on 235 acres (and in 5 service greenhouses). Essentially the station is involved in research, although it is educationally oriented. The plant collection, primarily tropical, consists of economic and ornamental plants suitable for the area. Monday, 7:30 A.M.–12:00 noon; 1:00 P.M.–4:30 P.M.

Note: There are many gardens in Puerto Rico, usually private, that sometimes may be visited through arrangements with the local garden clubs. A number of nurseries that deal in tropical plants and propagations for the continental United States are well worth visiting—as, also, are visits to the gardens of the governor's palace, the nearby rain forest, and the meadows and lowlands of southern Puerto Rico.

Virgin Islands

CHARLOTTE AMALIE: *St. Thomas Gardens and Orchidarium, 6-37 Contant, 00801*. Six acres of trees, palms, tropical flowers, and tropical foliage plants, with walks, benches for loitering and resting, waterfalls, and an extraordinarily large orchid greenhouse. The orchids are beautifully displayed among rocks and other plantings, all at table height, with hundreds of plants blooming every day of the year. Monday through Saturday: daily, 8:30 A.M.–5:00 P.M.

WATER ISLAND: *Water Isle Botanical Garden, 00801*. Orchids and cacti, collections of agaves, succulents, bromeliads, and Virgin Island native plants. Poincianas and bougainvillea grow very flamboyantly here. On 25 acres, with 3 greenhouses and 3,000 kinds of plants. Daily, 8:00 A.M.–2:00 P.M. (The island is reached by a very short boat trip from the harbor.)

Queen Victoria Park

Canada

ALDERGROVE (British Columbia): *Commercial bulb growers.* The areas around both Aldergrove and Bradner in the Fraser Valley are noted for their fields of flowering bulbs in spring; some growers stage a display with daffodils. The fields are usually small and family-owned, but nonetheless colorful. The largest acreage is that of P. J. Warmerdam, who grows gladioli on 11 acres, flowering from late June to October. Most spring bulbs come into flower around Easter.

BOISSEVAIN (Manitoba): *International Peace Garden.* This is the Canadian half of the United States' garden at Dunseith in North Dakota, the world's largest garden devoted to peace. Attractive buildings shared by both Canadians and Americans; formal gardens and flower beds, terraced panels surrounding a series of lakes that are drained by ornamental spillways. The Canadian garden clubs have also installed a small arboretum. April through November: daily.

BURNABY (British Columbia): *Century Gardens. Rhododendron Gardens.*

EDMONTON (Alberta): *Botanic Garden and Field Laboratory, University of Alberta, Highway 60.* A relatively young garden, but one with considerable display plantings. At present, there are 2,450 kinds of plants on 80 acres. Collections of primulas, alliums, peonies, Tibetan poppies, iris, and a flowering shrub garden. There are several plant trial gardens, since hardiness in Canada is an important attribute of plants and the garden has practical interest in introducing plants and shrubs that can withstand the Canadian winters. Under construction at this time is an herb garden, a rock garden of considerable interest (well-grown Canadian rock gardens are almost always beautiful beyond description), a group of shrubby roses (and species). Greenhouses. May through August: Saturday, 1:00 P.M.–7:00 P.M. Other times *by appointment only.*

ESTEVAN (Saskatchewan): *Prairie Nurseries Ltd. and Estevan Greenhouses and Nurseries, off Highway 47.* Both nurseries stock the hardy varieties of shelterland stock; trees (including plums, lilacs, flowering crab apples), ornamental shrubs (dogwood, caragana [pea shrubs], cotoneaster, honeysuckle), rugosa hybrids, perennials (30 kinds), some climbing vines, and fruiting shrubs. The stock is indicative of an area that can do so much

Butchart Gardens

gardening with so few available plant materials. Daily, during weekly working hours.

GRAND MÉTIS (Québec): *Parc de Métis*. Sometimes it is referred to as the Jardin Botanique de Grand Métis, or as the Reford Estate. Exotic plants from places like Tibet, the Himalayas, and alpine peaks are grown; such plants can thrive in the Canadian climate and soils. There is a remarkable collection of plants and shrubs (lilies, rock plants, and small shrubs), and excellent perennials (some unusual or unexpected), all surrounded by evergreens. Streams and rustic bridges. Madame Reford, the last owner of the estate, experimented with exotic plants (non-Canadian), bringing in all kinds of seeds, vegetables, and flowering plants for year-round bloom, succeeding beyond all expectations. Experts believe the gardens represent the only example of its type to be cultivated successfully so far north. The current inventory of plants, still incomplete, indicates that approximately 1,500 species may be found in the gardens. Daily, seasonal.

GUELPH (Ontario): *Arboretum, University of Guelph, Ontario Agricultural College*. Some 240 acres, recently developed (1968), of native woodlands and native shrubs and trees used ornamentally on the university campus. The university has completed a master plan for a 330-acre arboretum to be used for academic research and public service. Plans have been made to establish 47 major woody plant collections, and planting began in 1970. As of this time, there are 1,200 kinds of plants represented in the nursery and the arboretum.

HALIFAX (Nova Scotia): *Halifax Public Gardens*. A pleasant grouping of tulip beds around a bandstand, lawns, and ornamental shade trees; seasonal flowers—especially dahlias. The city also has a commons with plantings of annual flowers. Daily, seasonal.

HAMILTON (Ontario): *Royal Botanical Gardens, Highway 2*. The smaller gardens within the 2,000-acre area are often widely separated and an automobile is almost essential in order to visit many of the gardens in less than a day. Displays and collections include native trees, rhododendrons (and azaleas), flowering crab apples, day lilies, a hedge collection, late flowering tulips, lilacs (an excellent collection of French double-flowered hybrids—481 kinds), dogwood and redbud, lilies,

Nikka Yuka Centennial Garden

228

International Peace Garden

Halifax Public Gardens

Royal Botanical Gardens

magnolias, iris (600 cultivars), peonies, weeping hemlocks, flowering cherries and plums, roses (5,000 bushes, 250 varieties), plus a rock garden that is larger than usually seen, and which is colorful from spring to fall. Trial gardens for annuals (10,000); a children's garden in which there is a kitchen-herb section. The trees and shrubs are most likely to be natives, or hardy ornamentals from similar climatic regions. The greenhouse has an excellent collection of indoor house plants. The climate in Hamilton is about as mild as Canada has, and gardening possibilities are accordingly increased. The botanical gardens are well oriented toward public service, encouraging interest in home planting through a membership organization that is very active, and through lecture programs and botanical studies. Floral peaks in the gardens occur in mid-May, mid-June, full summer, and autumn (foliage). Daily, sunrise–sunset.

INDIAN HEAD (Saskatchewan): *Tree Nursery Division, P.F.R.A., SOG 2KD.* Although primarily a tree nursery (it has distributed 350 million trees since 1903), there are ornamental grounds for displaying annuals and perennials, lawns, hedges, lilies, peonies, roses, and chrysan-

themums. Collections include flowering crab apples, lilacs, and shrubby potentillas. The arboretum specializes in trees likely to survive the temperature extremes (to —34° F.) and be useful in prairie farm shelter belts. About 75 genera are represented. The remainder of the collection (from 100 to 150 species and cultivars) represents new types of plants being tested, or plant improvements and new introductions. A display house and a greenhouse. Daily, 8:00 A.M.–5:00 P.M.

KIMBERLEY (British Columbia): *Cominco Gardens, Hospital Hill.* Outstanding displays of massed flowers, usually one of a kind in separate beds, grass walkways. Kimberley is the highest city in Canada (3,661 feet) and has a background of mountains and pines for its floral displays. Daily during the season.

LADYSMITH (British Columbia): *Crown Zellerback Arboretum.*

LETHBRIDGE (Alberta): *Nikka Yuka Centennial Garden.* The largest Japanese garden of its kind outside of Japan (4 acres), authentic in design and planning. The pavilions, tea house, bell tower, waterfalls, streams, bridges, dwarf trees, and walks are scaled exactly

Jardin Botanique de Montréal

according to Japanese practice.

MACDONALD COLLEGE P.O.: (Québec), *Morgan Arboretum, MacDonald College, Ste. Marie Road (Ste.-Anne de Bellevue)*. Complete collection of native Canadian trees (particularly birch) on 600 acres; 170 kinds of trees. The total arboretum collection includes about 800 kinds of shrubs and trees that are displayed in an arboretum arrangement, with ample room to show their natural form and beauty. Under the jurisdiction of McGill University, it is intended primarily for research and educational purposes, so much emphasis is placed on conservation and resource husbandry. It is dedicated to the premise that "man will have to strike up a new acquaintance with this environment" and that man should view himself not as "a conqueror of the landscape, but, rather, as a trustee for it." There are 12 miles of excellent nature trails, and a children's program that permits nearly 8,000 children each year to visit the garden from nearby Montreal, learning at first hand the lessons of living with nature. Saturday and Sunday, 9:00 A.M.–5:00 P.M. Fee.

MONTRÉAL (Québec): *Jardin Botanique de Montréal,*
4101 Sherbrooke Street, East, 406. The Montréal Botanic Gardens occupy the same position in Canada as does the Missouri Botanical Gardens in the United States; both are rarely equalled and never surpassed. In the gardens at Montréal, scientific research and popular education go hand in hand, and the laboratories and supplemental facilities are the best of their kind. Although some areas of it are incomplete, the arboretum has a remarkable number of excellent gardens: a rock garden, a medicinal garden that includes a section for poisonous plants and another section for plants used by North American Indians, aquatic gardens (109 ponds), economic gardens (fruits and vegetables also), children's gardens, and home demonstration plots. Alpines, conifers, day lilies, hedges, iris, perennials (1,000 varieties), ornamental shrubs and trees, and trial or test gardens for various herbaceous and shrubby plants. The conservatory collections (9 display houses and 23 service greenhouses) and the displays are the equal of any gardens in North America. There is a tropical house with a rain forest and a display house for the three seasonal shows: in April, November, and December.

Cominco Public Gardens

Other greenhouses contain peerless collections of aroids, bromeliads, cacti and other succulents, ferns, orchids, tropical economic plants, and many begonias (tuberous) and columneas. The arboretum has just about everything that the people of Québec could be interested in, or, for that matter, should be interested in, and with ample information to support that interest. About 22,000 kinds of plants on 180 acres. There is never a best time to visit the Montréal gardens, because the marvelous display houses are always open. But for the outdoor gardens it is difficult to find a better time than from mid-May to to mid-June, although summer is also beautiful. Gardens: daily, 9:00 A.M.–dusk. Conservatories: daily, 9:00 A.M.–6:00 P.M.

MORDEN (Manitoba): *Experimental Farm, Research Center.* The Experimental Farm has made many real contributions to the Canadian home and farm economy by testing and introducing new varieties of ornamental and economic shrubs and trees. The climate variation in Manitoba is extremely difficult for plants (110° F to —40° F.) and the soil is excessively alkaline. Yet the farm maintains 3,000 kinds of plants on 627 acres,

featuring lilacs, the hardy rosybloom, flowering crab apples, hardy perennials and annuals, cold-resistant ornamental shrubs, flowering prunes, hardy roses, an excellent collection of chrysanthemums, very good hedge displays (dwarf to tall varieties), and 3 service greenhouses. The station has selected and introduced 79 new cultivars, among them small mums and asters, distinctive lilacs, and flowering crab apples. A continuous program of breeding and selection is helping to establish early-maturing sweet corn, tomatoes, cucumbers, and other commercial crops, including the oil-producing plants. Monday through Friday, 8:00 A.M.–8:00 P.M.

MOUNT UNIACKE (Nova Scotia): *Uniacke House and Gardens.* One of the early historic houses of Nova Scotia which possesses beautiful gardens. The original estate (1813) had a greenhouse among the outbuildings. From May 15 to October 15: daily, 9:30 A.M.–5:30 P.M.

NEW WESTMINSTER (British Columbia): *Garden of Friendship.* A pleasant 2½-acres garden next to the city hall, that was dedicated to New Westminster's sister city in Japan (Moriguchi), hence the name "Friendship." But the garden is a Western interpretation of classic

Niagara Parks Commission's Greenhouse

Jardin Botanique de Montréal

Experimental Farm, Morden

Japanese gardens, using native plant materials and informal plantings to achieve a similar classic simplicity and serenity. There are water-lily ponds and streams and cherry trees among the Canadian evergreens.

Queens Park. A rose garden and formal gardens, designed in the Shakespearean pattern, which are colorful from June to October.

NIAGARA FALLS (Ontario): *Niagara Parks Commission's School of Horticulture, North Parkway.* Some 100 acres of special campus gardens that are primarily maintained by the students in the school. The wide variety of plants (2,500 varieties) in the gardens is in part due to the needs of the students and to the methods of instruction, which are as practical as they are theoretic, providing an all-around sound professional training. The graduates of the school serve in responsible horticultural positions throughout the world. The special gardens: aquatic, alpine, annuals, perennials, evergreens, fruits, herbs, iris, lilacs, lilies, peonies, roses, vegetables, wildflowers, woody shrubs and trees. A floral fountain. A sort of something-for-everyone garden that is most delightfully arranged and immaculately maintained.

There is an annual fall exhibition of vegetables and berried shrubs. Daily, sunrise–sunset.

Oakes Garden Theater, Lakeshore Road. Colorful formal gardens that have combined the skills of both architects and horticulturists to create a Japanese garden, with sloping terraces, rock gardens, lily ponds, shrubbery, clipped hedges, and sculptured topiary—all of great beauty.

Queen Victoria Park, Queen Elizabeth Way. An extraordinary park that has a display of 300,000 daffodils in mid-May, a rock garden of considerable beauty, pillar roses, perennial beds that are unusually good, and a conservatory with excellent displays, which also handles all of the service plants for the park. At night the park is illuminated for casual strolling. Daily, until about 11:00 P.M.

NORTH VANCOUVER (British Columbia): *Park and Tilford Gardens, 1240 Colton Street.* A 2½-acre site on which six lovely gardens have been built. The Colonnade Garden: an intricate pattern of ground covers, annuals and perennials, and a reflection pool, surrounded by Romanesque arches. The Rhododendron Garden: rho-

Niagara Parks Commission's School of Horticulture

dodendrons and azaleas accented with magnolias, dogwoods (Japanese, Eastern, and Pacific), and thousands of spring bulbs such as hyacinths, crocus, daffodils, and Oriental lilies. The Flower Garden: 28 raised, circular planters in which unique annuals and perennials are placed; during Christmas eight of these planters have tropical displays protected by covers of plastic domes, warmed by forced air and electric soil cables. The Oriental Garden: tranquil and complete with moss-covered hummocks holding pines and maples and azaleas, red-lacquered bridges, lily pools, and a tea house. The Rose Garden: prize roses surrounding a fountain, and both in turn surrounded by a pergola and a thuja hedge. The Native Wood Garden: featuring the native trees, shrubs, and flowers of British Columbia. Daily, 8:00 A.M.–11:00 P.M.

ORSAINVILLE (Québec): *The Québec Zoological Gardens, Highway 54.* Although specializing in animals, the gardens have an excellent collection of exotics. Paths and areas between the animal displays are filled with rock gardens and other ornamental plantings. Daily. Fee.

OTTAWA (Ontario): *Dominion Arboretum and Botanic Gardens, Plant Research Institute, C.E.S., 3, Prince of Wales Highway.* The arboretum is responsible for a wide range of publications about horticultural subjects and as a result maintains both a large staff and an extraordinary range of plant materials (10,000 kinds) on 135 acres. The tree collection, one of the oldest in Canada, contains many specimens from other countries as well as Canadian natives. The test gardens for annuals and perennials are extensive, as, also, are the lovely display gardens—especially roses. The plant collections—featuring those most suitable for the climate—include flowering crab apples, lilacs, pea shrubs, shrubby cinquefoils, and hedge plants, as well as herbaceous plants such as day lilies, iris, lilies, and peonies. One greenhouse is used for display—the Mum Show; the other greenhouses are devoted to research and service. The arboretum not only promotes interest in gardening but also serves the city as a park and recreation area. May through June are good visiting months; somewhat later (toward September) for the fall foliage. Daily, sunrise–sunset.

Water Works Park

Rockcliffe Park has thousands of bulbs naturalized along its daffodil walk; and trilliums by the hundreds.

Tulip Gardens, Rideau Canal. More than 3 million tulips bloom in mid-May along the banks of the canal, and a festival is also provided for natives and visitors alike.

PORT ARTHUR (Ontario): *Sunken Gardens, Hillcrest Park.* The gardens, designed in geometric patterns—triangles centered on an oval—are considered to be masterpieces of floral display. Massed annuals and perennials, low-growing, are edged with grass and divided by wide paths.

REGINA (Saskatchewan): *Gardens of the Legislative Building.* An impressive and an extensive planting of spring bulbs, annuals, and perennials in the gardens fronting on the building.

SAANICHTON (British Columbia): *University of British Columbia Research Station.* Some good roses.

ST. JOHN'S (Newfoundland): *Agriculture Research Station, St. John's West.* There are a number of plants on trial here to determine their responses to the climate; roses have been grown for several years.

ST. THOMAS (Ontario): *Water Works Park.* One of the lovelier designs in parks. Lily ponds and rustic timbered bridges, small islands planted to grass with numerous small beds of annuals and perennials. Columnar and rounded cypress against a background of large trees. It is very much a westernized version of a Japanese garden, transformed with native plants, shrubs, and trees. Daily.

SHERWOOD (Prince Edward Island): *Valhalla Gardens.*

TORONTO (Ontario): *Civic Garden Center, 777 Lawrence Avenue, East.* A changing horticultural exhibition. Daily.

Edwards Gardens, Leslie Street and Lawrence Avenue, East. Beautiful floral displays all summer; rock gardens and arbors. Daily, 10:00 A.M.–9:00 P.M.

James Memorial Gardens, Edinbridge Drive. Ten acres of grass and native trees, streams, pools, and flower gardens. Daily, sunrise–sunset.

TRURO (Nova Scotia): *Victoria Park.* A natural woodland with paths edged by rock gardens, lily ponds, and bedding plants.

VANCOUVER (British Columbia): *Botanical Garden of the University of British Columbia, University Boulevard, 8.* A large collection of rhododendrons that, beginning in mid-April, is one of the garden pilgrimages of Vancouver.

234

Top: *Park and Tilford Gardens*. Above: *Québec Zoological Gardens*

A section of the garden is devoted to economic plants commonly used by Indians of the region. The rose garden is excellent, and the Japanese garden (Nitobe Memorial Garden) is a very good example of Oriental design transferred to Canada. The Nitobe Memorial Garden is actually two gardens: a tea garden of moss-covered rocks set in an abstract design, and a landscape garden built around a lake and a mini-mountain and its waterfall. The special delight of the second garden is the changing scene as one walks around the lake. There are also exotic gardens, medicinal gardens, a rock garden, an aquatic garden, a garden of native plants, and an arboretum of native shrubs and trees. One display greenhouse, 2 service houses. Gardens: daily, 10:00 A.M.–sunset. Greenhouse: daily, 8:30 A.M.–4:30 P.M. Fee.

Government House Gardens, 1401 Rockland Avenue. The sunken rose garden covers 1½ acres and is planted only with the finest cultivars. The formal lawns and gardens have perimeter beds of annuals and perennials, flowering shrubs, heather, azaleas, rhododendrons, lewisia, and clematis and ivy. There is a waterfall and a lily pond flanked with green and variegated bamboos. Daily.

Queen Elizabeth Park and Arboretums and the Bloedel Conservatory, Camden Street, Little Mountain. Magnificent gardens; 50 acres of beautiful lawns, weeping willows, colorful flower beds (annuals and perennials), woody shrubs and trees; an immaculately groomed sunken garden. The Bloedel Conservatory is as famous for its construction as for its collections of tropical plants and expertly managed displays.

Royal Roads Botanical Garden, Royal Roads Armed Services College, Sooke Road. Formerly a private estate (Hatley Park), the campus has a unique botanical garden in a beautiful setting. Daily, 1:00 P.M.–4:00 P.M.

Stanley Park, Georgia Street. A sanctuary in the heart of the city, the park has excellent roses and lush gardens, wide lawns, and the Lost Lagoon—Vancouver's counterpart of the lakes in New York City's Central Park. Dogwood, azaleas, and rhododendrons; hardy water lilies, weeping hemlocks, conifers, and many flowering cherry trees.

VERNON (British Columbia): *Japanese Gardens, Polsen Park.*

VICTORIA (British Columbia): *Bastion Square.* Just

Queen Elizabeth Park

Grand-Métis Botanical Garden

below the Maritime Museum, the square is designed in intricate parterres of annuals and perennials; pebbled walkways are edged with bricks and clipped dwarf hedges.

Beacon Hill Park. Little lakes, shaded walks, and masses of flowers, meandering streams, and flower-bordered duck ponds. Victoria, incidentally, is noted not only for its flowers, but almost equally so for its hanging flower baskets suspended from lampposts all over the city.

Butchart Gardens, Benvenuto Drive. One of the major attractions of western Canada, the 25-acre display gardens are unusual in both design and the brilliance of the floral arrangements. The gardens seem to contain the most colorful flowers in the world, in thousands and thousands of plants. These include 100 varieties of special tulips, wallflowers, myosotis, primroses, blue poppies, lupines, delphiniums, foxglove, iris, and many

annuals. There are also banks of rhododendrons. The perennial borders are extensive. The special gardens are: a Japanese garden, with maples, bridges, bamboos, waterfalls, dwarf trees, and ferns; an Italian garden, with pools, statues, and sculptured trees; an English rose garden, with many old favorites as well as new cultivars; and a sunken garden of great beauty and floral interest that is long remembered by visitors. Bulbs, particularly daffodils, are used for spring color; tuberous begonias may be seen in summer—hanging from trees or massed under lath and in the greenhouse. The many trees are both native and exotics, and grouped to form a background for the lawns and flowers. Woodland walks are edged with ferns and lily of the valley. Both the spectacular Ross fountain and the gardens are illuminated at night. Evening concerts and shows are also held here. Guide brochures are available in 11

Jackson's Gardens

Butchart Gardens

languages. Daily, summer, 9:00 A.M.–11:30 P.M.; other seasons, 9:00 A.M.–5:00 P.M. Fee
Japanese Gardens, Hatley Park.
VINELAND STATION (Ontario): *Horticultural Research Institute of Ontario.* The gardens, formal and informal, consist of large plantings of rhododendrons, test plantings of hollies, many shrubs and trees, annuals and perennials. Roses and day lilies are excellent, as are the many fruit trees and vegetables. The test gardens are very extensive, with many plants undergoing evaluation. Most of the planting is easily seen—about 20 acres well organized around the building of the research institute. Daily.
WINDSOR (Nova Scotia): *Haliburton Memorial Museum and Gardens.* The long driveway to the house is bordered with acacia, beech, white maple, poplar, and juniper. A fruit garden of considerable interest and a flower garden are enclosed with hawthorns and entered by boxwood-

edged paths. Coves and nooks of shrubbery provide welcome areas of quiet. From May 15 to October 15: daily, 9:30 A.M.–5:30 P.M.
WINDSOR (Ontario): *Jackson's Gardens.* One of the largest collections of roses in Canada. Fountains, ponds, and massed plantings of annuals and perennials.
WINNIPEG (Manitoba): *Arboretum, University of Manitoba.*
Assiniboine Park (362 acres). The English garden in the park probably has the largest collection of roses in the province (there are two other and smaller gardens of roses in the park). Daily.
Another planting of roses is maintained in nearby *Kildonan Park.*
YARMOUTH (Nova Scotia): *Rock Cottage Gardens.* Noted for its rhododendrons and rambler roses.
YORK (Prince Edward Island): *Jewell's Country Gardens.*

Plant Societies

AFRICAN VIOLET SOCIETY OF AMERICA, INC.: Box 1326, Knoxville, Tennessee 37901

AMERICAN BEGONIA SOCIETY, INC.: 1431 Coronado Terrace, Los Angeles, California 90026

AMERICAN BONSAI SOCIETY, 229 North Shore Drive, Lake Waukomis, Parksville, Missouri 64151

AMERICAN BOXWOOD SOCIETY, Box 85, Boyce, Virginia 22620

AMERICAN CAMELLIA SOCIETY: Box 212, Fort Valley, Georgia 31030

AMERICAN DAFFODIL SOCIETY, INC.: 89 Chichester Road, New Canaan, Connecticut 06840

AMERICAN DAHLIA SOCIETY, INC.: 92-21 W. Delaware Drive, Mystic Islands, Tuckerton, New Jersey 08087

AMERICAN FERN SOCIETY: Department of Botany, University of Tennessee, Knoxville, Tennessee 37916

AMERICAN FUCHSIA SOCIETY: 738-22nd Avenue, San Francisco, California 94121

AMERICAN GESNERIA SOCIETY: 11983 Darlington Avenue, Los Angeles, California 90049

AMERICAN GLOXINIA AND GESNERIAD SOCIETY, INC.: Department AHS, Eastford, Connecticut 06242

AMERICAN GOURD SOCIETY: RR 1, Box 274, Mt. Gilead, Ohio 43338

AMERICAN HIBISCUS SOCIETY: Box 98, Eagle Lake, Florida 33839

AMERICAN HEROCALLIS SOCIETY: Box 586, Woodstock, Illinois 60098

AMERICAN HOSTA SOCIETY: 4392 W. 20th Street Road, Oshkosh, Wisconsin 54901

AMERICAN IRIS SOCIETY: 2315 Tower Grove Avenue, St. Louis, Missouri 63110

AMERICAN MAGNOLIA SOCIETY: 2150 Woodward Avenue, Bloomfield Hills, Michigan 48013.

AMERICAN ORCHID SOCIETY: Botanical Museum of Harvard University, Cambridge, Massachusetts 02138

AMERICAN PENSTEMON SOCIETY: Box 64, Somersworth, New Hampshire 03878

AMERICAN PEONY SOCIETY: 107½ West Main Street, Van Wert, Ohio 45981

AMERICAN PLANT LIFE SOCIETY & AMERICAN AMARYLLIS GROUP: Box 150, La Jolla, California 92037

AMERICAN PRIMROSE SOCIETY: 10415-84th Avenue N.E., Bothell, Washington 98011

AMERICAN RHODODENDRON SOCIETY: 24450 S. W. Grahams Ferry Road, Sherwood Oregon 97140

AMERICAN ROCK GARDEN SOCIETY: 90 Pierpont Road, Waterbury, Connecticut 06705

AMERICAN ROSE SOCIETY: 4048 Roselea Place, Columbus, Ohio 43214

ARIL SOCIETY, INTERNATIONAL: 7802 Kyle Street, Sunland, California 91040

THE BROMELIAD SOCIETY: 1811 Edgecliffe Drive, Los Angeles, California 90026

THE CACTUS AND SUCCULENT SOCIETY OF AMERICA, INC.: Box 167, Reseda, California 91335

THE CANADIAN ROSE SOCIETY: 31 Learmont Drive, Weston, Ontario, Canada

CYMBIDIUM SOCIETY OF AMERICA, INC.: Box 4202, Downey, California 90242

EPIPHYLLUM SOCIETY OF AMERICA: 218 East Greystone Avenue, Monrovia, California 91016

HOLLY SOCIETY OF AMERICA, INC.: Box 8445, Baltimore, Maryland 21234

INTERNATIONAL GERANIUM SOCIETY: 1413 Shoreline Drive, Santa Barbara, California 93105

NATIONAL CHRYSANTHEMUM SOCIETY, INC.: 8504 La Verne Drive, Adelphi, Maryland 20763

NATIONAL OLEANDER SOCIETY: 22 S. Shore Road, Galveston, Texas 77550

NATIONAL TULIP SOCIETY, INC.: 250 West 57th Street, New York, New York 10019

THE NEW ENGLAND WILDFLOWER SOCIETY: Hemenway Road, Framingham, Massachusetts 10701

NORTH AMERICAN GLADIOLUS COUNCIL: 234 South Street, South Elgin, Illinois 60177

NORTH AMERICAN LILY SOCIETY, INC.: North Ferrisburg, Vermont 05473

SOCIETY FOR LOUISIANA IRISES: Box 175, University of Southwestern Louisiana Institute, Lafayette, Louisiana 70501

SPURIA IRIS SOCIETY (Spuria Section of the American Iris Society): Route 2, Box 35, Purcell, Oklahoma 73080

THE WILDFLOWER PRESERVATION SOCIETY, INC.: The New York Botanical Garden, Bronx, New York 10458

State Tourist Bureaus

ALABAMA: Bureau of Publicity and Information, State Capitol, Montgomery 36104.

ALASKA: Alaska Travel Division, Pouch E, Juneau 99801.

ARIZONA: Dept. of Economic Planning and Development, 3303 N. Central Ave., Phoenix 85012.

ARKANSAS: Publicity and Parks Commission, 149 State Capitol, Little Rock 72201.

CALIFORNIA: State Office of Tourism, 1400 Tenth St., Sacramento 95814.

COLORADO: State Division of Commerce and Development, 600 State Service Bldg., Denver 80203.

CONNECTICUT: Connecticut Development Commission, Research and Information Division, 102 State Office Bldg., Hartford 06115.

DELAWARE: State Development Dept., 45 The Green, Dover 19901.

DISTRICT OF COLUMBIA: Washington Convention and Visitors Bureau, 1616 K St., N.W., Washington 20006.

FLORIDA: Florida Dept. of Commerce, Tourist and Marketing—Caldwell Bldg., Tallahassee 32304.

GEORGIA: Dept. of Industry and Trade, Tourist Division, Box 38097, Atlanta 30334.

HAWAII: Hawaii Visitors Bureau, 609 5th Ave., New York, N.Y. 10017; 3440 Wilshire Blvd., Los Angeles, Calif. 90005; or 2270 Kalakaua Ave., Honolulu 96815.

IDAHO: Dept. of Commerce and Development, Room 108, Capitol Bldg., Boise 83701.

ILLINOIS: Division of Tourism, 222 College, Springfield 62706.

INDIANA: Dept. of Commerce, Tourist Div., 333 State House, Indianapolis 46204.

IOWA: Development Commission, 250 Jewett Bldg., Des Moines 50309.

KANSAS: Dept. of Economic Development, State Office Bldg., Room 122-S, Topeka 66612.

KENTUCKY: Dept. of Public Information, Travel Division, 410 Ann St., Frankfort 40601.

LOUISIANA: Tourist Development Commission, State Capitol, Baton Rouge 70804; Greater New Orleans Tourist Commission, 400 Royal St., Suite 203, New Orleans 70130.

MAINE: Maine Publicity Bureau, Gateway Circle, Portland 04102.

MARYLAND: Dept. of Economic Development, Travel Department Div., State Office Bldg., Annapolis 21401.

MASSACHUSETTS: Dept. of Commerce and Development, 100 Cambridge St., Boston 02202.

MICHIGAN: Michigan Tourist Council, Stevens T. Mason Bldg., Lansing 48926.

MINNESOTA: Dept. of Economic Development, 57 W. 7th St., St. Paul 55102.

MISSISSIPPI: Travel Department, Agricultural and Industrial Board, 1504 State Office Bldg., Jackson 39205.

MISSOURI: Division of Commerce and Industrial Development, Jefferson Bldg., Jefferson City 65101.

MONTANA: State Highway Commission, Advertising Dept., Helena 59601.

NEBRASKA: Nebraska Land, State Capitol, Lincoln 68509.

NEVADA: Dept. of Economic Development, Carson City 89701.

NEW HAMPSHIRE: Division of Economic Development, Box 856, Concord 03301.

NEW JERSEY: Dept. of Conservation and Economic Development, Box 1889, Trenton 08625.

NEW MEXICO: Tourist Division, Dept. of Development, 113 Washington Ave., Santa Fe 87501.

NEW YORK: Dept. of Commerce, Travel Bureau, 112 State St., Albany 12207; New York Convention and Visitors Bureau, 90 E. 42nd St., New York 10017.

NORTH CAROLINA: Dept. of Conservation and Development, Travel and Promotion Div., 211 Administration Bldg., Raleigh 27611.

NORTH DAKOTA: Greater North Dakota Association, Box 1781, Fargo 58102.

OHIO: Department of Development, 65 S. Front St., Box 1001, Columbus 43215.

OKLAHOMA: Industrial Development and Park Dept., Tourist Division, 500 Will Rogers Memorial Bldg., Oklahoma City 73105.

OREGON: Travel Information, State Highway Dept., 101 Highway Bldg., Salem 97310; Oregon Coast Assoc., 559 S.W. Coast Hwy., Newport 97365.

PENNSYLVANIA: Dept. of Commerce, Travel Development Bureau, 400 S. Office Bldg., Harrisburg 17120.

RHODE ISLAND: Tourist Promotion Division, Development Council, 49 Hayes St., Providence 02908.

SOUTH CAROLINA: State Development Board, Box 927, Columbia 29205.

SOUTH DAKOTA: Travel Division, Dept. of Highways, Highway Bldg., Pierre 57501.

TENNESSEE: Division of Tourist Promotion, Dept. of Conservation, 2611 W. End Ave., Nashville 37203.

TEXAS: Texas Highway Dept., Travel Division, Box 5064, Austin 78701.

UTAH: Utah Travel Council, Council Hall, Capitol Hill, Salt Lake City 84114.

VERMONT: Development Dept., Promotion and Travel, State Office Bldg., Montpelier 05602.

VIRGINIA: Virginia State Travel Service, 911 E. Broad St., Richmond 23219.

WASHINGTON: Tourist Promotion Div., Dept. of Commerce and Economic Development, General Administration Bldg., Olympia 98501.

WEST VIRGINIA: West Virginia Dept. of Commerce, Travel Development Div., Room E-404, State Capitol, Charleston 25305.

WISCONSIN: Dept. of Natural Resources, Vacation and Travel Service, Box 450, Madison 53701.

WYOMING: Travel Commission, 2320 Capitol Ave., Cheyenne 82001.

VIRGIN ISLANDS: Government Tourist Information Office, 16 W. 49th St., New York, N.Y. 10020.

CANADA

CANADIAN GOVERNMENT TRAVEL BUREAU: Ottawa, Ontario; 680 Fifth Ave., New York, N. Y. 10019.

ALBERTA: Government Travel Bureau, 1629 Centennial Bldg., Edmonton.

BRITISH COLUMBIA: Dept. of Travel and Industry, Parliament Bldgs., Victoria.

MANITOBA: Dept. of Tourism and Recreation, 408 Norquay Bldg., Winnipeg.

NEW BRUNSWICK: Travel Bureau, P. O. Box 1030, Fredericton.

NEWFOUNDLAND: Tourist Development Office, Confederation Bldg., St. Johns.

NOVA SCOTIA: Travel Bureau, Dept. of Industry and Trade, 5670 Spring Garden Rd., Halifax.

ONTARIO: Dept. of Tourism and Information, 185 Bloor St. E., Toronto 285.

PRINCE EDWARD ISLAND: Travel Bureau, P. O. Box 940, Charlottetown.

QUEBEC: Dept. of Tourism, Fish and Game, Parliament Bldgs., Quebec; Tourist Information Bureau, 48 Rockefeller Plaza, New York 10020.

SASKATCHEWAN: Dept. of Industry and Commerce, Power Bldg., Regina.

Photographic Credits

When the travel guide to the gardens of North America was completed, two observations were self-evident. Never before have there been so many lovely gardens; nor, never before, have so many organizations and individuals been concerned with them. And among them, I am especially indebted:

To the New York Horticultural Society;

To many garden club members, particularly the Visiting Chairmen;

To the officers and personnel of many Chambers of Commerce;

To the directors and information officers of each State Bureau of Tourism;

To the travel and tourism officers of each Canadian Province;

To the supervisors and horticulturists of many city, state, and federal parks;

To the directors, managers, and proprietors of many of the listed gardens.

And to each of the following agencies and individuals I acknowledge a debt and extend my gratitude for the use of their photographic illustrations:

BLACK AND WHITE PHOTOGRAPHS:
TITLE PAGE: Mynelle Gardens / Mynelle Hayward.
ALABAMA: page 2—Bellingrath Gardens / *Alabama Bureau of Publicity and Information.* 3—Ave Maria Grotto / *St. Bernard College.* 4—Oriental Gardens / *Gulf State Paper Company.* 5—Ivy Green / *Helen Keller Foundation.* 5—University of Alabama / *University News Bureau.*
ARIZONA: 7—Organ Pipe Cactus National Monument / *National Park Service.* 8—Mormon Temple Gardens / *Mormon Temple Information Service.* 8—San Xavier del Bac Mission Garden / *Tucson Chamber of Commerce.* 8—Dessert Botanical Garden / *W. H. Earle.* 9—Arizona-Sonora Desert Museum / *Tucson Chamber of Commerce.* 10—Boyce Thompson Southwestern Arboretum / *Phoenix Chamber of Commerce.*
ARKANSAS: 11—Arkansas Territorial Capitol / *Arkansas Department of Parks and Tourism.*
CALIFORNIA: 12, 13—Los Angeles State and County Arboretum / *Los Angeles State and County Arboretum.* 14—University of California Botanical Garden / *University of California, Berkeley.* 14—Mendocino Coast Botanical Garden / *Staff photograph-Eugene Memmler.* 15—Blake Garden / *University of California-Erwin Strohmaier.* 16—Muir Woods National Monument / *National Park Service.* 17—Native Plant Botanical Garden / *East Bay Regional Park District.* 17—Rancho Los Alamitos / *Long Beach Recreational Commission.* 18—Piedmount Park Cherry Tree Walk / *Mrs. G. Schoeneman.* 19—Oakland Museum Gardens / *Oakland Chamber of Commerce.* Marin Art and Garden Center / *Madison*

Devlin. 20—Eddy Arboretum / *U. S. Forest Service.* 21—Sea World Japanese Garden / *Sea World, Inc.* 21—Chinese Temple Garden / *J. P. Carpenter.* 22—Balboa Park / *City of San Diego.* 23—San Diego Zoo / *San Diego Zoo.* 24—Strybing Arboretum / *San Francisco Department of Parks.* 24—Hearst State Historical Monument / *California State Monument photograph.* 25—Japanese Tea Garden / *Redwood Empire Association.* 26—Joshua Tree National Monument / *National Park Service, D. M. Black.* 26—Shaffer's Tropical Gardens / *George Woodward.* 27—Luther Burbank Memorial Gardens / *Redwood Empire Association.* 28—Yosemite National Park / *National Park Service.* 28—Acres of Orchids / *Rod McLellan Company.*
COLORADO: 29—Denver Botanical Garden / *Staff photograph.*
CONNECTICUT: 30—Elizabeth Park; 31—Constitution Plaza; 32—Topping-Reeve House; 33—Harkness Memorial State Park / *Connecticut Development Commission.*
DELAWARE: 34—Winterthur Gardens Pinetum / *Winterthur Museum.* 35—Corbett-Sharp House / *Winterthur Museum.* 35—Winterthur Gardens / *Winterthur Museum.* 36—Josephine Gardens / *Delaware Bureau of Travel Development.* 36—Winterthur Gardens / *Winterthur Museum.*
DISTRICT OF COLUMBIA: 37, 38, 39—Dumbarton Oaks / *The Garden Library.* 40, 41—U. S. National Arboretum / *Education Office,* U. S. National Arboretum.
FLORIDA: 42—Mountain Lake Sanctuary / *Staff photograph.* 43—Cypress Gardens; 44—Everglades National

Park / *Florida News Bureau, Department of Commerce.* 44-45—Thomas A. Edison Winter Home Botanical Garden; 45—Koresham State Park / *Lee County News Bureau.* 46, 47—Vizcaya / *Vizcaya-Dade County Museum.* 47—Corkscrew Swamp Sanctuary / *Florida News Bureau, Department of Commerce.* 47—Fairchild Tropical Garden / *Metro-Dade County Park and Recreation Department.* 48, 49—Ca'd'Zan / *Ringling Brothers Museum.* 50—Sunken Gardens / *Delta Airlines.* 51—Caribbean Gardens / *Florida News Bureau, Department of Commerce.* 51—Highlands Hammock State Park / *Florida Department of Natural Resources.* 52—Alfred B. Maclay Gardens / *Florida Development Commission.* 53—Busch Gardens / *Florida News Bureau, Department of Commerce.*
GEORGIA: 56—Bonaventura Cemetery; 59—Forsyth Park / *Savannah Area Chamber of Commerce.*
HAWAII: 60, 61—Olu Pua Gardens / *Sta; photograph.* 62—Moanalua Gardens / *Hawaii Visitors Bureau.* 63—Alice Cooke Spaulding Gardens / *Honolulu Academy of Arts.*
IDAHO: 65—Lake Cœur d'Alene / *Idaho Department of Commerce and Development.* 66—Cedar Forests / *Moscow Chamber of Commerce.*
ILLINOIS: 67—Allerton House / *Illinois Department of Business and Economic Development.* 70, 71—Chicago Parks and Conservatory / *Chicago Park District.* 73—Butler Botanical Garden / *Butler University.* 74—Labyrinth / *Don Blair.* 74—Butler Botanical Garden / *Butler University.* 75—Hillsdale Rose Garden / *Hillsdale Nursery.* 75—Garfield Park Conservatory / *Indianapolis Department of*

Parks. 76—Butler Botanical Garden / *Butler University.*
IOWA: 77—Arie den Boer Arboretum / *Des Moines Water Works.* 78—Vander Veer Park / *Davenport Chamber of Commerce.* 78—Horticulture Gardens of Iowa State University / *University of Iowa.* 79—Kobes Garden / *Kobes Dist. Company.*
KANSAS: 80, 81—Meade Park Gardens; Reinisch Rose Garden / *Topeka Park Department.* 82—Memorial Rose Garden / *Fort Hays Kansas State College Information Services.*
KENTUCKY: 83, 85—Bernheim Forest Landscape Arboretum / *Isaac W. Bernstein Foundation.* 84—Tennessee Valley Environmental Education Center / *Tennessee Valley Authority.* 85—The Lexington Cemetery / *Lexington Herald Leader.*
LOUISIANA: 86, 87—Rip Van Winkle Gardens / *Michael Richards.* 88—Ira S. Nelson Horticultural Center / *University of Southwestern Louisiana Publication Bureau.* 88—Laurens Henry Cohn Memorial Arboretum / *Baton Rouge Recreation and Park Department.* 89, 95—Hodges Gardens / *Staff photograph.* 90—Jungle Gardens / *Frank Methe.* 95—The Shadows-on-the-Teche / *Louisiana Tourist Development Commission.*
MAINE: 97—Asticou Gardens / *Elinor Parker.*
MARYLAND: 98—Sherwood Gardens / *Baltimore Area Visitors Council.* 99, 100, 101—Brookside Botanical Garden / *Maryland-National Capitol Park and Planning Commission.*
MASSACHUSETTS: 102, 103—Arnold Arboretum / *Arnold Arboretum-P. Bruns.* 103—Garden in the Woods / *New England Wild Flower Preservation Society, Inc.* 106—Heritage Plantation of Sandwich / *Creamer, Trowbridge, Case, and Basford, Inc.* 107—Adams National Historical Site / *National Historical photograph.* 107—Bridge of Flowers / *Massachusetts Department of Commerce and Development.* 108—Stanley Park / *Stanley Park of Westfield, Inc.*
MICHIGAN: 109—Anna Scripps Whitcomb Conservatory / *Detroit Department of Parks and Recreation.* 110—Ford Arboretum / *Ford Motor Company.* 110, 111—Beal-Garfield Arboretum / *Michigan State University.* 112—Hidden Lake Garden / *Michigan State University.*
MINNESOTA: 113—Como Park / *Como Park Conservatory.* 114—University of Minnesota Landscape Arboretum / *Leon C. Snyder.* 114—Lake Harriet Garden Center / *Greater Minneapolis Chamber of Commerce.* 114—Lyndale Park / *Minneapolis Park and Recreation Board.* 115—Como Park Conservatory / *Como Park Conservatory.*
MISSISSIPPI: 116—Mynelle Gardens / *Mynelle Hayward.* 117—The Elms / *Pilgrimage Garden Club-Mabel Lane.* 118—White Arches / *Columbus-Lowndes Chamber of Commerce.* 118—Gloster Arboretum / *W. F. Gladney.* 119—D'Evereux / *Pilgrimage Garden Club-Mabel Lane.* 119—Natchez Trace Parkway / *National Park Service.* 119—Waverly Plantation / *Columbus-Lowndes Chamber of Commerce.* 120—Natchez Trace Parkway / *National Park Service.*
MISSOURI: 121—The Jewel Box / *St. Louis Convention and Publicity Bureau.* 122—Missouri Botanic Garden / *Chamber of Commerce of Metropolitan St. Louis.* 123—The Jewel Box / *Chamber of Commerce of Metropolitan St. Louis.* 124—Loose Park / *Convention and Tourist Bureau of Greater Kansas City.*
NEW HAMPSHIRE: 126—Alpine Gardens; 131—Fitzwilliam State Park; 132—Wentworth-Coolidge Mansion / *New Hampshire Planning and Development Commission.*
NEW JERSEY: 133—Delaware Water Gap National Recreation Area / *National Park Service.* 134—Frelinghuysen Arboretum / *Quentin Schlieder.* 135—Rutgers Display Garden / *Rutgers University.* 136—Prospect Gardens / *Princeton University.* 137—Skylands of New Jersey / *New Jersey Regional State Park System.* 138, 139—Duke Gardens / *Duke Gardens Foundation.*
NEW MEXICO: 140, 141—University of New Mexico / *University Information Office.* 142—Sandia Peak Botanic Garden / *Toppino, Golden, Lundberg, Inc.*
NEW YORK: 147—Brooklyn Botanic Garden / *Staff photograph.* The Cloisters / *Metropolitan Museum.* 149—Channel Gardens / *Rockefeller Center, Inc.* 149—Ford Foundation Indoor Garden / *Esto for the Ford Foundation, Inc.* 149—Courtyard Garden / *Ezra Stroller for the Frick Museum.* 150—New York Botanical Garden / *New York Convention and Visitors Bureau.* 151—Hammond Museum Oriental Stroll Garden / *New York State Department of Commerce.* 152—Bayard Cutting Arboretum / *Long Island State Park Commission.* 155—Old Westbury Gardens / *New York State Department of Commerce.* 156—Sterling Forest / *New York State Department of Commerce.*
NORTH CAROLINA: 157, 160, 161—Tryon Palace Restoration / *Michael W. Brantly.* 158—Elizabethan Garden / *Mrs. G. V. Chambley-Aycock Brown.* 159—Sarah P. Duke Memorial Garden / *Duke University.* 160—The Gourd Museum / *M. M. Johnson.* 160—Poets and Dreamers Garden / *Livingstone College-Walter G. Jones.* 160—North Carolina Botanical Garden / *University of North Carolina.* Reynolda Gardens / *Wake Forest University.*
NORTH DAKOTA: 167—International Peace Garden / *North Dakota Travel Department.*
OHIO: 168—Ault Park; 169—Mt. Airy Arboretum; 169—Sooty Acres / *Cincinnati Board of Park Commissioners.* 170—Western Reserve Herb Society Garden / *Garden Center of Greater Cleveland.* 170, 171—Franklin Park Conservatory / *Ohio Department of Industrial and Economic Development.* 172, 173—Kingwood Center / *R. C. Allen.* 174—Dawes Arboretum / *Allan D. Cook.* 175—Oldest Stone House / *Lakewood Historical Society.* 176—Secrest Arboretum / *Ohio Agricultural Research and Development Center.*
OKLAHOMA: 177—Will Rogers Horticultural Park and Arboretum / *Oklahoma City Parks and Recreation Department.*
OREGON: 179—Azalea State Park; 180—International Rose Test Garden; 181—Darlingtonia Wayside Preserve; 182—Shore Acres State Park / *Oregon State Highway Travel Division.*
PENNSYLVANIA: 183, 186—Longwood Gardens / *Longwood Gardens photographs.* 184—Haverford College / *Burgess Blevins.* 185—Hershey Rose Garden / *Hershey Estates.* 185—Mill Grove / *Edward W. Graham.* 185—Temple University Gardens / *George Manaker.* 187—Swiss Pines / *Anna Croyle.* 188—Masonic Homes Gardens / *Philadelphia Masonic Temple.*

188—Charles Ellis School / *J. H. MacGregor.* 189—18th-century Garden; 190—Magnolia Tribute Garden / *National Park Service.* 191—Japanese Garden / *City of Philadelphia photograph.* 194—Valley Forge State Park / *Montgomery County Tourist Bureau.* 194—Star Roses / *Conrad-Pyle Company.*
RHODE ISLAND: 195—The Elms / *The Preservation Society of Newport County.* 196—Wilcox Park / *Westerly Public Library.* 197—University of Rhode Island; 197—The Breakers; 197—Stephen Hopkins House; 198—Swann Point Cemetery / *Rhode Island Development Council.*
SOUTH CAROLINA: 202—Bomar Water Gardens; 203—Middleton Place Gardens; 205—Glencairn Gardens / *South Carolina Department of Parks, Recreation, and Tourism.*
SOUTH DAKOTA: 206—Pharmaceutical Gardens / *Brookings Area Chamber of Commerce.*
TENNESSEE: 207, 208, 209—Reflection Riding / *Sizer, Chamblis, Inc.*
TEXAS: 211—Fort Worth Botanic Garden; 211—Ima Hogg Home; 212—Cactus Garden-Judge Roy Bean Visitor Center; 212—Palmetto State Park; 213—Chrysanthemum Gardens; 214—Brackenridge Park / *Texas Highway Department.* 211—Memorial Park Rose Garden / *Southwestern Public Service Company.* 215—The Alamo Gardens / *San Antonio Convention and Visitors Bureau.* 216—Tyler Rose Farm / *Tyler Chamber of Commerce.*
UTAH: 217, 218—Temple Gardens / *Information Service, The Church of Jesus Christ of Latter Day Saints.* 219—International Peace Gardens; 219—Municipal Grounds / *Utah Travel Council.*
VERMONT: 220—Burklyn / *Elizabeth Brouha.*
VIRGINIA: 221—Bryan Park Azalea Garden / *Richmond Department of Recreation and Parks.* 222—Orland E. White Research Arboretum / *Russell L. Edwards-Frank R. Hupp.* 224, 225—The Mount Vernon Gardens / *The Mount Vernon Ladies Association.* 226—Norfolk Botanic Gardens / *George W. Baker.* 227—Maymount Park / *Richmond Department of Recreation and Parks.* 228, 229—Colonial

Williamsburg / *Press Bureau, Colonial Williamsburg photographs.*
WASHINGTON: 230—University of Washington Arboretum; 231—Peace Arch State Park; 232—Ohme Gardens / *Washington State Department of Commerce and Economic Development.* 231—University of Washington Arboretum / *Bill Eng.* 231—University of Washington Arboretum / *D. D. Methenn.* 232—Mount Rainier National Park; 233—Hurricane Ridge Flowers / *National Park Service.*
WEST VIRGINIA: 234—Cathedral State Park; 235—Cranberry Glades Botanical Area; 235—Holly River State Park / *West Virginia Department of Commerce-Gerald S. Ratliff.* 235—Huntington Galleries / *Robert Rodgers.* 236—Whelling Garden Center / *G. Randolph Worls.*
WISCONSIN: 237, 240—University of Wisconsin Arboretum / *Rodger Anderson.* 238—Olbrich Botanical Gardens / *Stan Hill.* 238—Kinn River Canyon Arboretum / *R. J. Matros.* 238, 239—Horticultural Conservator / *Milwaukee County Park Commission.*
CANADA: 242—Queen Victoria Park / *Niagara Parks Commission-Gordon Counsell.* 243—Butchart Gardens; 244—Nikka Yuka Centennial Gardens / *Canadian Government Travel Bureau.* 245—International Peace Garden / *Canadian Travel Bureau.* 245—Halifax Public Gardens / *Nova Scotia Information Service.* 245—Royal Botanical Society / *Canadian Government Travel Bureau.* 246—Jardin Botanique de Montréal / *Romeo Meloche.* 247—Cominco Public Gardens / *Canadian Government Travel Bureau.* 248—Niagara Parks Commissions Greenhouse / *Niagara Parks Commission.* 248—Experimental Farm, Morden / *Morden Research Station.* 249—Niagara Parks Commissions School of Horticulture / *Niagara Parks Commissions-Gordon Counsell.* 250—Water Works Park / *Ontario Ministry of Industry and Tourism.* 251—Park and Tilford Gardens / *Park and Tilford-Leblanc.* 251—Québec Zoological Gardens / *Province of Québec Film Bureau.* 252—Queen Elizabeth Park; 252—Grand-Métis Botanical Gardens / *Canadian Government Travel Bureau.* 253—Jackson's Gardens / *Ontario Ministry of Industry and Tourism.* 253—Butchart Gardens / *Butchart Gardens photograph.*

COLOR TRANSPARENCIES:

Page 58—McCullough Mansion / *McCullough Mansion Association, Inc.* Heritage Plantation of Sandwich / *Creamer, Trowbridge, Case, and Bradford.* Rockefeller Gardens / *Elinor Parker.* Watkins Iris Gardens / *New Hampshire Division of Economic Development.* Swiss Pines Gardens / *Anna E. Croyle.* Winterthur Gardens / *Winterthur Museum.*
Page 91—Oriental Gardens / *Gulf State Paper Corporation.* Hope Farm Plantation / *Pilgrimage Garden Club.* Elizabethan Gardens / *Mrs. Leo Midgette.* Mynelle Gardens / *Mynelle Hayward.* Rip Van Winkle Gardens / *Mitchel A. Richards.* Hodges Garden / *Staff Photograph.*
Page 94—Maclay Gardens / *Florida Department of Natural Resources.* Calloway Gardens / *Mrs. George Ray.* Sherwood Gardens / *Maryland Department of Economic Development-Bob Willis.* Miami Beach Gardens Center / *Miami Beach Publicity Department.* Chippokes Plantation / *Virginia Audio-Visual Services.*
Page 127—Rhododendron Society Gardens / *Travel Information, Oregon State Highway Department.* Organ Pipe Cactus National Monument / *Superintendent, Organ Pipe National Monument.* Desert Botanical Garden / *W. Earle.* Lilac Time / *Idaho Department of Commerce and Development.* Fort Worth Botanical Garden / *Travel Development, Texas Highway Department.* City of Rocks Botanical Garden / *Arizona State Park and Recreation Commission-Richard E. Cooper.* Hudsonian Meadows Garden / *Norman A. Bishop.*
Page 130—Pecos Botanical Garden / *Harold Meyer-Pecos Chamber of Commerce.* Marin Art and Garden Center / *Managing Director, Marin Art and Garden Center.* Marin Art and Garden Center / *Managing Director, Marin Art and Garden Center.* Japanese Garden / *Travel Information, Oregon State Highway Department.* Quail Botanic Garden / *Mrs. J. Von Pressig.*
Page 163—Kingwood Center / *R. C. Allen.* Missouri Botanic Garden / *St. Louis Convention and Tourist Board.* University of Minnesota Landscape Arboretum / *Leon C. Snyder.* University of Kansas Campus Gardens / *Alton C. Thomas-*

Architectural Services. Hayes Regional Arboretum / *Charles F. McGraw.* Page 166—Municipal Rose Garden / *Russell Studebaker.* Water Works Park / *Des Moines Water Works-Paul Ellerbrook.* The Lexington Cemetery / *The Lexington*

Cemetery-R. F. Wachs. Kinn River Arboretum / *R. J. Matros.* Page 199—Olu Pua Gardens / *Olu Pua Gardens photograph.* Jardin Botanique de Montréal / *Jardin Botanique-François Grignon.* Virgin Islands National Park /

National Park Service. Butchart Gardens / *Butchart Gardens photograph.* Olu Pua Gardens / *Olu Pua Gardens photograph.* Legislative Building Gardens / *Photographic Art Division, Regina.* St. Thomas Gardens / *Berger, Olson, Beaumont, Inc.*

Index